Lab Manual for MCSE Guide to
Planning a Microsoft® Windows® Server 2003 Network

Jennifer Guttormson

Kelly Reid

Byron Wright

THOMSON

COURSE TECHNOLOGY

Australia • Canada • Mexico • Singapore • Spain • United Kingdom • United States

THOMSON
™
COURSE TECHNOLOGY

Lab Manual for MCSE Guide to Planning a Microsoft Windows Server 2003 Network

by Jennifer Guttormson, Kelly Reid, Byron Wright

Managing Editor:
Will Pitkin III

Product Manager:
Nick Lombardi

Production Editor:
Brooke Booth

Development Editor:
Jill Batistick

Technical Edit/Quality Assurance:
Danielle Shaw
Marianne Snow

Associate Product Manager:
Mirella Misiaszek
David Rivera

Editorial Assistant:
Amanda Piantedosi

Senior Manufacturing Coordinator:
Trevor Kallop

Senior Marketing Manager:
Jason Sakos

Text Designer:
GEX Publishing Services

Compositor:
GEX Publishing Services

Cover Design:
Steve Deschene

TABLE OF
Contents

CHAPTER 2

CHAPTER 3

CHAPTER 4

Planning and Configuring Routing and Switching 75

CHAPTER 5

Planning, Configuring, and Troubleshooting DHCP   **111**

CHAPTER 9

CHAPTER 10

Planning and Managing IPSec   **285**

CHAPTER 11

CHAPTER 12

CHAPTER 13

CHAPTER 14

Problem Recovery   **395**

Introduction

The objective of this lab manual is to assist you in preparing for the Microsoft Certification Exam 70-293: Planning and Maintaining a Microsoft Windows Server 2003 Network Infrastructure by applying the objectives to relevant lab activities. This text is designed to be used in conjunction with *MCSE Guide to Planning a Microsoft Windows Server 2003 Network* (0–619–12025–8), and it should be noted that many of the labs rely upon activities from the book being completed first. Without completing those activities first, students may get different results from the labs. Although this manual is written to be used in a classroom lab environment, it also may be used for self-study on a home network.

Features

In order to ensure a successful experience for instructors and students alike, this book includes the following features:

- **Lab Objectives**—The goal of each lab is clearly stated at the beginning.

- **Materials Required**—Every lab includes information on hardware, software, and other materials that you will need to complete the lab.

- **Estimated Completion Time**—Every lab has an estimated completion time, so that you can plan your activities more accurately.

- **Activity Background**—Activity Background information provides important details and prepares students for the activity that follows.

- **Activity Sections**—Labs are presented in manageable sections and include figures to reinforce learning.

- **Step-by-Step Instructions**—Steps provide practice, which enhances technical proficiency.

- **Microsoft Windows Server 2003 MSCE Certification Objectives**—For each lab, the relevant objectives from MCSE Exam #70-293 are listed.

- **Review Questions**—Review reinforces concepts presented in the lab.

Hardware Requirements

All hardware in the computer should be listed on the Hardware Compatibility List available at *www.microsoft.com*.

Hardware	Description
CPU	Pentium III 533 or higher
Memory	256 MB RAM
Disk Space	Minimum 2 GB (3 GB if storing the installation files on local hard drive)
Drives	CD-ROM Floppy Disk
Networking	All labs assume a single instructor server acting as a domain controller. Two network cards are recommended to allow isolation from other networks. All student servers will be configured in pairs and must have two network cards to complete all of the exercises. The first network card is connected to the classroom network with the instructor server. The second network card is connected via crossover cable or hub to the other student server in the pair. Make sure to have Windows Server 2003-compatible network adapters. A connection to the Internet via some sort of NAT or Proxy server is assumed.

Software Requirements

The following software is needed for proper setup of the labs:

- Windows Server 2003 Enterprise Edition for each computer
- The latest Windows Server 2003 Service Pack (if available)

Setup Procedure

To successfully complete the lab exercises, set up the classroom computers as follows:

1. The instructor computer should initially be installed with default configuration options. The name of the server should be Instructor. The initial password should be Password!.

2. After installation, rename one of the network connections as Classroom with an IP address of 192.168.1.10, a subnet mask of 255.255.255.0, and 192.168.1.10 as the DNS server. Rename the other connection as External and configure it with the appropriate IP address, subnet mask, and default gateway to allow access to the Internet. Configure routing and remote access and network address translation (if

necessary) to allow access to the Internet. If network address translation is configured on this server, Classroom will be the internal interface, and External will be the external interface.

3. Configure the Instructor computer as a domain controller for the domain Arctic.local. When asked to create an Administrator password for the domain, use Password!. Allow the Active Directory installation wizard to automatically install DNS and create the domain. If the server does not detect Internet connectivity during the installation of Active Directory, it will create a root DNS domain on the instructor server. This prevents the server from performing Internet DNS lookups. Delete the root DNS domain if it is created.

4. Install IIS on the Instructor computer and enable the processing of ASP scripts.

5. After IIS is installed, create the file C:\inetpub\wwwroot\default.asp. The contents of this file should be as follows:

```
<html>
<body>
<p>Source IP address = <%=Request.ServerVariables("REMOTE_ADDR")%>
<p>Source TCP Port = <%=Request.ServerVariables("REMOTE_PORT")%>
<p>Server IP address = <%=Request.ServerVariables("LOCAL_ADDR")%>
<p>Server TCP Port = <%=Request.ServerVariables("SERVER_PORT")%>
</body>
</html>
```

6. Connect each pair of student computers with a crossover cable. Alternatively, they can be connected using straight cables and a hub or switch. During the course activities, each pair of computers is assigned a group number. For example, Student01 and Student02 are group 1, and Student03 and Student04 are group 2.

7. To make identification easier for students, consider placing a paper label on the monitor of each server indicating the name of the server and the group number for that pair of computers.

8. It is important to remember that when performing the activities included in this book that the student logs in as the Administrator for the Arctic.local domain. The local Administrator accounts on the student member servers do not have enough privileges to complete some of the activities.

Acknowledgements

The authoring team would like to thank the following reviewers for their insight and help as this book was written: Patty Gillilan, Sinclair Community College; John Hagle, Texas State Technical College; and Neal Zimmerman, CHI Institute.

1

OVERVIEW OF PLANNING A WINDOWS SERVER 2003 NETWORK

Labs included in this chapter:

♦ Lab 1.1 Installing Windows Server 2003

♦ Lab 1.2 Network Architecture: Viewing and Modifying Bindings

♦ Lab 1.3 Comparing Editions of Windows Server 2003

♦ Lab 1.4 Windows NT Workstation 3.51 and Windows Server 2003

♦ Lab 1.5 New and Updated Features on Windows Server 2003

Microsoft MCSE Exam #70-293 Objectives	
Objective	**Lab**
Evaluate and select the operating system to install on computers in an enterprise.	1.1, 1.3, 1.5
Identify the minimum configuration to satisfy security requirements.	1.3, 1.4
Diagnose and resolve issues related to client computer configuration.	1.2

Lab 1.1 Installing Windows Server 2003

Objectives

The goal of this lab is to install Windows Server 2003 with the configuration necessary to complete the labs as laid out in this manual.

Materials Required

This lab will require the following:

- Windows Server 2003 Enterprise Edition CD

- A computer meeting the hardware requirements outlined for this course

Estimated completion time: **60 minutes**

Activity Background

In order to deploy Windows Server 2003 on your network, you need to be familiar with the installation process. During the installation of Windows Server 2003, you must make several choices: selecting licensing modes, choosing a file system for the installation partition, planning partitions and volumes, configuring Transmission Control Protocol/Internet Protocol (TCP/IP) addresses and name resolution settings, and choosing between joining a workgroup or a domain.

ACTIVITY

Activity

1. Insert the Windows Server 2003 Enterprise Edition CD-ROM into your computer and reboot the system. When you see the message "Press any key to boot from CD," press any key on your keyboard. If you have inserted the CD-ROM and do not see this prompt, you will need to configure the BIOS on your system to boot from CD-ROM.

2. If your CD is the MSDN version you will have the option to select either Standard or Enterprise Edition. If this is the case, select the Enterprise Edition installation option. The Windows Setup screen appears. Setup loads all necessary files. When the Welcome to Setup page appears, press **Enter** to begin the Windows Server 2003 Enterprise Edition setup.

3. When the Windows Licensing Agreement page appears, press the **F8** key on your keyboard to indicate that you agree with the licensing agreement.

4. The Windows Server 2003 Enterprise Edition setup page appears. If your server has a previous installation of Windows Server 2003, you may be prompted to repair the existing installation. If given this option, press the **Esc** key to install a fresh copy of Windows without repairing.

1

5. Delete all partitions on your system to begin the fresh install. If only unpartitioned space is shown, skip to Step 6. Otherwise, for each existing partition, complete the following: Use the arrow keys to highlight the partition you want to delete. Press **D** to delete the selected partition. Press **Enter** to confirm the deletion of this partition. Press **L** to reconfirm the deletion of this partition. Repeat these actions to select and delete each remaining partition.

6. Press **C** to create a new partition. In the Create partition of size (in MB): text box, type **4096** and press **Enter**. This creates a 4 GB partition to install Windows Server 2003. It is a good practice to keep the operating system on a separate partition from data and applications. This ensures that if a data or application partition runs out of disk space, the operating system will be unaffected.

7. Select **C: Partition1[New (Raw)]** using the up/down arrow keys on your keyboard, and press **Enter** to install.

8. Press the letter **C** on the keyboard to continue setup using this partition.

9. Select **Format the partition using the NTFS file system (Quick)**, if necessary, and press **Enter** to continue.

10. Setup formats drive C:, examines the disks on the computer, and then copies files to the Windows Installation folders. This may take several minutes to complete.

11. Once the file copy completes, you will be prompted to remove the CD-ROM and the system will reboot. Remove your CD-ROM and allow the system to reboot. If you accidentally leave your CD-ROM in the system, be sure not to press a key when the message "Press any key to boot from CD" appears. When the system reboots, a graphical installation screen appears. If the screen blinks now and again, it is most likely detecting your system hardware devices. On the Regional and Language Options page, click **Next** to accept the default language setting of English (United States) and the default text input language and method of the U.S. keyboard layout.

12. On the Personalize your Software page, type **Your Name** in the Name field, and type **Arctic University** in the Organization field. Click **Next**.

13. In the Product Key text box, type the product key (which is written on your evaluation copy CD or provided by your instructor), and click **Next**.

14. On the Licensing Modes page, confirm that Per server is selected in the Number of concurrent connections field and then type **50**. Click **Next**.

15. On the Computer Name and Administrator Password page, type **StudentXX** for the server name (where *XX* is your assigned student number).

16. In the Type an Administrator Password field, type **Password!** in both the Administrator password and Confirm password fields. Click **Next**.

17. On the Date and Time Settings page, ensure that the date, time, and time zone are correct, and then click **Next**.

18. On the Network Settings page, ensure that **Typical Settings** is selected. This will automatically detect and install the network drivers for your network cards. By default, each card will be configured to obtain an IP address automatically. Later on in this lab activity, you will modify these settings. Click **Next** to continue.

19. On the Workgroup or Computer Domain page, select **No, this computer is not on a network, or is on a network without a domain**, if necessary. Click **Next** to continue. Finalizing installation completes and the system restarts.

20. After your server reboots, log on as **Administrator**. The first time you log on to your server, the Manage Your Server window appears. Click **Don't display this page at logon** and close the Manage Your Server window.

21. Next you are going to rename the network connections to help identify each network connection for the lab activities that follow. First, disconnect the crossover cable that connects your server to your partner's server. Click **Start**, point to **Control Panel**, and double-click **Network Connections**. There will be two network connections. One of them shows the status Network cable unplugged. This is the private connection between your server and your partner's server. The network connection with the status Enabled is connected to the classroom network.

22. Right-click the network connection with the status Enabled, click **Rename**, type **Classroom**, and press **Enter**.

23. Right-click the network connection with the status Network cable unplugged, click **Rename**, type **Private**, and press **Enter**.

24. Now you need to configure the IP address on your Classroom connection. Right-click **Classroom** and click **Properties**. Click **Internet Protocol (TCP/IP)** and click the **Properties** button.

25. Click **Use the following IP address**. In the IP address text box, type **192.168.1.1XX**, where *XX* is your assigned student number. In the Subnet mask text box, type **255.255.255.0**.

26. In the Default gateway text box, type **192.168.1.10**, unless the instructor specifies otherwise. (Depending on how the classroom has been configured for Internet access, this may vary.)

27. In the Preferred DNS server text box, type **192.168.1.10** and click **OK**. Click **Close**. Close the Network Connections window.

28. Reconnect the crossover cable that connects your server to your partner's server.

29. Next you are going to join your computer to the Arctic.local domain. Click **Start**, right-click **My Computer**, and click **Properties**.

30. In the System Properties dialog box, click the **Computer Name** tab.

31. Click **Change**.

32. In the Member of field in the Computer Name Changes dialog box, click **Domain**. Type **Arctic.local** and click **OK**.

33. In the Computer Name Changes dialog box, type **Administrator** in the User name field, type **Password!** in the Password field, and click **OK**. This account has the necessary permissions to add computers to the domain.

34. A message appears, welcoming you to the Arctic.local domain. Click **OK**.

35. A message appears, indicating that you must restart this computer for the changes to take effect. Click **OK**.

36. Click **OK** to close the System Properties dialog box. Click **Yes**.

37. After your computer has rebooted and the Welcome to Windows dialog box appears, press **Ctrl+Alt+Delete** to begin the logon process.

38. In the Log on to Windows dialog box, type **Password!** in the Password field. Click **Options**. Click the **Log on to** drop-down arrow, and click **ARCTIC**. Click **OK**.

39. In the Manage Your Server window, click the **Don't display this page at logon** check box, and then close the window.

40. Right-click **Start** and click **Explore**.

41. Click the CD-ROM drive that contains your Windows Server 2003 Enterprise Edition CD. Right-click the **i386** directory on the CD, and click **Copy**.

42. Right-click **Local Disk (C:)** and click **Paste**.

43. Close Windows Explorer.

Certification Objectives

Objective for Microsoft Exam #70-293: Planning a Microsoft Windows Server 2003 Network:

- Evaluate and select the operating system to install on computers in an enterprise.

REVIEW QUESTIONS

1. What is the default licensing mode on Windows Server 2003?

    a. Per Device

    b. Per User

    c. Per Device or User

    d. Per Server

2. Which file system is recommended for the installation partition?

   a. FAT

   b. FAT32

   c. NTFS

   d. all of the above

3. What is the minimum amount of RAM that is recommended for a Windows Server 2003 installation?

   a. 64 MB

   b. 128 MB

   c. 256 MB

   d. 512 MB

4. Which of the following recommendations should you follow before installing Windows Server 2003?

   a. running a preinstallation compatibility check from the CD

   b. checking hardware and software compatibility information from Microsoft

   c. checking drivers and system bios or firmware

   d. all of the above

5. Which of the following steps could you follow when joining your Windows Server 2003 system to an Active Directory domain?

   a. Log onto the local computer as a member of the local Administrators group and open the system applet in Control Panel.

   b. Use the runas command to open the system from a command line as an Administrator.

   c. Provide credentials of a user with permissions to create a computer account or to join a computer to the domain.

   d. all of the above

LAB 1.2 NETWORK ARCHITECTURE: VIEWING AND MODIFYING BINDINGS

Objectives

The goal of this lab is to gain an understanding of this specification by installing protocols and modifying the binding order of installed protocols.

Materials Required

This lab will require the following:

- Windows Server 2003 installed and configured according to Lab 1.1

Estimated completion time:**15 minutes**

Activity Background

Network Driver Interface Specification (NDIS) allows multiple transport protocols to be bound to a single network adapter card. For this reason, network driver development is improved because programmers no longer have to create drivers to interact with each individual protocol. Instead, drivers need only interact with NDIS.

Activity

1. To view the default bindings prior to installing additional protocols, click **Start**, point to **Control Panel**, and double-click **Network Connections**.

2. In the Network Connections window, click **Advanced** on the menu bar, and click **Advanced Settings**. The Adapters and Bindings tab in the Advanced Settings dialog box should now be visible, as shown in Figure 1-1.

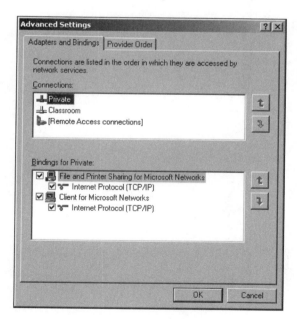

Figure 1-1   Advanced Settings dialog box

3. As indicated in the Bindings for Classroom section, the Internet Protocol TCP/IP protocol is bound to both File and Printer Sharing for Microsoft Networks and Client for Microsoft Networks. Next, you are going to install another protocol to see how the Adapters and Bindings tab is modified as a result. Click the **Cancel** button to close the Advanced Settings dialog box.

4. In the Network Connections window, right-click the **Classroom** connection, and click **Properties**.

5. In the Classroom Properties dialog box, shown in Figure 1-2, click **Install**.

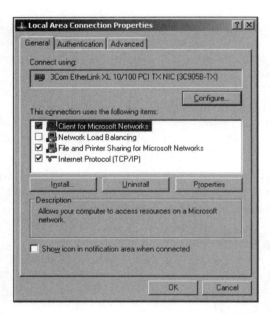

Figure 1-2   Classroom Properties dialog box

6. In the Select Network Component Type dialog box, click **Protocol** (as shown in Figure 1–3), and then click **Add**.

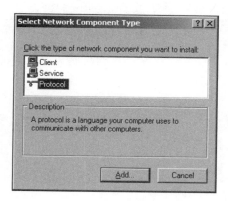

Figure 1-3   Select Network Component Type dialog box

7. In the Select Network Protocol dialog box, click **NWLink IPX/SPX/NetBIOS Compatible Transport Protocol** (as shown in Figure 1–4), and click **OK**.

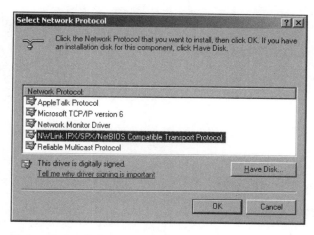

Figure 1-4   Select Network Protocol dialog box

8. Click **Close** to exit the Classroom Properties dialog box.

9. In the Network Connections window, click **Advanced** on the menu bar, and click **Advanced Settings**. As indicated on the Adapters and Bindings tab, the NWLink IPX/SPX/NetBIOS Compatible Transport Protocol is bound to both File and Printer Sharing for Microsoft Networks and Client for Microsoft Networks. See Figure 1-5.

Figure 1-5   Modified Classroom connection bindings

10. Under the File and Printer Sharing for Microsoft Networks option, click
NWLink IPX/SPX/NetBIOS Compatible Transport Protocol. The
down arrow is now green, as shown in Figure 1-6, indicating that it is now
available to use to change the order in which the protocols are implemented.

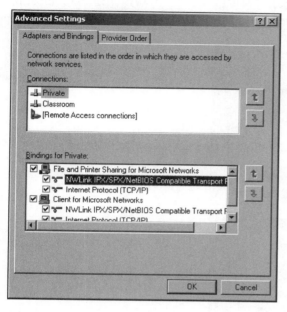

Figure 1-6   NWLink IPX/SPX/NetBIOS Compatible Transport Protocol at the top of the
binding order

11. Click the **down arrow**. The NWLink protocol moves below Internet Protocol TCP/IP, as shown in Figure 1-7. You have just changed the binding order for this service. With the current settings, Internet Protocol TCP/IP will be the first protocol attempted when accessing files or printers on other computers. If the protocol is unsuccessful, NWLink IPX/SPX/NetBIOS Compatible Transport Protocol would be attempted next.

Figure 1-7   Internet Protocol (TCP/IP) at the top of the binding order

12. Under the Client for Microsoft Networks option, click to deselect the **NWLink IPX/SPX/NetBIOS Compatible Transport Protocol** check box, as shown in Figure 1-8.

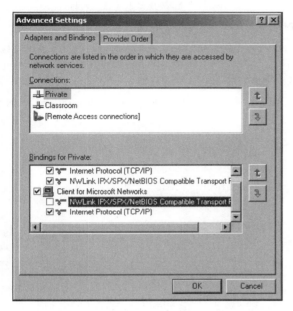

Figure 1-8   Unbinding NWLink IPX/SPX/NetBIOS Compatible Transport Protocol from Client for Microsoft Networks

13. Click the **question mark** in the upper-right corner of the Advanced Settings dialog box. A question mark will appear with the cursor as you move your mouse. Move the cursor next to the check box you cleared in the previous step and then click. A comment appears, as shown in Figure 1-9, that explains the configuration settings. If you did not want a protocol enabled or to be used with a particular service, you would click to deselect the check box.

> Lists the bindings for the selected connection. A binding is enabled if the check box is selected.

Figure 1-9   Bindings explained

14. Click **OK** to close the Advanced Settings dialog box.

15. You will now uninstall the NWLink IPX/SPX/NetBIOS Compatible Transport Protocol. In the Network Connections window, right-click **Classroom** and select **Properties**.

16. Click **NWLink IPX/SPX/NetBIOS Compatible Transport Protocol** and click **Uninstall**. A message appears, indicating that uninstalling a component removes it from all network connections. Click **Yes** to indicate you want to uninstall NWLink IPX/SPX/NetBIOS Compatible Transport Protocol.

17. Click **Close** to exit the Classroom Properties dialog box.

18. In the Network Connections window, click **Advanced** on the menu bar, and click **Advanced Settings**. The binding order has now changed back to what you started with at the beginning of this Activity.

19. Click **OK** to close the Advanced Settings dialog box. Then close the Network Connections window.

Certification Objectives

Objective for Microsoft Exam #70-293: Planning a Microsoft Windows Server 2003 Network:

- Diagnose and resolve issues related to client computer configuration.

REVIEW QUESTIONS

1. Which of the following services will all installed protocols be bound to by default?

   a. Client for Microsoft Networks

   b. File and Printer Sharing for Microsoft Networks

   c. Network Load Balancing

   d. all of the above

2. If multiple protocols are bound to a service, which protocol will be attempted first?

   a. the protocol highest in the binding order

   b. the protocol lowest in the binding order

   c. the fastest protocol

   d. none of the above

3. If you do not want a protocol bound to File and Printer Sharing for Microsoft Networks, what should you do?

   a. In the Advanced Settings dialog box, under the File and Printer Sharing for Microsoft Networks option, click to select the protocol.

   b. In the Advanced Settings dialog box, under the File and Printer Sharing for Microsoft Networks option, click to deselect the protocol.

   c. Do nothing; by default, the File and Printer Sharing for Microsoft Networks option is not bound to any protocol.

   d. none of the above

4. Which of the following can be installed by clicking the Install button on the General tab in the Local Area Connection Properties dialog box?

   a. a client

   b. a protocol

   c. a service

   d. all of the above

5. Which of the following protocols is installed by default on a Windows Server 2003 system?

   a. Appletalk

   b. Microsoft TCP/IP version 6

   c. Internet Protocol (TCP/IP)

   d. NWLink IPX/SPX/NetBIOS Compatible Transport protocol

LAB 1.3 COMPARING EDITIONS OF WINDOWS SERVER 2003

Objectives

The goal of this lab is to identify the unique features supported by the various editions of Windows Server 2003 to meet the requirements of a given network environment.

Materials Required

This lab will require the following:

- Internet access

- A Windows Server 2003 setup, as directed at the front of this lab manual

Estimated completion time: **10 minutes**

Activity Background

Much like its predecessors, Windows Server 2003 is available in multiple versions. One of the fundamental choices you need to make prior to implementing a Windows Server 2003 solution is deciding which version best suits the functionality you require. There are four versions: Web Edition, Standard Edition, Enterprise Edition, and Datacenter Edition.

Activity

1. Click the **Launch Internet Explorer Browser** shortcut on your Quick Launch taskbar to open Internet Explorer. The Internet Explorer Enhanced Security Configuration is enabled page appears in your browser window. A message may appear indicating that Microsoft Internet Explorer's Enhanced Security Configuration is currently enabled on your server. This enhanced level of security reduces the risk of attack from Web-based content that is not secure, but it may also prevent Web sites from displaying correctly and restrict access to network resources. Click **OK** to close the message box.

2. In the Address bar, type **www.microsoft.com/technet**, and then press **Enter**. Another message box appears, indicating that content from the Web site that you have entered into your browser window is being blocked by the Internet Explorer Enhanced Security Configuration. Uncheck the **Continue to prompt when Web site content is blocked** check box. Click **Close**.

3. The Web page appears. Click the **Products and Technologies** link and then scroll down under Products and Technologies and click the **Windows Server 2003** link.

4. On the Windows Server 2003 Resources page, under the Related Sites section, click the **Windows Server 2003 Site** link.

5. Point to **How to Buy** and then click the **Choosing the Right Operating System** link. The Compare the Editions of Windows Server 2003 page is displayed.

6. Read the information and take notes. Prepare a short report on one of the versions. Close Internet Explorer.

Certification Objectives

Objectives for Microsoft Exam #70-293: Planning a Microsoft Windows Server 2003 Network:

- Evaluate and select the OS to install on computers in an enterprise.

- Identify the minimum configuration to satisfy security requirements.

REVIEW QUESTIONS

1. Which v   ort for Intel Itanium
based co

   a. Standa

   b. Enterp

   c. Datace

   d. Web E

2. Which ve   Metadirectory Services (MM

   a. Standar

   b. Enterpr

   c. Datacen

   d. Web Edition

3. Which version of Windows Server 2003 does not support Internet Authentication
Service (IAS)?

   a. Standard Edition

   b. Enterprise Edition

   c. Datacenter Edition

   d. Web Edition

4. Which of the following features is not found in all versions of Windows Server
2003?

   a. Remote Desktop for Administration

   b. Terminal Server

   c. Network Load Balancing

   d. IPv6

5. Which of the following features is only partially supported in the Standard Edition
of Windows Server 2003?

   a. Active Directory

   b. public key infrastructure (PKI), certificate services, and smart cards

   c. Terminal Server Session Directory

   d. virtual private network (VPN) support

LAB 1.4 WINDOWS NT WORKSTATION 3.51 AND WINDOWS SERVER 2003

Objectives

The goal of this lab is to review the steps that must be taken in order to enable systems running Windows for Workgroups, Windows 95, and Windows NT 4.0 to log on and access resources on a Windows Server 2003 domain.

Materials Required

This lab will require the following:

- A Windows Server 2003 setup, as directed at the front of this lab manual

Estimated completion time: **15 minutes**

Activity Background

Some features and services of Windows Server 2003 are only available by default to newer Windows clients, such as Windows 2000, Windows XP, and Windows Server 2003. In order for older Windows clients to take advantage of the advanced security and Active Directory functionality, you may have to install service packs and the Active Directory client software. For example, Windows NT Workstation 3.51 is not a supported client OS with Windows Server 2003; therefore, you must install the service pack and Active Directory software.

ACTIVITY

Activity

1. Click **Start** and then click **Help and Support**. In the Help and Support Center window, type **Alphabetical List of features** in the Search field and then click the **green arrow**.

2. Under Help Topics in the Search Results window, click the **Alphabetical list of features: Getting Started** topic. Read the list of features supported in the Windows Server 2003 product family, and then click the **Operating system migration, support, and integration** topic.

3. Note that Windows NT Workstation 3.51 is not listed as a supported client. To determine why it has been excluded, type **"compatibility with previous operating systems"** (be sure to include the quotation marks because you want to obtain an exact match for this phrase) in the Search field, and then click the **green arrow**.

4. Under Help Topics, click the **Compatibility with previous operating systems: Active Directory** topic. Read the information provided in the details pane. Explore any related topics linked to this page. Close the Help and Support Center window.

Certification Objectives

Objective for Microsoft Exam #70-293: Planning a Microsoft Windows Server 2003 Network:

- Identify the minimum configuration to satisfy security requirements.

REVIEW QUESTIONS

1. Which of the following actions can be performed so a client computer running Windows 95 can successfully log on to the domain and access domain resources? (Choose all that apply.)

   a. install the Active Directory Client

   b. upgrade the operating system

   c. install service pack 4 or later

   d. install the Domain 95 service pack

2. Which of the following client computers can, by default, connect to domain controllers running Windows Server 2003? (Choose all that apply.)

   a. Windows for Workgroups

   b. Windows 95 without the Active Directory Client

   c. Windows 95 with the Active Directory Client

   d. Windows NT 4.0 service pack 2

3. Although it is *not* recommended that you take this action, you can prevent domain controllers from requiring SMB signing by editing the Default Domain Controllers Policy and disabling the _____ settings under the Security Options section.

   a. Microsoft network client: digitally sign communications (if server agrees)

   b. Microsoft network client: digitally sign communications (always)

   c. Microsoft network server: digitally sign communications (if server agrees)

   d. Microsoft network server: digitally sign communications (always)

4. Which of the following is not a supported feature with the Active Directory client on Windows 95, Windows 98, and Windows NT 4.0?

   a. site awareness

   b. NTLM version 2 authentication

   c. mutual authentication

   d. Active Directory search capability

5. Which of the following statements is false?

   a. Domain controllers running Windows Server 2003 require that all secure channel communications be either encrypted or signed.

   b. Client computers running Windows NT 4.0 service pack 3 (or earlier) support signing or encrypting secure channel communications.

   c. Trusts between domains with domain controllers running Windows NT 4.0 service pack 3 (or earlier) and domains with domain controllers running Windows Server 2003 may fail.

   d. Installing Windows Server 2003 domain controllers into the same domain as Windows 2000 domain controllers will not affect existing domain controller security settings.

LAB 1.5 NEW AND UPDATED FEATURES ON WINDOWS SERVER 2003

Objectives

The goal of this lab is to use the Help and Support Center to identify the improvements that have been made since Windows NT 4.0 and Windows 2000 Server platforms were released.

Materials Required

This lab will require the following:

- Windows Server 2003 installed and configured according to the instructions at the beginning of this lab manual

Estimated completion time: **5 minutes**

Activity Background

When rolling out a new server operating system, you should be familiar with the features and capabilities of that server platform in order to address the requirements of your network environment. As with all newer versions of software and operating systems on the market today, Windows Server 2003 offers many features that were previously unavailable with earlier Windows server platforms.

Activity

1. Click **Start** and click **Help and Support**, if necessary.

2. In the Help and Support Center window, type **network protocols and technologies** in the Search field, and then click the **green arrow**.

3. In the Search Results field, under Help Topics, click **Network protocols and technologies: Getting Started**. The details pane displays the information related to the selected topic. Note that Windows Server 2003 offers new and updated features that were previously unavailable for both Windows NT 4.0 and Windows 2000.

4. Review the advancements that have been made with the Windows Server 2003 operating system. Close the Help and Support Center window.

Certification Objectives

Objectives for Microsoft Exam #70-293: Planning a Microsoft Windows Server 2003 Network:

- Evaluate and select the operating system to install on computers in an enterprise.

REVIEW QUESTIONS

1. Which of the following network protocols is no longer available on editions of Windows Server 2003? (Choose all that apply.)

   a. Data Link Control (DLC) protocol

   b. Internet Protocol (TCP/IP)

   c. NetBIOS Extended User Interface (NetBEUI)

   d. NWLink IPX/SPX/NetBIOS-compatible transport protocol

2. Which of the following protocols is not available on the 64-bit version of Windows Server 2003? (Choose all that apply.)

   a. Internet Protocol (TCP/IP)

   b. Internetwork Packet Exchange/Sequenced Packet Exchange (IPX/SPX)

   c. Open Shortest Path First (OSPF)

   d. all of the above

3. Which of the following editions of Windows Server 2003 supports infrared (IR) networking?

   a. Web Edition

   b. Standard Edition

   c. Enterprise Edition

   d. Datacenter Edition

4. Which version of Windows Server 2003 does not support Internet Connection Sharing (ICS)? (Choose all that apply.)

   a. Web Edition

   b. Standard Edition

   c. Enterprise Edition

   d. Datacenter Edition

5. Which of the following features is not supported on Windows 2000?

   a. configuring IAS to forward radius authentication and accounting requests to another radius server

   b. 802.1x authentication enabled by default

   c. IP version 6

   d. all of the above

CHAPTER 2

TCP/IP ARCHITECTURE

Labs included in this chapter:

- ◆ Lab 2.1 Demonstrating APIPA and the Alternate Configuration Tab
- ◆ Lab 2.2 ARP and Network Monitor
- ◆ Lab 2.3 Using Network Monitor to Capture APIPA Traffic
- ◆ Lab 2.4 Local Area Connection Troubleshooting
- ◆ Lab 2.5 Using Netsh Interface IP

Microsoft MCSE Exam #70-293 Objectives	
Objective	Lab
Diagnose and resolve issues related to client computer configuration.	2.1, 2.4, 2.5
Diagnose and resolve issues related to DHCP server address assignment.	2.1, 2.5
Plan network traffic monitoring. Tools might include Network Monitor and System Monitor.	2.2, 2.3

Lab 2.1 Demonstrating APIPA and the Alternate Configuration Tab

Objectives

The goal of this lab is to investigate both the APIPA and User configured options on the Alternate Configuration tab.

Materials Required:

This lab will require the following:

- Windows 2003 Server installed and configured according to the instructions at the beginning of this lab manual

Estimated completion time: **15 minutes**

Activity Background

The Alternate Configuration tab provides portable computers with the flexibility to be used on more than one network without their TCP/IP protocol settings being manually reconfigured. The Alternate Configuration tab becomes available when a computer is configured to obtain an IP address automatically. Should a DHCP (Dynamic Host Configuration Protocol) server not be available on the network, the system can use either an APIPA address or a manually configured IP address.

APIPA (Automatic Private IP Addressing) is the default setting. Should a DHCP server not respond, the client computer will assign its own IP address. One option that will not be assigned with this method is a default gateway. As a result of not being configured with a default gateway, these systems will be restricted to communicating with other systems on that subnet that are also configured with APIPA addresses. As you would expect, this feature works well only on single subnet networks and on networks that do not require Internet access.

Using the User configured option on the Alternate Configuration tab, you can manually configure additional settings such as a default gateway, DNS addresses, and WINS server addresses.

Activity

ACTIVITY

1. Log on as **Administrator** to the Arctic.local domain with the password **Password!**.

2. Click **Start**, point to **Control Panel**, and then double-click **Network Connections**. In the Network Connections window, right-click the **Classroom** connection and click **Properties**. Click **Internet Protocol (TCP/IP)** and click **Properties** to open the Internet Protocol (TCP/IP) Properties dialog box.

3. Click to select the **Obtain an IP address automatically** option, as shown in Figure 2-1. The Alternate Configuration tab becomes visible. Click the **Obtain DNS server address automatically** option.

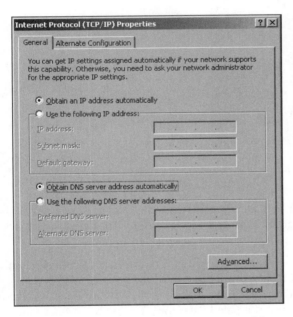

Figure 2-1   Selecting the Obtain an IP address automatically option

4. Click the **Alternate Configuration** tab. Unless you have already configured a User configured address on the Alternate Configuration tab, it will default to the setting Automatic private IP address, as shown in Figure 2-2.

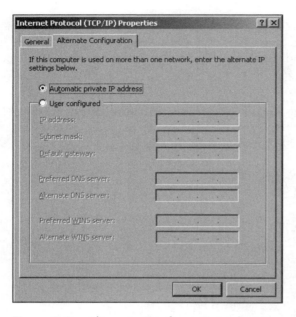

Figure 2-2 Alternate Configuration tab

5. Click the **Automatic private IP address** radio button, if necessary, and click **OK** to close the Internet Protocol (TCP/IP) Properties dialog box. Click **Close** to close the Classroom Properties dialog box.

6. To observe what this setting does to your IP address, click **Start**, click **Run**, type **cmd**, and click **OK**. In the Command Prompt window, type **ipconfig /renew** and press **Enter**. After a while, the message "An error occurred while renewing interface Classroom: unable to contact your DHCP server. Request has timed out" appears.

7. In the Command Prompt window, type **ipconfig** and press **Enter**. It may take a few seconds for your computer to configure itself with an IP address. Your IP configuration settings should appear, as shown in Figure 2-3. Note the IP address that you have obtained. The first two octets of your IP address should be 169.254 and should identify your computer as being on the 169.254.0.0 subnet. The last two octets of your IP address are generated by your computer in such a way so as to ensure that you have a unique IP address on the network. If your classmates are performing this exercise at the same time, each privately generated IP address will be unique on the subnet.

```
Command Prompt                                                    _ □ ×

C:\Documents and Settings\Administrator>ipconfig

Windows IP Configuration

Ethernet adapter Classroom:

        Connection-specific DNS Suffix  . :
        Autoconfiguration IP Address. . . : 169.254.26.134
        Subnet Mask . . . . . . . . . . . : 255.255.0.0
        Default Gateway . . . . . . . . . :

C:\Documents and Settings\Administrator>
```

Figure 2-3   An autoconfiguration IP address

 NOTE Consider the scenario where you have a laptop computer. The corporate office has Windows Server 2003 running DHCP, so your laptop can obtain an IP address from the server. At the remote office where you work from time to time, there is no DHCP server; therefore, a static IP address needs to be configured in order to communicate on that network.

 NOTE In the next part of this lab, you will modify the TCP/IP configuration settings to set up a laptop so regardless of which network that it is connected to, you will be able to access resources on the local network.

8. In the Network Connections window, right-click the **Classroom** connection, and click **Properties**. In the Classroom Properties dialog box, click **Internet Protocol (TCP/IP)** and click **Properties**. Click the **Alternate Configuration** tab, and then click the **User configured** option button, shown in Figure 2-4.

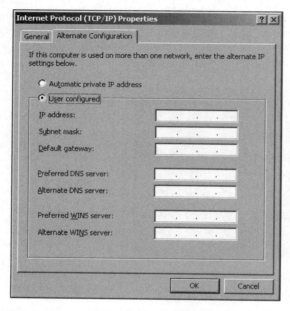

Figure 2-4   Selecting the User configured option

9. To configure a static IP address for your laptop (your computer), type the following information:

IP address	**192.168**.x.x (where x is your assigned student number)
Preferred DNS server	**192.168.x.10**
Preferred WINS server	**192.168.x.10**

10. Click **OK** to close the Internet Protocol (TCP/IP) Properties dialog box, and then click **Close** to close the Classroom Properties dialog box.

11. In the Command Prompt window, type **ipconfig** and press **Enter**. Your TCP/IP configuration information should reflect the values you just entered. When the laptop is started in the remote office, it will automatically assign itself this address if no DHCP server is available. Close the Command Prompt window.

12. You will now change the configuration information back to the original settings. In the Network Connections window, right-click the **Classroom** connection, and click **Properties**. Click **Internet Protocol (TCP/IP)** and click **Properties**. On the General tab, click the **Use the following IP address** option button, and then enter the following information:

IP address	192.168.1.1*XX* (where *XX* is your assigned student number)
Subnet mask	255.255.255.0
Default gateway	192.168.1.10
Preferred DNS server	192.168.1.10

13. When you are finished, click **OK** to close the dialog box, and then click **Close** to close the Classroom Properties dialog box. Close the Network Connection window.

Certification Objectives

Objectives for Microsoft Exam #70-293: Planning a Microsoft Windows Server 2003 Network:

■ Diagnose and resolve issues related to client computer configuration.

■ Diagnose and resolve issues related to DHCP server address assignment.

REVIEW QUESTIONS

1. To view the Alternate Configuration tab, click the _____ option on the General tab of the Internet Protocol (TCP/IP) Properties dialog box.

   a. Obtain an IP address automatically

   b. Use the following IP address

   c. Obtain DNS server address automatically

   d. Use the following DNS server addresses

2. If a DHCP server offers a lease, what will be the result?

   a. If the client computer is configured to obtain an IP address automatically, it will obtain an IP address through DHCP.

   b. The client computer will use a static IP address configured on the Alternate Configuration tab instead.

   c. The client computer will be assigned an IP address in the range 169.254.*x*.*y*.

   d. none of the above

3. When your computer obtains an automatic private IP address, which of the following options are not assigned? (Choose all that apply.)

   a. IP address

   b. Subnet mask

   c. Default gateway

   d. DNS Server

4. When your computer obtains an automatic private IP address, with which of the following subnets would your computer be able to communicate? (Choose all that apply.)

   a. 192.168.1.0

   b. 10.0.0.0

   c. 172.30.0.0

   d. 169.254.0.0

5. In order to make TCP/IP configuration changes and to renew and release TCP/IP addresses, you need to belong to which of the following groups? (Choose all that apply.)

   a. Administrators

   b. DHCP Users

   c. Network Configuration Operators

   d. Power Users

LAB 2.2 ARP AND NETWORK MONITOR

Objectives

The goal of this this lab is to use Network Monitor to view the information that is transmitted through the ARP protocol.

Materials Required

This lab will require the following:

- Windows Server 2003 installed and configured according to the instructions at the beginning of this lab manual

2

Estimated completion time: **30 minutes**

Activity Background

Network Monitor is a tool that you can use to capture and analyze traffic when trouble-shooting problems on a network. The ARP (Address Resolution Protocol) is one of the protocols in the TCP/IP protocol stack. Its function is to resolve IP addresses to MAC addresses. To ensure that a network adapter card is able to identify which packets have been sent to it, the MAC address is included in all packets sent to remote systems on the network. After an ARP request is received, the destination computer adds an IP address to MAC address mapping for the sending computer to its local ARP cache and responds to the request. When the sending computer receives the reply, it adds the mapping for the destination computer to its local ARP cache.

ACTIVITY

Activity

NOTE

If you have not already installed Network Monitor, you need to complete Part A of this lab. If Network Monitor is already installed, you can skip to Part B.

Part A:

1. Log on as **Administrator** to the Arctic.local domain with the password **Password!**.

2. Click **Start**, point to **Control Panel**, and double-click **Network Connections**.

3. In the Network Connections window, click **Advanced** on the menu bar, and then click **Optional Networking Components**.

4. In the Windows Optional Networking Components Wizard dialog box, click **Management and Monitoring Tools**, if necessary (as shown in Figure 2-5).

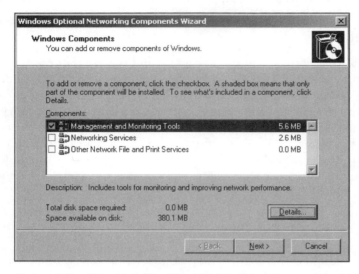

Figure 2-5   Windows Optional Networking Components Wizard dialog box

5. Click **Details** to display the Management and Monitoring Tools dialog box. Check the **Network Monitor Tools** check box (as shown in Figure 2-6) and click **OK**.

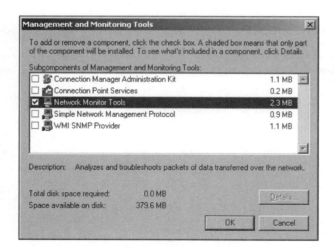

Figure 2-6   Selecting Network Monitor Tools in the Management and Monitoring Tools dialog box

6. In the Windows Optional Networking Components Wizard dialog box, click **Next**. When the Insert Disk dialog box appears, click **OK**.

7. In the Files Needed dialog box, click **Browse** to select the location from which you will be copying the necessary files. In the Locate File dialog box, navigate to the **C:\I386** directory and click **Open**. Click the file named **BHSUPP.DL_**, as shown in Figure 2-7. Click **Open**.

Figure 2-7   Locating the file to install Network Monitor tools

8. In the Files Needed dialog box, verify that the location in the Copy Files From field displays C:\I386, then click **OK**.

9. Close the Network Connections window.

Part B:

1. If necessary, log on as **Administrator** to the Arctic.local domain with a password of **Password!**.

2. Click **Start**, point to **Administrative Tools**, and click **Network Monitor**.

3. If you receive the Microsoft Network Monitor message, indicating that you need to specify the network on which you want to capture data, click **OK**. If you do not receive this message, you will need to verify that the appropriate network card has been selected. In Microsoft Network Monitor, click **Capture** on the menu bar and then click **Networks**.

4. In the Select a network dialog box, click the **plus sign** next to Local Computer. Under Local Computer, click **Classroom**, as shown in Figure 2-8, and click **OK**. The Microsoft Network Monitor window opens, as shown in Figure 2-9.

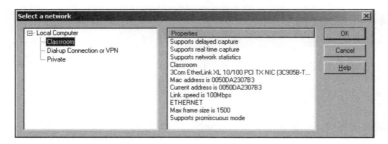

Figure 2-8   Selecting the Classroom connection in the Select a network dialog box

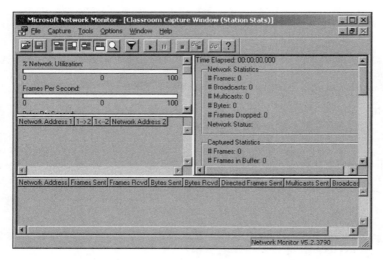

Figure 2-9   Microsoft Network Monitor

5. Click **Start**, click **Run**, type **cmd**, and click **OK**.

6. In the Microsoft Network Monitor window, click **Capture** on the menu bar, and click **Start**.

7. Switch to the Command Prompt window, type **ping 192.168.1.1XX** (where XX represents another student's assigned number), and press **Enter**. As soon as you see the Reply from 192.168.1.1XX response, switch to the Microsoft Network Monitor window.

8. In the Microsoft Network Monitor window, click the **Stop and View Capture** shortcut (the icon looks like eyeglasses next to a square). The capture results now display, as shown in Figure 2-10. You will now analyze the contents of these frames.

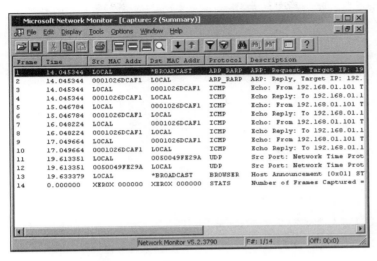

Figure 2-10   Capture results

9. In the Microsoft Network Monitor window, look for the ARP_RARP protocol in the Protocol column and click the frame that was captured. You will now filter the frames captured to display only the ARP_RARP frames. Click the **Edit Display Filter** button on the shortcut menu (the icon looks like a funnel). (If you move your mouse over this icon for a few seconds, the tip will read Edit Display Filter.) The Display Filter dialog box opens.

10. Click **Protocol==Any** and click **Edit Expression**.

11. In the Expression dialog box, click **Disable All**. Under Disabled Protocols, click **ARP_RARP** and click **Enable**. See Figure 2-11. Click **OK** to close the Expression dialog box. The Display Filter dialog box refreshes.

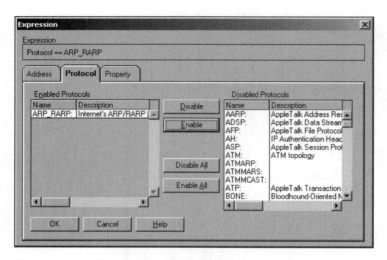

Figure 2-11   Filtering for ARP_RARP

12. The Display Filter dialog box displays Protocol==ARP_RARP (as shown in Figure 2-12). Click **OK** to close the Display Filter dialog box. Only ARP traffic should now be displayed in the Microsoft Network Monitor window.

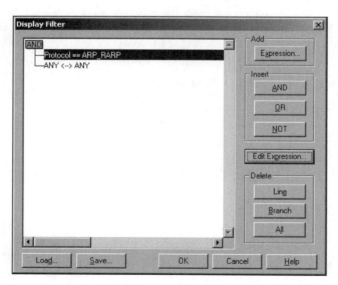

Figure 2-12   Display Filter dialog box

2

13. In the Description column, find the frame with the text "ARP: Request Target IP: 192.168.1.*XX*" (where *XX* completes the unique IP address of the computer you have just pinged), as shown in Figure 2-13. Double-click this frame. In the middle panel of the window, double-click **Ethernet: EType=ARP**. Notice that the Destination address is FFFFFFFFFFFF. The Source address field displays the MAC address for the network adapter card, as shown in Figure 2-14.

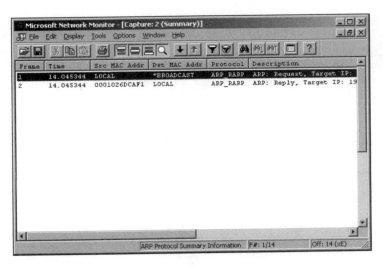

Figure 2-13 ARP Request frame

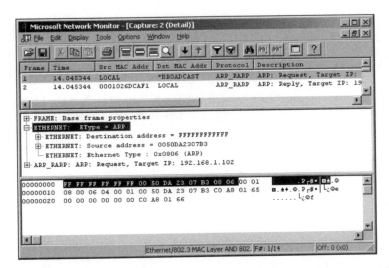

Figure 2-14 Examining the Destination address and Source address fields

14. Double-click the last entry in the middle panel of the Microsoft Network Monitor window, which displays as ARP_RARP ARP: Request, Target IP: 192.168.1.*XX*, where *XX* completes the IP address of the computer you just pinged. Note that the Sender's Hardware Address is the MAC address of your network adapter card. The Sender's Protocol Address is your IP address. The Target's Hardware Address is presently all zeroes because this is the information the ARP protocol is trying to obtain. The Target's Protocol Address is the IP address of the computer you just pinged. See Figure 2-15.

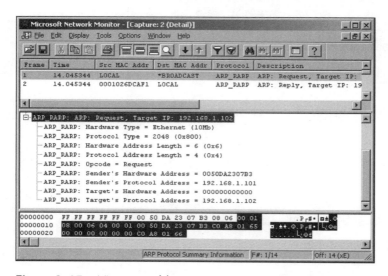

Figure 2-15   Viewing addresses

15. Next, you will look at the ARP: Reply message. In the top panel in the Microsoft Network Monitor window, click **ARP: Reply, Target IP: 192.168.1.*XX* Target Hdwr Addr: XXXXXXXXXXXX**. The contents of the frame are displayed in the middle panel of the Network Monitor window.

16. In the middle panel of the display, double-click **Ethernet: EType=ARP**. This is the reply from the computer you just pinged. The Destination address is the MAC address of the server at which you are sitting. The Source address is the MAC address of the network card on the server you just pinged. See Figure 2-16.

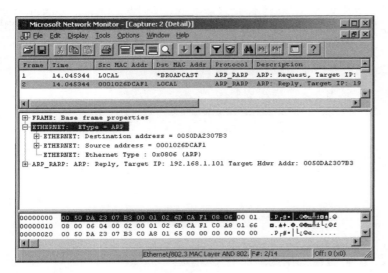

Figure 2-16   ARP Reply packet

17. In the middle panel, double-click **ARP_RARP: ARP: Reply, Target IP: 192.168.1.1XX Target Hdwr Addr: XXXXXXXXXXXX** to expand it, if necessary. Note that the Sender's Hardware Address is the MAC address of the network card on the computer you pinged. The Sender's Protocol Address is the IP address on the network card of the computer you just pinged. The Target's Hardware Address is the MAC address of your computer's network card. The Target's Protocol Address is your computer's IP address. See Figure 2-17.

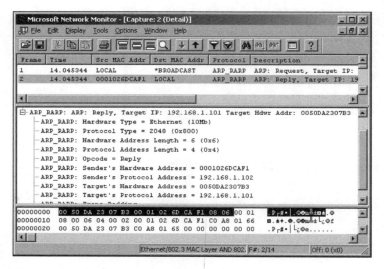

Figure 2-17   Viewing a capture

18. To save this capture for further analysis, click **File** on the menu and click **Save As**. In the Save As dialog box in the File name field, type **Lab 2–2 ARP Traffic** and click **Save**.

19. Close the Microsoft Network Monitor window, and then close the Command Prompt window.

Certification Objectives

Objectives for Microsoft Exam #70-293: Planning a Microsoft Windows Server 2003 Network:

- Plan network traffic monitoring. Tools might include Network Monitor and System Monitor.

REVIEW QUESTIONS

2

1. In an ARP Request frame, which of the following is unknown?

    a. sender's hardware address

    b. sender's protocol address

    c. target's hardware address

    d. target's protocol address

2. Static entries remain in the ARP cache ____. (Choose all that apply.)

    a. until the computer is restarted

    b. for 2 minutes

    c. for a maximum of 10 minutes

    d. until the interface is reinitiated

3. Which of the following events causes an interface to be reinitiated? (Choose all that apply).

    a. The interface is disabled and then enabled.

    b. The Repair feature is used.

    c. The computer awakes from a suspend or hibernation state.

    d. You removed or replugged a network cable, or a computer was moved out of and back into wireless range.

    e. The commands ipconfig /release and ipconfig /renew are given.

4. Which command would you use to remove static entries from the ARP cache?

    a. arp −a

    b. arp −d

    c. arp −g

    d. arp −s

5. Which of the following statements are true? (Choose all that apply.)

    a. If a dynamic entry is not reused within 2 minutes of being added, it expires and is removed from the ARP cache.

    b. Multiple network adapters share a single ARP cache.

    c. The ARP cache contains both static and dynamic entries.

    d. An entry that keeps getting used can stay in the ARP cache for a maximum lifetime of 10 minutes.

Lab 2.3 Using Network Monitor to Capture APIPA Traffic

Objectives

The goal of this lab is to view the information transmitted when a Windows Server 2003 system attempts to configure itself with an automatic private IP address.

Materials Required

This lab will require the following:

- Windows Server 2003 installed and configured according to the instructions at the beginning of this lab manual

Estimated completion time: **30 minutes**

Activity Background

APIPA (Automatic Private IP Addressing) is a feature used by TCP/IP to provide automatic IP configuration to Windows Server 2003 systems in the event that a DHCP server is not available on that subnet. You can use Network Monitor to capture and analyze traffic on your network.

Activity

1. Log on as **Administrator** to the Arctic.local domain with a password of **Password!**.

2. If necessary, install Network Monitor. If you are unsure of how to do so, refer to Part A of Lab 2.2.

3. Click **Start**, point to **Control Panel**, and double-click **Network Connections**.

4. In the Network Connections window, right-click the **Private** connection, and click **Disable**.

5. Right-click the **Classroom** connection and click **Properties**.

6. In the Classroom Properties dialog box, click **Internet Protocol (TCP/IP)** and click **Properties**.

7. In the Internet Protocol (TCP/IP) Properties dialog box, you will see that your computer is now configured with the Use the following IP address option. Take note of the IP address that has been assigned to your computer; you will be configuring your Classroom connection properties back to these settings at the end of this lab. Click the **Obtain an IP address automatically** option button. Click the **Alternate Configuration** tab, click the **Automatic private IP address** option, and then click **OK**. Click **Close** to close the Classroom Properties dialog box.

8. Click **Start**, point to **Administrative Tools**, and then click **Network Monitor**.

9. In the Microsoft Network Monitor window, click **Capture** on the menu bar, and click **Start**.

10. Click **Start**, click **Run**, type **cmd**, and click **OK**.

11. In the Command Prompt window, type **ipconfig /release** and press **Enter**.

12. In the Command Prompt window, type **ipconfig /renew** and press **Enter**. You are trying to obtain an IP address from a DHCP server. Because there is no DHCP server configured on the network at this point in time, your system will need to configure an APIPA address. After a while, a message displays, indicating that an error occurred. This behavior is to be expected when there are no DHCP servers available on the network. Close the Command Prompt window.

13. Switch to the Microsoft Network Monitor window, and click the **Stop and View Capture** icon on the shortcut bar (or press the **Shift + F11** keys).

14. In the Microsoft Network Monitor window, look at the Protocol column to view the DHCP traffic. Double-click on the first frame in your capture that matches the following fields:

Src MAC Addr	Dst MAC Addr	Protocol	Description	Src Other Addr	Dst Other Addr
LOCAL	*BROADCAST	DHCP	Discover	0.0.0.0	255.255.255.255

Note that under the Description column, the entry for this frame will begin with Discover.

15. In the middle panel in the Microsoft Network Monitor screen, double-click **ETHERNET: EType – Internet IP (IPv4)**. The Destination address of the frame is listed as FFFFFFFFFFFF, and the source address is the MAC address of your network adapter card.

16. Double-click **IP: Protocol=UDP – User Datagram** (the third component of the frame, which can be analyzed, located in the middle panel of the screen). Under the IP Source Address field, the IP address is 0.0.0.0 and the IP Destination Address is 255.255.255.255 (a broadcast). These discover packets are sent by your Windows Server 2003 system as it looks for a DHCP server from which to obtain an IP address.

17. In the top panel of the Microsoft Network Monitor window, find the packet that matches the following criteria, and then double click the frame:

Src MAC Addr	Dst MAC Addr	Protocol	Description
LOCAL	*BROADCAST	ARP_RARP	ARP: Request, Target IP: 169.254.x.y

18. In the middle panel of the Microsoft Network Monitor window, click the **+** next to ETHERNET: EType=ARP. The Destination address is FFFFFFFFFFFF. This message is being broadcast on the network. The Source address is the MAC address of your Classroom connection network adapter card.

19. Click the **+** next to ARP_RARP: ARP: Request, Target IP: 169.254.*x.y*. The sender's hardware address is the MAC address of your Classroom connection network adapter card. The Sender Protocol Address and the Target Protocol Address fields are the same. In this packet, your system is attempting to verify if the IP address it has selected is currently in use on the network. In the top panel of the Microsoft Network Monitor window, you will notice that there are three frames. If you were to expand each of these, you could verify that the Sender Protocol Address and the Target Protocol Address fields display the automatic private IP address that your system has assigned to itself.

20. In the top panel of the Microsoft Network Monitor window, find the frame that matches the following criteria, and then double-click the frame:

Src MAC Addr	Dst MAC Addr	Protocol	Description	Src Other Addr	Dst Other Addr
LOCAL	*BROADCAST	NBT	NS: Registration req. for StudentX	169.254.x.y	169.254.255.255

21. In the middle panel of the Microsoft Network Monitor window, click the **+** next to ETHERNET: EType=Internet IP (IPv4). The Destination address field displays FFFFFFFFFFFF. The Source address field displays the MAC address of your Classroom connection network adapter card.

22. In the middle panel, click the **+** next to the IP: Protocol = UDP - User Datagram. The Source address field displays the automatic private IP address that your system has assigned to itself. The Destination address field displays 169.254.255.255. In this frame, your system is attempting to register its NetBIOS name STUDENTX to the IP address that it has just assigned to itself.

23. In the middle panel, click the **+** next to NBT: NS: Registration req. for STUDENTX. The Resource Record Name field displays the name of your computer (STUDENTX), and the Owner IP field displays the automatic private IP address that your system has assigned to itself.

24. To save this capture for further analysis, click **File** on the menu and click **Save As**. In the Save As dialog box in the File name field, type **Lab 2-3 APIPA Traffic**, and click **Save**.

25. Close the **Microsoft Network Monitor** window.

26. Click **Start**, point to **Control Panel**, and double-click **Network Connections**.

27. In the Network Connections window, right-click the **Classroom** connection and click **Properties**.

28. In the Classroom Properties dialog box, click **Internet Protocol (TCP/IP)** and click **Properties**.

29. In the Internet Protocol (TCP/IP) Properties dialog box, click **Use the following IP address**. Tab down to the IP address field and type **192.168.1.1XX** (where *XX* is your assigned student number). Tab down to the Default Gateway field and type **192.168.1.10**. Tab down to the Preferred DNS server field and type **192.168.1.10**. Click **OK** to close the Internet Protocol (TCP/IP) Properties dialog box.

30. Click **Close** to exit the Classroom Properties dialog box.

31. In the Network Connections window, right-click the **Private** connection and click **Enable**.

32. Close the **Network Connections** window.

Certification Objectives

Objectives for Microsoft Exam #70-293: Planning a Microsoft Windows Server 2003 Network:

■ Plan network traffic monitoring. Tools might include Network Monitor and System Monitor.

REVIEW QUESTIONS

1. Which of the following best describes the functionality of the version of Network Monitor that comes with Windows Server 2003?

   a. It captures frames sent to the computer on which Network Monitor is installed.

   b. It captures frames sent to or from the computer on which Network Monitor is installed.

   c. It captures frames sent to any computer with the Network Monitor driver installed.

   d. It captures frames sent to or from any computer with the Network Monitor driver installed.

2. Which of the following information can be found within a frame? (Choose all that apply.)

   a. source address

   b. destination address

   c. header information

   d. data

3. In Network Monitor, you can create a ____ so that, if Network Monitor detects a particular set of conditions on the network, it can start a capture, end a capture, or start a program.

   a. buffer

   b. capture

   c. capture filter

   d. capture trigger

4. To which group must you belong on the local computer to install Network Monitor?

   a. Administrators

   b. Network Configuration Operators

   c. Performance Monitor Users

   d. Power Users

5. If you want to capture data from multiple local networks at the same time, which of the following best describes the actions you would take?

   a. Start Network Monitor, open the Select a network dialog box, use the Control key to select all necessary adapters, and click OK.

   b. Install all necessary adapters. Start an instance of Network Monitor for each network, and select Networks on the Capture menu to select the network you want to monitor for each instance of network monitor.

   c. Start all additional instances of Network Monitor from other Windows Server 2003 systems.

   d. none of the above (captures for multiple local networks is a feature that is supported only in the version of Network Monitor that comes with Systems Management Server)

LAB 2.4 LOCAL AREA CONNECTION TROUBLESHOOTING

Objectives

The goal of this lab is to walk through steps that you can use to troubleshoot a problem with a network connection.

Materials Required

This lab will require the following:

- Windows Server 2003 installed and configured according to the instructions at the beginning of this lab manual

Estimated completion time: **10 minutes**

Activity Background

When Windows Server 2003 is installed, a local area connection is created for all network adapters that are detected on the system. The local area connection icon can be viewed in the Network Connections folder, or on the taskbar (if the option has been selected). Occasionally you may need to troubleshoot your system's network connections. That process will start with checking these connections.

Activity

1. Log on as **Administrator** to the Arctic.local domain with a password of **Password!**.

2. Click **Start**, point to **Control Panel**, and double-click **Network Connections**.

3. In the Network Connections window, right-click the **Classroom** connection, and click **Disable**.

4. In the Network Connections window, click **Help** on the menu bar, and click **Help and Support Center**.

5. In the details pane, double-click **Network Connections** to expand it, if necessary, and click **Troubleshooting**.

6. Click **Troubleshooting Network and dial-up connections**.

7. Under What problem are you having? click **When using a local area connection, there is no response**. You are advised to check the appearance of the Local Area Connection icon. Depending on the status of the connection, the icon may appear differently in the Network Connections folder.

8. Click **Use Device Manager** to verify that your network adapter is working correctly. In the Device Manager window, note that your network adapter appears with a red X.

9. Right-click the network adapter that appears with the red X, and click **Properties**. Note that the Device status field indicates that the device is disabled (code 22). Click **Enable Device** to enable this device.

10. In the Device Problems Troubleshooting Wizard on the Enabling a Device page, review the information provided, click **Next**, and then click **Finish**.

11. Click **Close** to close the Network Card Properties dialog box.

12. Close Device Manager.

13. Right-click the **Classroom** connection, and then click **Status**. In the Classroom Status dialog box, click the **Support** tab. Note the Internet Protocol (TCP/IP) settings. Click **Details** to open the Network Connection Details dialog box. Review the connection information and then click **Close**.

14. Click **Repair**. The Repair operations completed message appears, indicating that, if the problem persists, you should contact your network administrator or ISP. Click **OK**.

15. Click **Close** to close the Classroom Status dialog box.

16. In the Network Connections Help window, click **Local Area Connections** in the details pane. Review the Help documentation regarding using local area connections. Click the **Network connection icons** link at the bottom of the details pane. This page displays the different network connection icons that may appear in the Network Connections folder and on the taskbar. Familiarizing yourself with these icons can assist you in troubleshooting connectivity problems on your network.

17. Close the Network Connections Help window and the Help and Support Center window.

Certification Objectives

Objectives for Microsoft Exam #70-293: Planning a Microsoft Windows Server 2003 Network:

- Diagnose and resolve issues related to client computer configuration.

REVIEW QUESTIONS

1. Which of the following is true regarding local area connections?

   a. By default, they are always activated.

   b. They appear in the Network Connections folder.

   c. They are the only type of connection that is automatically created and activated.

   d. all of the above

2. Which of the following is true?

   a. If you disable your local area connection, it is also disabled in the hardware profile.

   b. Your computer displays a local area connection icon for each adapter installed.

   c. Local area connections can be manually added to the Network Connections folder.

   d. all of the above

3. Which of the following are examples of LAN connections? (Choose all that apply.)

   a. Ethernet

   b. Token ring

   c. cable modem

   d. wireless

4. Which of the following options can be viewed from the General tab in the Local Area Connection Status dialog box?

   a. status

   b. speed

   c. bytes sent and received

   d. all of the above

5. If a local area connection icon displays on your taskbar with a red question mark, what does this indicate?

   a. The media is disconnected.

   b. The adapter has an invalid IP address.

   c. The connection is active.

   d. The driver is disabled.

LAB 2.5 USING NETSH INTERFACE IP

Objectives

The goal of this lab is to investigate the Netsh interface ip context for configuring and managing your IP settings.

Materials Required

This lab will require the following:

- Windows Server 2003 installed and configured according to the instructions at the beginning of this lab manual

Estimated completion time: **15 minutes**

Activity Background

Netsh (Net Shell) is a command-line utility that enables you to view and modify the configuration settings for your network adapter cards. There are various contexts in which Netsh can be run. This command can be executed from the Command Prompt window. After you have launched the Netsh utility, you can select the context for which you want to configure.

Activity

1. Log on as **Administrator** of the Arctic.local domain with a password of **Password!**.

2. Click **Start**, click **Run**, type **cmd**, and click **OK**.

3. In the Command Prompt window, type **netsh** and press **Enter**.

4. Type **Help** and press **Enter**. The options that are available with the Netsh command-line utility are listed.

5. Type **interface ip** and press **Enter**.

6. Type **add address private 10.0.0.XX 255.0.0.0** (where *XX* is your assigned student number) and press **Enter**.

7. Type **show address private** and press **Enter**. The configuration for interface "private" appears.

8. Type **add dns private 10.0.0.100** and press **Enter**.

9. Type **show dns private** and press **Enter**. Configuration for interface "private" appears, displaying the DNS configuration settings.

10. Type **delete dns private all** and press **Enter**.

11. Type **show dns private** and press **Enter**. The statically configured DNS servers field displays "None."

12. Type **show address private** and press **Enter**. Your IP address information appears.

13. Type **show config private** and press **Enter**. Your configuration information appears.

14. Type **reset private** and press **Enter**. Your IP address on your private connection is set to obtain an IP address automatically.

15. Type **show address private** and press **Enter**. DHCP enabled displays as "Yes."

16. To test whether you have obtained a new IP address, you need to exit the utility. Type **bye** and press **Enter**.

17. Type **ipconfig** and press **Enter**. You now have an automatic private IP address.

18. Type **netsh** and press **Enter**.

19. Type **interface ip** and press **Enter**.

20. Type **diag** and press **Enter**.

21. Type **ping** and press **Enter**. Type **help** and press **Enter**. The available options are displayed.

22. Type **ping adapter** and press **Enter**. This command pings all of your configured IP addresses showing replies and ping statistics.

23. Type **ping dns** and press **Enter**. This command pings your configured DNS servers showing replies and ping statistics.

24. Type **ping ip** and press **Enter**. This command pings all configured IP addresses for all network adapters.

25. Type **bye** and press **Enter**.

26. Type **exit** and press **Enter** to close the Command Prompt window.

Certification Objectives

Objectives for Microsoft Exam #70-293: Planning a Microsoft Windows Server 2003 Network:

■ Diagnose and resolve issues related to client computer configuration.

■ Diagnose and resolve issues related to DHCP server addresses.

REVIEW QUESTIONS

1. What do you type in a command prompt window to exit the Netsh utility but to remain in the Command Prompt window?

   a. bye

   b. quit

   c. exit

   d. any of the above

2. Which of the following can be configured using the Netsh interface ip command-line utility? (Choose all that apply.)

   a. IP addresses to an interface

   b. DNS servers to an interface

   c. WINS servers to an interface

   d. DHCP servers to an interface

3. Which of the following would be the correct syntax to use with Netsh interface ip if you wanted to reset the private connection to obtain both the IP address and the DNS server settings automatically?

   a. delete DNS private

   b. reset DNS private

   c. reset private

   d. all of the above

4. Which of the following would be the correct syntax to use with Netsh interface ip if you wanted to view the Internet Protocol (TCP/IP) configuration for the private connection?

   a. show private

   b. show address private

   c. view private

   d. none of the above

5. On your computer, you haven't renamed the local area connection in the Network Connections folder. It is presently configured to obtain an IP address automatically; however, you want to add the DNS server configuration settings manually using the Netsh utility. Which of the following will allow you to configure a DNS server address of 192.168.1.10 for that connection?

   a. add DNS local area connection 192.168.1.10

   b. add DNS "local area connection" 192.168.1.10

   c. add DNS 192.168.1.10

   d. none of the above

3

PLANNING AND MANAGING A TCP/IP NETWORK

Labs included in this chapter:

♦ Lab 3.1 How to Use Network Monitor to Select a Different Network Adapter Card to Capture Network Data

♦ Lab 3.2 Installing the Network Monitor Driver

♦ Lab 3.3 An Introduction to System Monitor

♦ Lab 3.4 Performance Logs and Alerts: Configuring an Alert

♦ Lab 3.5 Support Tools: An Introduction to Netdiag

Microsoft MCSE Exam #70-293 Objectives	
Objective	Lab
Plan network traffic monitoring. Tools might include Network Monitor and System Monitor.	3.1, 3.2
Troubleshoot TCP/IP routing. Tools might include the route, tracert, ping, pathping, and netsh commands and Network Monitor.	3.1, 3.2, 3.5
Identify system bottlenecks, including memory, processor, disk, and network related bottlenecks.	3.3, 3.4
Identify system bottlenecks by using System Monitor.	3.3
Troubleshoot connectivity to the Internet.	3.5
Diagnose and resolve issues related to client configuration.	3.5
Troubleshoot TCP/IP addressing.	3.5
Diagnose and resolve issues related to client computer configuration.	3.5
Troubleshoot host name resolution.	3.5

Lab 3.1: How to Use Network Monitor to Select a Different Network Adapter Card to Capture Network Data

Objectives

The goal of this lab is to demonstrate how to modify settings in Network Monitor.

Materials Required

This lab will require the following:

■ Windows Server 2003 installed and configured according to the instructions at the beginning of this lab manual

Estimated completion time: **5 minutes**

Activity Background

The first time you launch Network Monitor, you are asked to select a network adapter card for the subnet from which you want to capture data. If your computer is connected to more than one subnet, there may come a point in time where you need to capture frames from the other subnet or additionally from multiple subnets simultaneously. This will necessitate selecting a different network adapter card. This lab will show you how.

Activity

1. If necessary, log on as **Administrator** to the Arctic.local domain with a password of **Password!**.

2. Click **Start**, point to **Administrative Tools**, and then click **Network Monitor**. The Microsoft Network Monitor window opens.

3. In the Microsoft Network Monitor window, click **Capture** on the menu bar, and click **Networks**.

4. In the Select a network dialog box, click the **plus sign** next to Local Computer to expand this option and display its related options.

5. Under Local Computer, click **Private**, as shown in Figure 3-1.

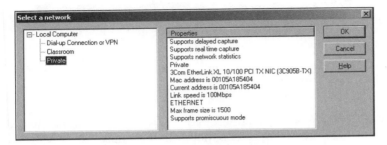

Figure 3-1   Select a network dialog box

6. Click **OK** to close the Select a network dialog box, and then close the Microsoft Network Monitor window.

Certification Objectives

Objectives for Microsoft Exam #70-293: Planning a Microsoft Windows Server 2003 Network:

- Plan network traffic monitoring. Tools might include Network Monitor and System Monitor.

- Troubleshoot TCP/IP routing. Tools might include the route, tracert, ping, pathping, and netsh commands and Network Monitor.

REVIEW QUESTIONS

1. To install Network Monitor, you must belong to which of the following groups?

   a. Administrators

   b. Network Configuration Operators

   c. Server Operators

   d. all of the above

2. Which of the following are features of the version of Network Monitor that ships with Windows Server 2003? (Choose all that apply.)

   a. captures traffic to and from the network adapter on which it is installed

   b. captures traffic to and from remote computers on which the Network Monitor driver is installed

   c. can be used to capture and analyze traffic to help solve network problems

   d. can set up triggers to capture or stop a capture under particular conditions

3. Which of the following actions can be configured to occur after trigger criteria has been met?

   a. The computer beeps.

   b. Network Monitor stops capturing frames.

   c. A command that you specify runs.

   d. all of the above

4. Which of the following properties of your network card can be viewed from the Select a network dialog box? (Choose all that apply.)

   a. whether the network configuration supports delayed capture

   b. whether the network configuration supports real-time capture

   c. the type of network connection (i.e., a dial-up connection)

   d. the MAC address of your network adapter

5. Which of the following would be the most appropriate option to select in the Microsoft Network Monitor window if you want to exclude traffic from a certain network address from being captured?

   a. Capture trigger

   b. Capture filter

   c. Display filter

   d. none of the above

Lab 3.2 Installing the Network Monitor Driver

Objectives

This goal of this lab is to describe how to install the Network Monitor Driver as a single component for monitoring remote systems.

Materials Required

This lab will require the following:

- Windows Server 2003 installed and configured according to the instructions at the beginning of this lab manual

Estimated completion time: **10 minutes**

Activity Background

The Network Monitor Driver is one of the components that is installed automatically when Network Tools are installed. The Network Monitor Driver enables your system to receive frames from all installed local network adapters and then analyze this captured traffic when troubleshooting network connectivity problems. Should the Microsoft Network Monitor utility not be required, you can install the Network Monitor Driver as a single component. You will learn how to accomplish this through this lab activity.

Activity

1. If necessary, log on as **Administrator** to the Arctic.local domain with a password of **Password!**.

2. Click **Start**, point to **Control Panel**, and then double-click **Network Connections**. In the Network Connections window, right-click **Classroom** and click **Properties**.

3. In the Classroom Properties dialog box, look in the This connection uses the following items list box to see if the Network Monitor Driver is installed. If the Network Monitor Driver is installed, click **Network Monitor Driver** and click **Uninstall**. (If it isn't installed, proceed to Step 13.)

4. A message appears explaining that uninstalling a component will remove it from all network connections. Click **Yes** to indicate that you are sure you want to uninstall Network Monitor Driver.

5. A message appears explaining that the Network Monitor Driver component cannot be uninstalled because it is still required by Network Monitor Tools. See Figure 3-2. Click **OK** to close this message.

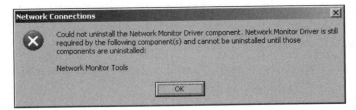

Figure 3-2   Network Monitor Driver is required by Network Monitor Tools

6. Click **Close** to exit the Classroom Properties dialog box.

7. In the Network Connections window, click **Advanced** on the menu bar, and click **Optional Networking Components**. The Windows Optional Networking Components Wizard starts.

8. In the Windows Optional Networking Components Wizard, click **Management and Monitoring Tools**, if necessary, and then click **Details**.

9. In the Management and Monitoring Tools dialog box, uncheck the **Network Monitor Tools** check box, as shown in Figure 3-3.

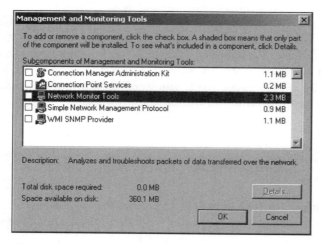

Figure 3-3   Deselecting Network Monitor Tools

10. Click **OK** to close the dialog box, and then click **Next** in the Windows Optional Networking Components Wizard dialog box.

11. If the System Settings Change message box appears, indicating that you must restart this computer for the new settings to take effect, click **Yes**.

12. If necessary, log in as **Administrator** of the Arctic.local domain with a password of **Password!**.

13. Click **Start**, point to **Control Panel**, and then double-click **Network Connections**. In the Network Connections window, right-click **Classroom** and click **Properties**. In the Classroom Properties dialog box, the Network Monitor driver is no longer listed as installed.

14. Click the **Install** button.

15. In the Select Network Component Type dialog box, click **Protocol** and click **Add**.

16. In the Select Network Protocol dialog box, click **Network Monitor Driver**, as shown in Figure 3-4.

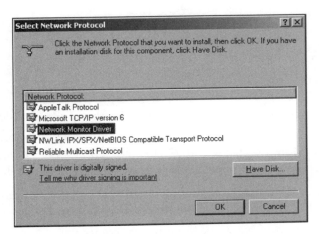

Figure 3-4 Installing the Network Monitor Driver

17. Click **OK** to close the dialog box. The Network Monitor Driver should now appear on the General tab of the Classroom Properties dialog box.

18. Click **Close** to exit the Classroom Properties dialog box, and then close the Network Connections window.

Certification Objectives

Objectives for Microsoft Exam #70-293: Planning a Microsoft Windows Server 2003 Network:

- Plan network traffic monitoring. Tools might include Network Monitor and System Monitor.

- Troubleshoot TCP/IP routing. Tools might include the route, tracert, ping, pathping, and netsh commands and Network Monitor.

REVIEW QUESTIONS

1. When the No Networks Found dialog box appears, what does this indicate?

a. Network Monitor cannot find the installed network drivers on the local machine.

b. Network Monitor driver is not installed.

c. You do not have the necessary permissions to run Network Monitor.

d. none of the above

2. Network Monitor Capture is a command-line utility that can be run on which of the following operating systems?

   a. Windows 2000

   b. Windows XP

   c. Windows Server 2003

   d. all of the above

3. If you want to capture data from multiple local networks simultaneously, how could this be done?

   a. Open Network Monitor, click Capture, click Networks, click all local area network connections in the Select a network dialog box, and then click OK.

   b. Install a second adapter, open up a second instance of Network Monitor, and then use the Select a network dialog box to select the second adapter.

   c. You need the version of Network Monitor that comes with SMS in order to accomplish this.

   d. none of the above

4. In the Capture window, which pane provides an overall view of network traffic sent to or from the local computer?

   a. Graph pane

   b. Session statistics pane

   c. Station statistics pane

   d. Total statistics pane

5. In the Frame Viewer window, which pane displays a list of the frames in the order in which they were captured?

   a. Summary pane

   b. Detail pane

   c. Hexadecimal pane

   d. none of the above

LAB 3.3 AN INTRODUCTION TO SYSTEM MONITOR

Objectives

The goal of this lab is to describe System Monitor.

Materials Required

This lab will require the following:

■ Windows Server 2003 installed and configured according to the instructions at the beginning of this lab manual

Estimated completion time: **15 minutes**

Activity Background

System monitor enables you to monitor the performance of either local or remote computers on your network. Using this built-in utility, you can view and analyze either real-time data or data that has been gathered using a counter log. System Monitor offers many customizable options for gathering data such as which performance objects, performance counters, or instance to gather data on. Collected data can be displayed using three different views, all of which can be customized to meet your specific needs: Graph, Histogram, or Report View.

Activity

1. If necessary, log on as **Administrator** of the Arctic.local domain with a password of **Password!**.

2. Click **Start**, point to **Administrative Tools**, and then click **Performance**. In the Performance window, you can see that System Monitor is gathering data, as shown in Figure 3-5.

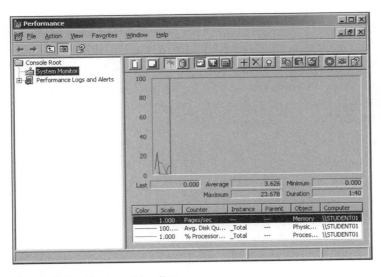

Figure 3-5   System Monitor

In the right pane of the screen, position your pointer over the View Current Activity button on the toolbar, which is currently selected.

3. Click the **View Log Data** button on the toolbar. The System Monitor Properties dialog box appears with the Source tab selected. The data source is set to Current activity, as shown in Figure 3–6. This indicates that the System Monitor window is displaying real-time activity.

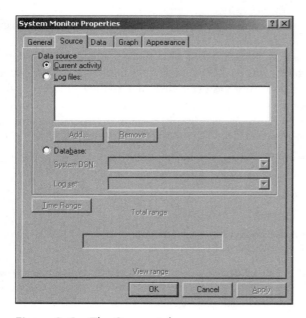

Figure 3-6   The Source tab

4. Click **Cancel** to close the System Monitor Properties dialog box and return to the Performance dialog box.

5. Click the **View Histogram** button on the toolbar. The data is now displayed as a histogram or a bar chart. This may not always be the best method of displaying counter values.

6. Click the **View Report** button on the toolbar. The view has again changed so you can now see the average values that are calculated for the default counters of Memory, Physical Disk, and Processor. See Figure 3-7.

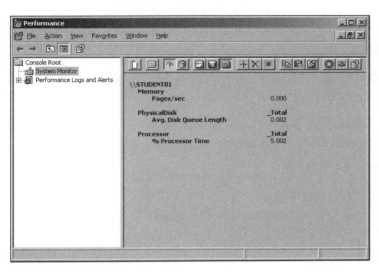

Figure 3-7   Report view

7. Click the **Add** button on the toolbar. The Add Counters dialog box appears, as shown in Figure 3-8. You can use the options in this dialog box to add more counters to the System Monitor display. Note that the default setting is "Select counters from computer" and that the computer name in the display is that of your server.

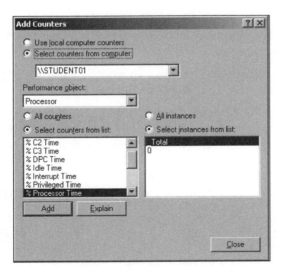

Figure 3-8   The Add Counters dialog box

8. Click the **Performance object** list arrow to display the options that are available. These are the available performance objects about which you can gather data. Scroll the list if necessary, and then click **IPSec v4 Driver** in the list of performance objects. Under Select counters from list, the available counters for IPSec v4 Driver are now displayed (as shown in Figure 3-9).

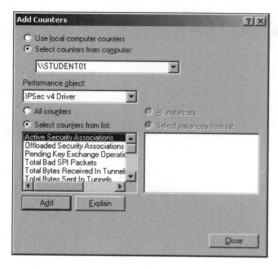

Figure 3-9   IPSec v4 Driver performance object counters

9. Click **Explain**. The Explain Text dialog box appears, providing background information about what the Active Security Associations counter gathers. Close the Explain Text dialog box.

10. Click **Add** to select the Active Security Associations counter into your display.

11. Click **Close** to close the Add Counters dialog box. The IPSec v4 Driver appears in the System Monitor display.

12. You will now delete the counter you have just added. Click the **View Graph** button on the toolbar. The view changes to show a line graph.

13. You will adjust the size of the Counter column at the bottom of the display. Place your pointer on the line between the Counter and Instance fields. When the two-headed arrow pointer appears, click and drag the line to the left until the Counter column is the size that you want. At the bottom of the screen, select **Active Security Associations** in the list of counters, and then click the Delete button on the toolbar. The Active Security Associations counter has now been removed from the counters displayed.

14. Click the **New Counter Set** button on the toolbar. Notice that no activity is taking place in the System Monitor window. If you wanted to select only particular counters to be displayed, you would use this feature to make your selections.

Certification Objectives

Objectives for Microsoft Exam #70-293: Planning a Microsoft Windows Server 2003 Network:

- Identify system bottlenecks, including memory, processor, disk, and network related bottlenecks.

- Identify system bottlenecks by using System Monitor.

3

REVIEW QUESTIONS

1. Where can you find the Help documentation for System Monitor?

   a. Right-click System Monitor and click Help on the shortcut menu.

   b. In the Performance console, click the question mark on the menu bar.

   c. In the Performance console, click Help from the menu and then click Help Topics.

   d. From the System Monitor toolbar, click the Help button.

2. Which of the following increases the monitoring overhead when using System Monitor?

   a. running System Monitor in Graph view

   b. sampling at very frequent intervals (less than three seconds apart)

   c. selecting many different objects and counters

   d. all of the above

3. You receive an error message while trying to export log data to Microsoft Excel as the Performance Logs and Alerts service is actively collecting data for that log. How can you view this log data in Excel?

   a. Apply the latest service pack.

   b. Microsoft Excel requires exclusive access to the log file; stop the log before trying to access the data using Microsoft Excel.

   c. Log data is not in a compatible format and cannot be viewed in Microsoft Excel.

   d. none of the above

4. Which groups have the ability to delete counters from System Monitor?

   a. Administrators

   b. Performance Log Users

   c. Performance Monitor Users

   d. none of the above

5. Which of the following are true with regards to System Monitor?

   a. The extension for log files is .blg.

   b. Log files created on Windows Server 2003 cannot be read on earlier operating system versions.

   c. A user must be logged on to the computer being monitored.

   d. all of the above

Lab 3.4 Performance Logs and Alerts: Configuring an Alert

Objectives

The goal of this lab is to create and configure an alert.

Materials Required

This lab will require the following:

- Windows Server 2003 installed and configured according to the instructions at the beginning of this lab manual

Estimated completion time: **15 minutes**

Activity Background

One of the features available in the Performance console is Performance Logs and Alerts. Performance Logs and Alerts enable you to monitor local or remote computers either according to a defined schedule or initiated manually. Alerts can be configured to send a message to a particular user or system, run a specific program, or gather information to a log file, once a particular condition has been met. By taking advantage of this function, you can automate the monitoring of servers and workstations on your network. In this lab activity, you will create and configure an alert.

Activity

1. If necessary, log on as **Administrator** of the Arctic.local domain with a password of **Password!**.

2. Click **Start**, right-click **My Computer**, and then click **Manage**. The Computer Management window opens. Maximize the window if necessary.

3. Expand **Storage**, if necessary, and then click **Disk Management**.

4. In the top-right pane of the window, find the % Free column for Drive C: and record this value. You will need it later in this lab activity.

5. In the Computer Management window, expand **System Tools**, if necessary, and then expand **Performance Logs and Alerts**. There are three options available: Counter Logs, Trace Logs, and Alerts. See Figure 3-10.

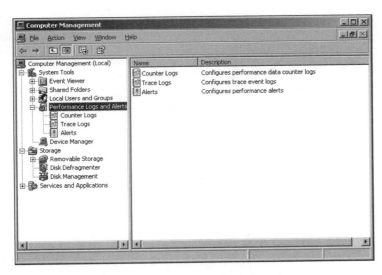

Figure 3-10   Performance Logs and Alerts options

6. Under Performance Logs and Alerts, select and right-click **Alerts**, and then click **New Alert Settings**.

7. In the New Alert Settings dialog box, type **Free Disk Space on C** and click **OK**.

8. In the Free Disk Space on C dialog box in the Comment field, type **Free Disk Space on C**, and then click the **Add** button.

9. Click the **Performance object** list arrow, and then click **LogicalDisk**.

10. Under Select counters from list, click **% Free Space**, and then click **C:** under Select instances from list. The Add Counters dialog box should now appear, as shown in Figure 3-11.

Figure 3-11 Adding the % Free Space LogicalDisk counter

11. Click **Add** and then click **Close** to close the Add Counters dialog box.

12. In the Free Disk Space on C dialog box, click the drop-down arrow next to the Alert when the value is field, and click **Under**.

13. Type **The value you wrote down in Step 4 of this lab activity.** in the Limit field.

14. Click the **Action tab** in the Free Disk Space on C Properties dialog box. The Log an entry in the application event log check box is already selected. Check the **Send a network message to** check box and then type **StudentXX** (where XX is your assigned student number). See Figure 3-12.

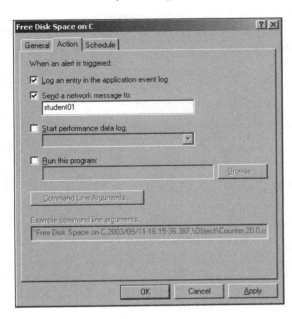

Figure 3-12   The Action tab

15. Click the **Schedule** tab in the Free Disk Space on C dialog box, check the default settings, and then click **OK** to close the Free Disk Space on C dialog box.

16. Right-click the **Free Disk Space on C** alert, and then click **Stop**.

17. Close the Computer Management console.

Certification Objectives

Objectives for Microsoft Exam #70-293: Planning a Microsoft Windows Server 2003 Network:

■ Identify system bottlenecks, including memory, processor, disk, and network related bottlenecks.

REVIEW QUESTIONS

1. Which of the following is a default counter in the System Monitor console?

   a. Pages/sec

   b. Avg. Disk Queue Length

   c. % Processor Time

   d. all of the above

2. Which of the following command-line utilities do you use to write performance counter data to the command window or to a supported log file format?

   a. Logman

   b. Perfmon

   c. Typeperf

   d. Unlodctr

3. Which of the following command-line utilities do you use to manage and schedule performance counter and event trace log collections on local and remote systems?

   a. Logman

   b. Perfmon

   c. Relog

   d. Typeperf

4. You are unable to log performance counters from a remote computer. Which of the following are possible reasons? (Choose all that apply.)

   a. You may not have administrative credentials to view the counters on the remote computer.

   b. The Performance Logs and Alerts service may not have permission to log on to the remote computer or to create and update the log file.

   c. The size limit of the log file may not be large enough to collect your requested data.

   d. The Remote Registry service is not running on the remote computer.

5. Which of the following are considered to be causes of bottlenecks? (Choose all that apply.)

   a. Insufficient resources may need to be upgraded, or components may need to be added.

   b. A program may be monopolizing a resource and needs to be replaced, rewritten, or run when demand is low.

   c. Resource configuration settings may need to be modified.

   d. Resources may be malfunctioning and need to be replaced.

LAB 3.5 SUPPORT TOOLS: AN INTRODUCTION TO NETDIAG

Objectives

The goal of this lab activity is to use the netdiag command-line utility to gather information about your system.

Materials Required

This lab will require the following:

- Windows Server 2003 installed and configured according to the instructions at the beginning of this lab manual

Estimated completion time: **15 minutes**

Activity Background

Netdiag is a command-line diagnostic utility available on the Windows Server 2003 CD that can be used to identify and isolate network connectivity problems. Once Netdiag is installed, you can use this utility to test the state of your network client.

Activity

1. If necessary, log on as **Administrator** for the Arctic.local domain with a password of **Password!**.

2. Insert the Windows Server 2003 CD, navigate to the \Support\Tools directory, and then double-click **SUPTOOLS.MSI** to install the Support Tools on your server. You must be logged on as an administrator in order to complete this action.

3. On the Welcome to the Windows Support Tools Setup Wizard page, click **Next**.

4. On the End User License Agreement page, click the **I Agree** option button, and then click **Next**.

5. On the User Information page, type **Administrator** in the Name field, type **Arctic University** in the Organization field and then click **Next**.

6. On the Destination Directory page, accept the default setting and click **Install Now**.

7. If a message appears, indicating that the CiceroUIWndFrame application has been detected, click **OK**. Close all other programs and then restart the installation of the Support Tools. If not, continue to Step 8.

8. On the Completing the Windows Support Tools Setup Wizard page, click **Finish**.

9. Click **Start**, click **Run**, type **cmd**, and then click **OK**.

10. In the Command Prompt window, type **netdiag /?** and press **Enter**. View the different switches that are available for the netdiag utility.

11. Type **netdiag** and press **Enter**. Scroll through the Command Prompt window, and view the results.

12. Type **netdiag /v /l** and press **Enter**.

13. Close the Command Prompt window.

14. Right-click **Start** and click **Explore**.

15. Navigate to the C:\Documents and Settings\Administrator.ARCTIC directory.

16. Open **NetDiag.log** and view the results of the tests performed.

17. Close the log file, and then close Windows Explorer.

Certification Objectives

Objectives for Microsoft Exam #70-293: Planning a Microsoft Windows Server 2003 Network:

- Troubleshoot TCP/IP routing. Tools might include the route, tracert, ping, pathping, and netsh commands and Network Monitor.

- Troubleshoot connectivity to the Internet.

- Diagnose and resolve issues related to client configuration.

- Troubleshoot TCP/IP addressing.

- Diagnose and resolve issues related to client computer configuration.

- Troubleshoot host name resolution.

REVIEW QUESTIONS

1. Which of the following is true of the Netdiag utility?

   a. It is a command-line diagnostic tool.

   b. It is available on the Windows Server 2003 CD-ROM.

   c. TCP/IP must be installed in order to use Netdiag.

   d. all of the above

2. Which of the following can be accomplished using the Netdiag utility? (Choose all that apply.)

   a. along with the Scheduler service, generating reports at regularly scheduled intervals

   b. testing whether APIPA is in use for the network adapters

   c. obtaining a list of domain controllers for the domain

   d. enumerating the TCP/IP configuration information for each adapter

3. Which of the following switches do you use with Netdiag to find a domain controller in a specified domain?

   a. /d

   b. /dcAccountEnum

   c. /l

   d. /test

4. Which of the following is true about Netdiag?

   a. You can use Netdiag along with dcdiag.exe to troubleshoot client computers that cannot locate a domain controller.

   b. You can use Netdiag to help determine both server and client DNS misconfigurations.

   c. If you receive the Domain not found, Server not available, or RPC server is unavailable error messages, you can use Netdiag with the /debug command to evaluate the registration of NetBIOS, DNS, and services.

   d. all of the above

5. Which of the following is true about Netdiag?

   a. To run the utility, you must be a member of the Administrators local group on that computer.

   b. Each version of netdiag.exe is customized to run on a different version of the Windows operating system and can be run only on a computer running the Windows operating system for which it has been specifically designed.

   c. If you run a version of netdiag.exe that has been designed for Windows 2000 or Windows XP in a Windows Server 2003 domain, it might not report the correct operating system version of the domain.

   d. all of the above

4

PLANNING AND CONFIGURING ROUTING AND SWITCHING

Labs included in this chapter:

♦ Lab 4.1 ANDing Decimal Values with a Calculator

♦ Lab 4.2 Installing and Configuring a RIP Router

♦ Lab 4.3 Demand-dial Routing: Configuring Dial-out Hours

♦ Lab 4.4 An Introduction to the Basic Firewall Component

♦ Lab 4.5 An Introduction to ICS (Internet Connection Sharing)

Microsoft MCSE Exam #70-293 Objectives	
Objective	Lab
Plan an IP routing solution.	4.2
Create an IP subnet scheme.	4.1
Plan an Internet connectivity strategy.	4.4, 4.5
Troubleshoot connectivity to the Internet.	4.4, 4.5
Diagnose and resolve issues related to Network Address Translation (NAT).	4.4, 4.5
Plan a routing strategy.	4.2
Identify routing protocols to use in a specified environment.	4.2
Plan routing for IP multicast traffic.	4.2
Implement secure access between private networks.	4.3

LAB 4.1 ANDING DECIMAL VALUES WITH A CALCULATOR

Objectives

The goal of this lab activity is to explore how to use the Windows Calculator to calculate the network ID of a remote system. To accomplish this, you will first need to switch your Windows Calculator from Standard view (which is the default setting) to Scientific view.

Materials Required

This lab will require the following:

- Windows Server 2003 installed and configured according to the instructions at the beginning of this lab manual

Estimated completion time: **10 minutes**

Activity Background

By default, the Windows Calculator uses the decimal number system. However, once in Scientific view, you can convert to the hexadecimal, octal, and binary number systems as well. Additionally, the And operator in the Windows Calculator can be used to determine the network address of remote systems when troubleshooting network connectivity.

ACTIVITY

Activity

1. If necessary, log on as **Administrator** to the Arctic.local domain with a password of **Password!**.

2. Click **Start**, point to **All Programs**, point to **Accessories**, and then click **Calculator**.

3. In the Calculator window, click **View** on the menu bar, and then click **Scientific**. Your screen should like the one shown in Figure 4-1.

Figure 4-1   Scientific view

4. Your system is configured with IP address 192.168.1.1xx and subnet mask of 255.255.255.0. You need to calculate the network ID for your subnet. First you are going to use the Windows Calculator to compare the values in the first octet of your IP address against the value in the first octet in the subnet mask. In the Calculator window, type **192**, click the **And** button, type **255**, and then click the = button. Record the value returned.

5. Next you will use Windows Calculator to compare the value in the second octet of your IP address against the value in the second octet of the subnet mask. In the Calculator window, type **168**, click the **And** button, type **255**, and then click the = button. Record the value returned.

6. Next you will use Windows Calculator to compare the value in the third octet of your IP address with the value in the third octet of the subnet mask. In the Calculator window, type **1**, click the **And** button, type **255**, and then click the = button. Record the value returned. Do you see a pattern of what happens when you AND numbers with the value 255? Whenever a number is ANDed with 255, the value that is returned is the number you started with.

7. Compare the value in the fourth octet of your IP address with the fourth octet value in the subnet mask. In the Calculator window, type **1XX** (where XX is the unique value in the last octet of your Classroom connection IP address), click the **And** button on, type **0**, and then click the = button. Record the value returned. Any value ANDed with 0 returns 0. Your network address is 192.168.1.0. Any computer that resides on this subnet will return the same network address when compared with this subnet mask.

8. Close Calculator.

Certification Objectives

Objectives for Microsoft Exam #70-293: Planning a Microsoft Windows Server 2003 Network:

- Create an IP subnet scheme.

REVIEW QUESTIONS

1. Which of the following computers would be on the same subnet as a computer having an IP address of 192.168.99.100 with a subnet mask of 255.255.224.0? (Choose all that apply.)

   a. 192.168.96.100

   b. 192.168.65.100

   c. 192.168.128.100

   d. 192.168.100.100

2. Which of the following computers would be on the same subnet as a computer having an IP address of 192.168.99.100 with a subnet mask of 255.255.248.0?

   a. 192.168.96.100

   b. 192.168.100.100

   c. 192.168.104.100

   d. All of the above

3. Which of the following computers would be on the same subnet as a computer having an IP address of 192.168.99.100 with a subnet mask of 255.255.192.0? (Choose all that apply.)

   a. 192.168.90.100

   b. 192.168.128.100

   c. 192.168.192.100

   d. 192.168.232.100

4. Which of the following computers would be on the same subnet as a computer having an IP address of 192.168.99.100 with a subnet mask of 255.240.0.0? (Choose all that apply.)

   a. 192.160.84.100

   b. 192.168.127.100

   c. 192.172.168.100

   d. 192.182.0.46

5. Which of the following computers would be on the same subnet as a computer having an IP address of 192.168.99.100 with a subnet mask of 255.224.0.0? (Choose all that apply.)

a. 192.160.84.100

b. 192.172.127.100

c. 192.192.168.100

d. 192.224.0.46

4

LAB 4.2 INSTALLING AND CONFIGURING A RIP ROUTER

Objectives

The goal of this lab is to install and configure RIP (Routing Information Protocol) and investigate some of the configurable options available with RIP routing on Windows Server 2003.

Materials Required

This lab will require the following:

- Two Windows Server 2003 servers installed and configured according to the instructions at the beginning of this lab manual

- A lab partner; if none is available, complete the lab activity steps in sequence on both Windows Server 2003 systems

Estimated completion time: **25 minutes**

Activity Background

RIP is one of the routing protocols supported on Windows Server 2003. RIP routers are best suited in small to medium-sized networks where multiple paths are available for a packet to move from one endpoint to another. RIP is usually suited for networks having somewhere between 10 and 50 subnets.

Activity

To be completed by both partners:

1. If necessary, log on as **Administrator** for the Arctic.local domain with a password of **Password!**.

2. Click **Start**, point to **Administrative Tools**, and click **Routing and Remote Access**. The Routing and Remote Access window opens.

3. If Routing and Remote Access has already been enabled on your system, a green arrow will appear next to your server name in the Routing and Remote Access window. If Routing and Remote Access is enabled, right-click **STUDENTXX (local)** (where *XX* is your assigned student number), and click **Disable Routing and Remote Access**. Disabling the service ensures that your computer and that of your partner's are configured the same.

4. Right-click **STUDENTXX** (where *XX* is your assigned student number), and click **Configure and Enable Routing and Remote Access**.

5. On the Welcome to the Routing and Remote Access Server Setup Wizard page, click **Next**.

6. On the Configuration page, click **Custom configuration** and click **Next**.

7. On the Custom Configuration page, click **LAN routing** and click **Next**.

8. On the Completing the Routing and Remote Access Server Setup Wizard page, click **Finish**.

9. A message dialog box appears, indicating that the Routing and Remote Access Service has now been installed and asking if you would like to start the service. Click **Yes**.

10. In the Routing and Remote Access window, review the instructions in the details pane regarding how to make changes to the current configuration. Then, under IP Routing, right-click **General** and click **New Routing Protocol**.

11. The New Routing Protocol dialog box appears. The available routing protocols are displayed. Click **RIP Version 2 for Internet Protocol** and click **OK**.

12. RIP now appears under IP Routing. Right-click **RIP** and click **Properties**. The RIP Properties dialog box opens.

13. Under Event logging, click the **Log the maximum amount of information** option button, and then click **OK** to close the RIP Properties dialog box. By turning on the maximum amount of logging, you can check the system log in Event Viewer to monitor RIP activity.

14. Right-click **RIP** and click **New Interface**.

15. In the New Interface for RIP Version 2 for Internet Protocol dialog box, click **Private** and click **OK**.

To be completed by Partner One only:

1. In the RIP Properties – Private Properties dialog box, read the information provided on the General tab. The Operation mode is configured to Periodic update mode, which is the default setting for LAN interfaces.

2. The default setting for the Outgoing packet protocol option is RIP version 2 broadcast. Click the drop-down arrow and click **Silent RIP**, as shown in Figure 4-2. For the purposes of this lab, one router will advertise its routes to another. The default setting for the Incoming packet protocol option is RIP version 1 and 2.

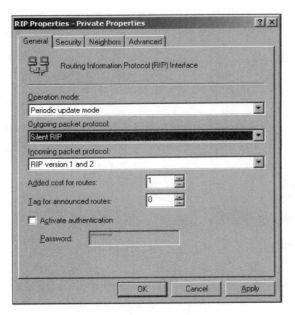

Figure 4-2   Configuring a silent RIP router

3. Click the **Security** tab, verify that the Action list box displays **For incoming routes**, click the **Ignore all routes in the ranges listed** option button In the From field, type **192.168.1XX.0** (where *XX* is your assigned student number). In the To field, type **192.168.1XX.255** (where *XX* is your assigned student number). Click **Add**. See Figure 4–3.

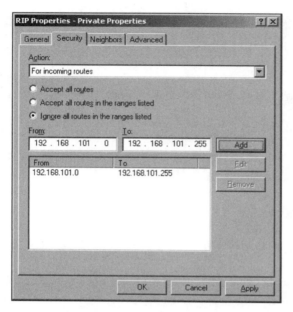

Figure 4-3   Filtering incoming routes

4. Click **OK** to close the RIP Properties – Private Properties dialog box.

5. Under IP Routing, right-click **Static Routes** and click **New Static Route**. In the Static Route dialog box, select **Classroom** as the interface, if necessary. In the Destination field, type **172.1XX.0.0** (where *XX* is your assigned student number). In the Network mask field, type **255.255.0.0**. In the Gateway field, type **192.168.1.10** and click **OK**.

6. Right-click **Static Routes** and click **Show IP Routing table**. The static route you just entered appears in the Protocol column in the table (non demand-dial). Close the table. Leave the Routing and Remote Access window open. The next activity must be completed by your partner.

To be completed by Partner Two only:

1. In the RIP Properties – Private Properties dialog box, view the information provided on the General tab. The Operation mode is configured to Periodic update mode, which is the default setting for LAN interfaces. You are accepting all default settings on the General tab.

2. Click the **Security** tab. Click the Action drop-down arrow, and click **For outgoing routes**. Click the **Do not announce all routes in the ranges listed** option button. In the From field, type **192.168.1XX.0** (where *XX* is your assigned student number). In the To field, type **192.168.1XX.255** (where *XX* is your assigned student number). Click **Add**. See Figure 4-4.

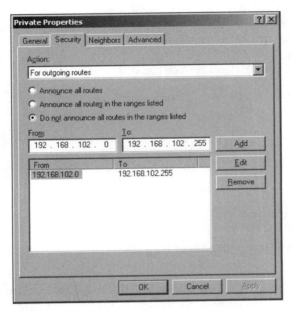

Figure 4-4   Filtering outgoing routes

3. Click **OK** to close the RIP Properties - Private Properties dialog box.

4. Right-click **Static Routes** and click **New Static Route**. In the Static Route dialog box, select **Classroom** as the interface, if necessary. In the Destination field, type **192.168.1XX.0** (where *XX* is your partner's assigned student number). In the Network mask field, type **255.255.255.0**. In the Gateway field, type **192.168.1.10**. Click **OK** to close the Static Route dialog box.

5. Right-click **Static Routes** and click **New Static Route**. In the Static Route dialog box, select **Classroom** as the interface, if necessary. In the Destination field, type **192.168.1XX.0** (where *XX* is your assigned student number). In the Network mask field, type **255.255.255.0**. In the Gateway field, type **192.168.1.10**. Click **OK** to close the Static Route dialog box.

6. Right-click **Static Routes** and click **New Static Route**. In the Static Route dialog box, select **Classroom** as the interface, if necessary. In the Destination field, type **192.168.254.0**. In the Network mask field, type **255.255.255.0**. In the Gateway field, type **192.168.1.10**. Click **OK** to close the Static Route dialog box. You should now have three static entries, as shown in Figure 4-5.

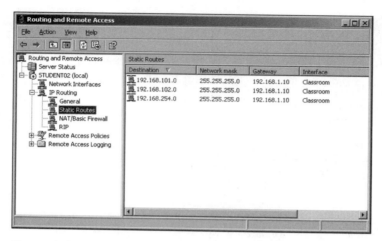

Figure 4-5   Viewing static routes

7. Right-click **Static Routes** and click **Show IP Routing Table**. The entry Static (non demand–dial) should now appear in the Protocol column for each of the three static routes that you have just added.

8. Close the table.

To be completed by both partners:

You will now check the routing tables to see if the static routes have been announced to your partner's routing table. Note that you and your partner must complete this series of steps at the same time.

NOTE

1. Right-click **Static Routes** and click **Show IP Routing Table**. Because the RIP protocol is installed, your routing table is updated with entries announced by other routers.

   a. On partner one's routing table, in the Destination column, the 192.168.254.0 destination network entry has been added. The route that was marked as blocked is not in the routing table. Also note that the route entries that your partner specified not to announce are also missing from the table.

   b. On partner two's routing table, all static routes that were added appear. The 172.1XX.0.0 subnet entry that was added to partner one's routing table does not appear because partner one's system has been configured as a silent RIP router. This router will listen, but not advertise its own routes.

2. Close IP Routing Tables and then right-click **STUDENTXX (local)** (where *XX* is your assigned student number) and click **Disable Routing and Remote Access**.

3. A message appears, indicating that you are disabling the router and removing its configuration and that you will have to reenable it and reconfigure it later. Click **Yes** to indicate that you want to continue.

4. Close the Routing and Remote Access window.

Certification Objectives

Objectives for Microsoft Exam #70-293: Planning a Microsoft Windows Server 2003 Network:

- Plan an IP routing solution.

- Plan a routing strategy.

- Identify routing protocols to use in a specified environment.

- Plan routing for IP multicast traffic.

REVIEW QUESTIONS

1. Which of the following are advantages of the RIP protocol?

   a. simple to configure and deploy

   b. scaleable to larger networks

   c. low recovery time

   d. all of the above

2. Which of the following are true statements about RIP?

   a. Maximum hop count used by RIP routers is 15.

   b. If authentication is configured, passwords will be encrypted.

   c. By default, RIP announcements from all sources are accepted.

   d. all of the above

3. Which of the following are true with regards to authentication and RIP?

   a. With authentication enabled, RIP announcements that don't match the configured password will be discarded.

   b. RIP v2 interface passwords can be captured and viewed with network sniffers.

   c. All RIP v2 interfaces on the same network must be configured with the same password.

   d. all of the above

4. Which of the following is a reason why RIP routers may not receive expected routes? (Choose all that apply.)

   a. You have deployed variable length subnetting.

   b. Not all RIP v2 interfaces on the network are using the same password.

   c. RIP route filtering has not been configured properly.

   d. RIP peer filtering has not been configured properly.

5. What is the default ope

   a. Silent RIP

   b. Ignore incoming pa

   c. Periodic update mo

   d. Auto-static update

LAB 4.3 DEMAND-DIAL ROUTIN

Objectives

The goal of this lab is to explore one of the features supported by Routing and Remote Access in Windows Server 2003—demand-dial routing.

Materials Required

This lab will require the following:

- Two Windows Server 2003 servers installed and configured according to the instructions at the beginning of this lab manual

NOTE

This lab also requires that each student work with a partner. There are sections of this activity that need to be completed by both partners, and others that need to be completed by only one partner.

Estimated completion time: **30 minutes**

Activity Background

Demand-dial routing is also commonly referred to as dial-on-demand routing. When data needs to be sent to remote networks, a demand-dial interface can be initiated by the router that receives the packet. By default, demand-dial interfaces are configured as demand-dial connections and hang up after the connection has been idle for five minutes. However, demand-dial interfaces may also be configured as persistent connections.

When implemented, demand-dial connections can help to reduce connection costs to remote networks. There are also two configurable parameters that you can use to achieve this goal: 1) set IP Demand-dial filters, which allow you to specify the type of traffic that will initiate a connection, and 2) set dial-out hours, which allow you to specify when demand-dial connections can be made.

ACTIVITY

Activity

For both partners:

1. If necessary, log on as **Administrator** to the Arctic.local domain with a password of **Password!**.

2. Click **Start**, point to **Administrative Tools**, and click **Routing and Remote Access**.

3. In the Routing and Remote Access window, right-click **STUDENTXX (local)** (where *XX* is your assigned student number) and click **Configure and Enable Routing and Remote Access**.

4. On the Welcome to the Routing and Remote Access Server Setup Wizard page, click **Next**.

5. On the Configuration page, click **Custom configuration** and click **Next**.

6. On the Custom Configuration page, check both the **VPN access** check box and the **Demand-dial connections (used for branch office routing)** check box and then click **Next**.

7. On the Completing the Routing and Remote Access Server Setup Wizard page, verify that **VPN access** and **Demand-dial connections** appear in the Summary of selections list, and click **Finish**.

8. A message appears, indicating that the Routing and Remove Access service has been installed and asking you if you want to start the service. Click **Yes**.

9. In the Routing and Remote Access window, right-click **STUDENTXX (local)** (where *XX* is your assigned student number) and click **Properties**. As indicated on the General tab, your server is configured as both a router for LAN and demand-dial routing, as well as a remote access server. Click **OK** to close the STUDENT*XX* (local) Properties dialog box.

10. Under STUDENT*XX* (local) (where *XX* is your assigned student number), right–click **Network Interfaces** and click **New Demand–dial Interface**.

11. On the Welcome to the Demand-Dial Interface Wizard page, click **Next**.

12. It is a common practice to name interfaces after the network to which you are connecting. On the Interface Name page, click in the Interface name field, then type **Student*XX*** (where *XX* is your partner's assigned student number). The Interface Name field should now read Student*XX* (where *XX* is your partner's assigned student number). See Figure 4-6.

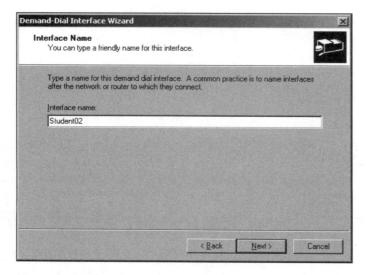

Figure 4-6   Creating a demand-dial interface to Student*XX*

13. Click **Next** to go to the next step in the wizard.

14. On the Connection Type page, verify that the default option **Connect using virtual private networking (VPN)** is selected, and click **Next**.

15. On the VPN Type page, verify that the default option **Automatic selection** is selected, and click **Next**.

16. On the Destination Address page, type **192.168.1.1*XX*** (where *XX* is your partner's assigned student number), and click **Next**.

17. On the Protocols and Security page, verify that the **Route IP packets on this interface** check box is selected, and then check the **Add a user account so a remote router can dial in** check box to select it, as shown in Figure 4–7. Click **Next**.

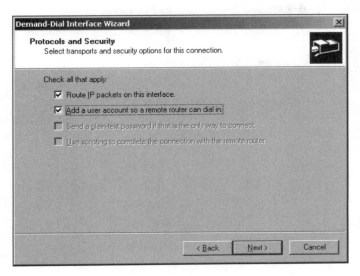

Figure 4-7   Creating a dial-in account for the remote router

18. On the Static Routes for Remote Networks page, click **Add**. In the Static Route dialog box, type **192.168.1XX.0** (where *XX* is your partner's assigned student number), type **255.255.255.0** in the Network Mask field, verify that the default Metric setting is **1**, and then click **OK**. Click **Next**.

19. On the Dial In Credentials page, the user name is already configured and grayed out. Type **Password!** in both the Password and Confirm password fields. Your password is displayed using asterisks, as shown in Figure 4-8. Click **Next**.

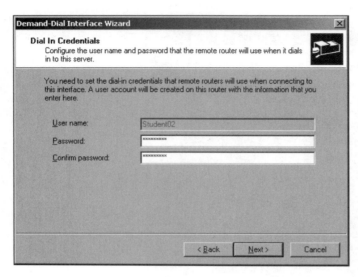

Figure 4-8   Configuring dial-in credentials for the remote router

20. On the Dial Out Credentials page, type **StudentXX** (where *XX* is your assigned student number). When configuring the Dial In Credentials page in the Demand–Dial Interface Wizard, your partner has to set up this account for your server.

It is important that these particular steps are followed precisely; otherwise, your demand-dial connections will not work when you test them.

21. In the Domain field, type **STUDENTXX** (where *XX* is your partner's assigned student number).

Note that, if there are no spaces between STUDENT and *XX* in your server name, you must be sure that there are no spaces in the Domain field either.

22. Verify that the User name field displays the name of your server and that the Domain field displays the name of your partner's server. Type **Password!** in both the Password and Confirm password fields. See Figure 4-9.

Demand-Dial Interface Wizard   ☒

Dial Out Credentials
Configure the user name and password to be used when connecting to the remote router.

You need to set the dial out credentials that this interface will use when connecting to the remote router. These credentials must match the dial in credentials configured on the remote router.

User name:	Student01
Domain:	STUDENT02
Password:	✕✕✕✕✕✕✕✕
Confirm password:	✕✕✕✕✕✕✕✕

< Back   Next >   Cancel

Figure 4-9   Configuring dial-out credentials to the remote router

23. Click **Next** to go to the last step of the wizard. On the Completing the Demand-Dial Interface Wizard page, click **Finish**.

CAUTION Wait until your partner has completed all previous steps before continuing with this lab.

24. Click **Network Interfaces**. In the details pane of the Routing and Remote Access window, a new network interface has been created, "Demand-dial" appears in the Type column, and "Disconnected" appears in the Connection State column. In the next part of this lab, you will test the connection you have created.

25. In the Routing and Remote Access window under Network Interfaces, right-click **STUDENTXX LAN and Demand-dial Interface** (where *XX* is your partner's assigned student number), and click **Connect**. The Interface Connection dialog box should appear briefly. Under Network Interfaces, the demand-dial interface should now appear as Connected.

26. Right-click the **StudentXX** demand-dial connection (where *XX* is your partner's assigned student number) and click **Disconnect**.

27. Click **Start**, click **Run**, type **cmd**, and then click **OK**.

28. In the command prompt window, type **ping 192.168.1XX.1XX** (where *XX* is your partner's assigned student number), and press **Enter**. When you created the demand-dial interface, you also created a static route to the 192.168.1*XX*.0 subnet (where *XX* is your partner's assigned student number). By pinging an IP address on the 192.168.1*XX*.0 subnet, you are trying to initiate the demand-dial connection.

29. In the command prompt window, you should see the Destination host unreachable message and then the Request timed out message. Switch to the Routing and Remote Access window, and press the **F5** key. The connection state of the demand-dial connection should now appear as Connected. The ping will have failed because there is no computer with the IP address that you pinged in the previous step. You only wanted to initiate the demand-dial connection.

30. Right-click the **Student*XX*** demand-dial connection (where *XX* is your partner's assigned student number) and click **Disconnect**. The connection state changes to Disconnected.

31. Right-click the **Student*XX*** demand-dial connection (where *XX* is your partner's assigned student number) and click **Dial-out Hours**.

32. In the Dial-out Hours dialog box, click the current day of the week, and click the **Denied** option button, as shown in Figure 4–10.

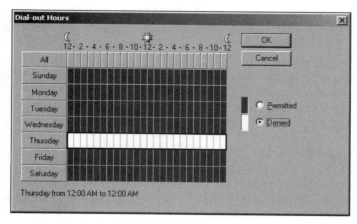

Figure 4-10   Configuring dial-out hours filters

33. Click **OK** to close the Dial-out Hours dialog box.

34. Switch to the command prompt window. Type **ping 192.168.1XX.1XX** (where *XX* is your partner's assigned student number). Again you are pinging for the static route that you created earlier when you were testing the demand-dial connection. (If you can't remember what the last step you pinged was, press the F3 key and then press Enter.) This time you will receive the Request timed out error message.

35. In the Routing and Remote Access window, right-click the **StudentXX** demand-dial connection (where *XX* is your partner's assigned student number), and click **Dial-out Hours**. In the Dial-out Hours dialog box, click **All** and click the **Permitted** option button. All the times in the Dial-out Hours dialog box should now appear in blue. Click **OK** to close the Dial-out Hours dialog box.

36. Switch to the command prompt window, press the **F3** key, and then press **Enter**. You are pinging to establish the demand-dial connection again.

37. Close the command prompt window.

38. Switch back to the Routing and Remote Access window, and then press the **F5** key to refresh the display. The connection state of the demand-dial connection appears as Connected.

39. Right-click the **StudentXX** demand-dial connection (where *XX* is your partner's assigned student number), and click **Disconnect**.

40. Right-click **STUDENTXX (local)** (where *XX* is your assigned student number), and click **Disable Routing and Remote Access**. A message appears, indicating that you are disabling the router and removing its configuration and that you will have to re-enable and reconfigure it later. Click **Yes** to indicate that you want to continue.

41. Close the Routing and Remote Access window.

Certification Objectives

Objectives for Microsoft Exam #70-293: Planning a Microsoft Windows Server 2003 Network:

- Implement secure access between private networks.

REVIEW QUESTIONS

1. Which of the following are not true about demand-dial connections?

   a. They can reduce your connection costs.

   b. Static routing is recommended for on-demand connections.

   c. Demand-dial filters are applied after a connection is made.

   d. all of the above

2. A demand-dial connection fails to connect. Which of the following is a possible explanation? (Choose all that apply.)

   a. IP routing is not enabled.

   b. Dial-out hours prevent th~~~~~~~~

   c. Demand-~

   d. Static rou~

3. Which of the~~~~~~~~~~~~~~-dial routing to work?

   a. Both rout~~~~~~~~~~~outers.

   b. There mu~

   c. The user n~~~~~~~~~the demand-dial interface o~~~~~~~~~~~~~~~for both sides.

   d. all of the above

4. Which of the following must be configured for an account used for initiating a demand-dial interface? (Choose all that apply.)

   a. User must change password at next logon must be cleared.

   b. User must change password at next logon must be selected.

   c. Password never expires must be cleared.

   d. Password never expires must be selected.

5. Once you have created a demand-dial interface, how do you modify the dial-out credentials on the connection?

   a. Right-click Network Interfaces and click Set Credentials.

   b. Right-click the demand-dial interface and click Set Credentials.

   c. Right-click the demand-dial interface and click Properties. On the Networking tab, click Set Credentials.

   d. all of the above

Lab 4.4 An Introduction to the Basic Firewall Component

Objectives

The goal of this lab is to configure and enable Basic Firewall.

Materials Required

This lab will require the following:

- Two Windows Server 2003 servers installed and configured according to the instructions at the beginning of this lab manual

NOTE

This lab also requires that each student work with a partner. There are sections of this activity that need to be completed by both partners, and others that need to be completed by only one partner.

Estimated completion time: **30 minutes**

Activity Background

One of the new features available in Routing and Remote Access on Windows Server 2003 is Basic Firewall. The Basic Firewall option is only available on public interfaces and can help to secure your network from unsolicited traffic. With this component enabled, all traffic passing though the interface is monitored according to the firewall rules. As with other firewall implementations, Basic Firewall also offers the ability to configure exceptions as to which traffic will be blocked by the firewall. By default, echo requests from an external network are not allowed to pass through the firewall and onto the private network.

ACTIVITY

Activity

Partner One only:

1. If necessary, log on as **Administrator** for the Arctic.local domain with a password of **Password!**.

2. Click **Start**, point to **Administrative Tools**, and click **Routing and Remote Access**.

3. In the Routing and Remote Access window, right-click **STUDENTXX (local)** (where *XX* is your assigned student number), and click **Configure and Enable Routing and Remote Access**.

4. On the Welcome to the Routing and Remote Access Server Setup Wizard page, click **Next**.

5. On the Configuration tab, click the **Custom Configuration** option and click **Next**.

6. On the Custom configuration page, check the **NAT and basic firewall** check box and click **Next**.

7. On the Completing the Routing and Remote Access Server Setup Wizard page, verify that NAT and basic firewall appears under the Summary of selections list, and click **Finish**.

8. A message appears, indicating that Routing and Remote Access is installed and asking you if you want to start the service. Click **Yes**.

9. If necessary, expand IP Routing, and then right-click **NAT/Basic Firewall** and click **New Interface**.

10. In the New Interface for Network Address Translation (NAT) dialog box, click **Classroom** and click **OK**.

11. In the Network Address Translation Properties - Classroom Properties dialog box, the Interface Type setting defaults to the Private interface connected to private network option. Click the **Basic firewall only** option button. Once you have selected this option, the Address Pool, Services and Ports, and ICMP tabs now appear, as shown in Figure 4-11.

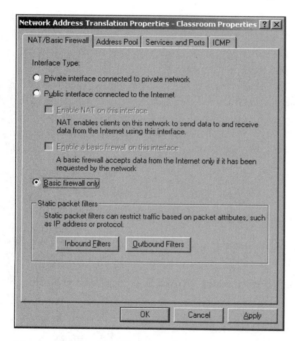

Figure 4-11   Configuring the Basic firewall only option

12. Click **OK** to close the Network Address Translation Properties - Classroom Properties dialog box.

Partner Two only:

1. Click **Start**, click **Run**, type **cmd**, and click **OK**.

2. In the command prompt window, type **Ping 192.168.1.1XX** (where *XX* is your partner's assigned student number), and press **Enter**. The message Request timed out is displayed.

Partner One only:

1. Under IP Routing, click **NAT/Basic Firewall,** right-click the **Classroom** interface and click **Properties**. Click the ICMP tab, then check the **Incoming echo request** check box to select it, and then click **Apply**.

2. Click **OK** to close the Network Address Translation Properties - Classroom Properties dialog box.

Partner Two only:

1. In the command prompt window, press the **F3** key and press **Enter**. You should receive a reply from your partner's IP address.

Partner One only:

1. In the Routing and Remote Access window, right-click **STUDENTXX (local)** (where *XX* is your assigned student number), and click **Properties**.

2. In the STUDENT*XX* (local) Properties dialog box (where *XX* is your assigned student number), check the **Remote access server** check box to select it, and then click **OK**. You are now going to enable VPN access to your server to test the firewall settings.

3. A message appears, indicating that you made changes to the router configuration that requires the router to be restarted and asking you if you would like to continue. Click **Yes**.

4. Right-click **Ports** and click **Properties**. On the Ports Properties dialog box, click **WAN Miniport (PPTP)** and click **Configure**.

5. In the Configure Device - WAN Miniport (PPTP) dialog box, check the **Remote access connections (inbound only)** check box to select it, as shown in Figure 4-12.

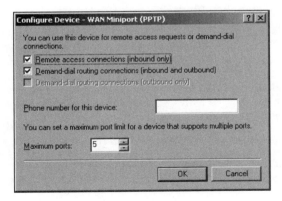

Figure 4-12   Configuring WAN Miniport (PPTP) for remote access

6. Click **OK** to close the Configure Device - WAN Miniport (PPTP) dialog box, and then click **OK** to close the Ports Properties dialog box.

7. The WAN Miniport (PPTP) entries under Ports now show RAS/Routing under the Used By column. You are now going to create a user account on this server that your partner can use to connect to the VPN server. Click **Start**, right-click **My Computer**, and click **Manage**.

8. In the Computer Management window, expand Local Users and Groups. Right-click **Users** and click **New User**. Type **FirewallVPNTest** as the user name. Type **Password!** in both the Password and Confirm password fields. Uncheck the **User must change password at next logon** check box, and then click the **User cannot change password** option button to select this option. Click **Create** to create the new user, and then click **Close** to close the New User dialog box.

9. Expand the Users folder, if necessary, then right-click the **FirewallVPNTest** account, and click **Properties**. In the FirewallVPNTest Properties dialog box, click the **Dial-in** tab. Under Remote Access Permission (Dial-in or VPN), click the **Allow access** option button, and then click **OK** to close the Firewal-lVPNTest Properties dialog box.

10. Close the Computer Management window.

Partner Two only:

1. Click **Start**, point to **Control Panel**, point to **Network Connections**, and then click **New Connection Wizard**.

2. In the Welcome to the New Connection Wizard dialog box, click **Next**.

3. On the Network Connection Type page, click **Connect to the network at my workplace**, and click **Next**.

4. On the Network Connection page, click **Virtual Private Network connection**, and click **Next**.

5. On the Connection Name page, type **StudentXX** (where *XX* is your partner's assigned student number), and click **Next**.

6. On the VPN Server Selection page under Host name or IP address, type **192.168.1.1XX** (where *XX* is your partner's assigned student number), and then click **Next**.

7. On the Connection Availability page, leave at the default For My use only and click **Next**.

8. On the Completing the New Connection Wizard page, click the **Add a shortcut to this connection to my desktop** option button, and click **Finish**.

9. In the Connect StudentXX dialog box, type **FirewallVPNTest** in the User name field, type **Password!** in the Password field, and then click **Connect**.

10. The Error Connecting to Student*XX* message (where *XX* is your partner's assigned student number), as shown in Figure 4-13, is displayed. This error indicates that it was unable to establish the VPN connection and that the VPN server may be unreachable or that security parameters may not be configured properly for this connection.

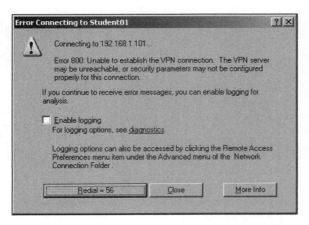

4

Figure 4-13   Error message when basic firewall not configured to allow VPN access

11. Click **More Info** to view more information on Error 800, and then review the information provided.

12. Click **Close** to close the Error Connecting to Student*XX* message box (where *XX* is your partner's assigned student number).

Partner One only:

1. In the Routing and Remote Access window, click **NAT/Basic Firewall**.

2. Right-click the **Classroom** interface and click **Properties**.

3. In the Classroom Properties dialog box, click the **Services and Ports** tab. In the list of services for which you can create exceptions on your firewall, scroll down and click to select **VPN Gateway (PPTP)**. The Edit Service dialog box opens.

4. Click in the Private address field, type **192.168.1.1XX** (where *XX* is your assigned student number), as shown in Figure 4-14. Click **OK**.

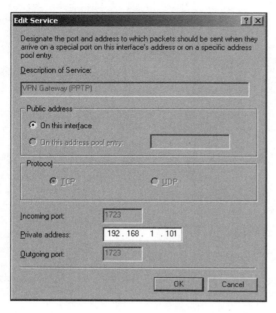

Figure 4-14 Configuring VPN Gateway (PPTP)

5. In the Classroom Properties dialog box, verify that **VPN Gateway (PPTP)** is selected, as shown in Figure 4-15, and then click **OK** to close the Classroom Properties dialog box.

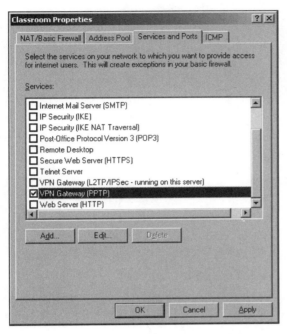

Figure 4-15   Selecting VPN Gateway (PPTP)

Partner Two only:

1. Click **Start**, point to **Control Panel**, and double-click **Network Connections**. In the Network Connections window, double-click the **Student*XX*** Virtual Private Network Connection (where *XX* is your partner's assigned student number). In the Connect Student*XX* window, type **FirewallVPNTest** in the User name field, type **Password!** in the password field, and then click **Connect**. When the Connect Student*XX* dialog box appears indicating that Windows was unable to connect to the network using the username and password you provided, re-enter the username and password. Verify that FirewallVPNTest appears in the User name field, and that Student*XX* (where *XX* is your partner's student number) appears in the Domain field. Click **OK** to close the Connect Student*XX* dialog box.

Partner One only:

1. In the Routing and Remote Access window, the Total mappings, Inbound packets translated, Inbound packets rejected, Outbound packets translated, and Outbound packets rejected columns now show values.

2. Refresh the Routing and Remote Access window, and then click **Remote Access Clients (1)**. Note that in the details pane, the Student*XX*\ FirewallVPNTest connection (where *XX* is your assigned student number) appears in the User Name column, as shown in Figure 4-16.

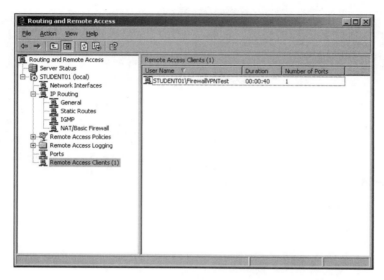

Figure 4-16   Viewing Remote Access Clients connections

3. Right-click the **STUDENT*XX*\FirewallVPNTest** connection (where *XX* is your assigned student number), and click **Disconnect**.

4. Right-click **STUDENT*XX* (local)** (where *XX* is your assigned student number), and click **Disable Routing and Remote Access**. A message appears, indicating that you are disabling the router and removing its configuration and that you will have to re-enable and reconfigure it later. Click **Yes** to indicate that you want to continue.

Certification Objectives

Objectives for Microsoft Exam #70-293: Planning a Microsoft Windows Server 2003 Network:

- Plan an Internet connectivity strategy.

- Troubleshoot connectivity to the Internet.

- Diagnose and resolve issues related to Network Address Translation (NAT).

REVIEW QUESTIONS

1. Which of the following statements are true?

   a. If using private addresses on an intranet and you require connectivity to the Internet, address translation is required.

   b. Basic firewall can be enabled without NAT.

   c. Traffic can be allowed or blocked using static packet filters.

   d. all of the above

2. Where would you configure the Basic Firewall option?

   a. Right-click the network connection and click the Advanced tab.

   b. Right-click the network connection, click Internet Protocol (TCP/IP), click Properties, and click the Advanced tab.

   c. Open Routing and Remote Access, right-click NAT/Basic Firewall, and click Properties.

   d. none of the above

3. What is the default set to for event logging?

   a. Log errors only

   b. Log errors and warnings

   c. Log the maximum amount of information

   d. Disable event logging

4. Which ICMP options are allowed by default when just the basic firewall option has been configured? (Choose all that apply.)

   a. Incoming echo request

   b. Incoming router request

   c. Outgoing source quench

   d. Outgoing parameter problem

5. Which of the following selections, if selected on the NAT/Basic Firewall tab, provides the interface with basic firewall?

   a. Private interface connected to private network

   b. Public interface connected to the Internet

   c. Basic firewall only

   d. all of the above

4

LAB 4.5 AN INTRODUCTION TO INTERNET CONNECTION SHARING (ICS)

Objectives

The goal of this lab is to connect to the Web server running on the instructor computer. To accomplish this goal, you will explore the two alternative methods provided by Windows Server 2003 for connecting SOHOs to the Internet: routing and translation.

Materials Required

This lab will require the following:

- Two Windows Server 2003 servers installed and configured according to the instructions at the beginning of this lab manual

NOTE

This lab also requires that each student work with a partner. One student computer must be connected to the other student computer with a crossover cable.

Estimated completion time: **15 minutes**

Activity Background

Implementing routing requires that you have some knowledge of IP addressing and routing configuration information; whereas translation offers a somewhat simpler implementation.

One way that you can access the Internet is to configure Internet Connection Sharing (ICS) on the properties of a network connection. Once Internet Connection Sharing is enabled, all computers on your internal network can use that interface to gain access to the Internet. In order to implement ICS, you must make sure that your system has a public connection that connects your network to the Internet and a private connection that communicates with systems in your internal network.

Unlike the NAT protocol, ICS does not offer configurable options. Once enabled, the interface is assigned a specific IP address (192.168.0.1) and then assigns hosts on your network IP addresses on that same subnet. This configuration cannot be modified. Should these settings not work on your internal network, you need to implement NAT instead.

ACTIVITY

Activity

Partner One only:

1. If necessary, log on as **Administrator** of the Arctic.local domain with a password of **Password!**.

2. Click **Start**, point to **Control Panel**, and double-click **Network Connections**.

3. In the Network Connections window, right-click **Classroom** and click **Properties**.

4. In the Classroom Properties dialog box, click the **Advanced** tab. On the Advanced tab under Internet Connection Sharing, check the **Allow other network users to connect through this computer's Internet connection** check box, as shown in Figure 4-17. Click **OK** to close the Classroom Properties dialog box.

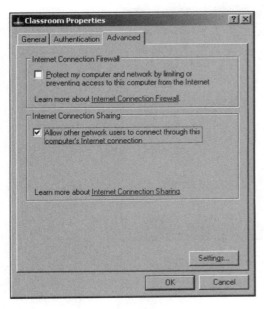

Figure 4-17   Enabling ICS

5. If you receive the message, indicating that your LAN adapter will be set to use IP address 192.168.0.1, that your computer may lose connectivity with other computers on your network, and that if those other systems have static addresses then you should configured them to obtain their IP addresses automatically, click **Yes** to indicate that you are sure you want to enable Internet Connection Sharing. In the Network Connections window, the Classroom connection should now appear as Enabled, Shared, as shown in Figure 4–18.

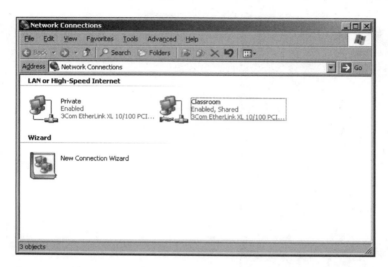

Figure 4-18   ICS enabled on the Classroom connection

Partner Two only:

1. Log on as **Administrator** of the Arctic.local domain with a password of **Password!**.

2. Click **Start**, point to **Control Panel**, and double-click **Network Connections**.

3. In the Network Connections window, right-click **Classroom** and click **Disable**.

4. Click **Start**, click **Run**, type **cmd**, and click **OK**.

5. In the command prompt window, type **ipconfig /release** and press **Enter**.

6. In the command prompt window, type **ipconfig /renew** and press **Enter**. Notice that the connection-specific DNS suffix now appears as mshome.net. Your IP address is 192.168.0.*x* (where *x* is a random number between 1 and 254), your subnet mask is now 255.255.255.0, and your default gateway has been set to 192.168.0.1. See Figure 4-19.

Figure 4-19   New IP configuration settings for Partner Two

7. Click the **Internet Explorer** shortcut on the Quick Launch toolbar.

8. In Internet Explorer, type **http://192.168.1.10** in the Address bar, and then press **Enter**. You connect to the Web server running on your instructor's computer. The source IP address appears as the IP address on the Classroom connection of your partner's server, as shown in Figure 4-20.

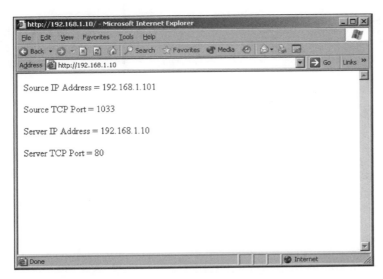

Figure 4-20   Source IP address of packets sent to instructor Web page

9. Close Internet Explorer, and close the command prompt window.

10. In the Network Connections window, right-click **Classroom** and click **Enable**.

11. Close the Network Connections window.

Partner One only:

1. In the Network Connections window, right-click **Classroom** and click **Properties**. Click the **Advanced** tab, uncheck the **Allow other network users to connect through this computer's Internet connection** check box, and then click **OK**.

2. If the Private connection appears as an Invalid Address (as shown in Figure 4-21), right-click the **Private** connection and click **Repair**. (This may take a while. A message will appear, indicating that it was unable to renew an IP address from the DHCP server and that it will not have an automatic private address to connect to computers on the same private network; click **OK**.) Close the Network Connections window.

Figure 4-21   Private connection with an invalid address

Certification Objectives

Objectives for Microsoft Exam #70-293: Planning a Microsoft Windows Server 2003 Network:

- Plan an Internet connectivity strategy.

- Troubleshoot connectivity to the Internet.

- Diagnose and resolve issues related to Network Address Translation (NAT).

REVIEW QUESTIONS

1. Which of the following is true about ICS?

   a. To configure, you check just one box.

   b. It offers a single public IP address.

   c. It offers a configurable address range.

   d. all of the above

2. Both ICS and NAT provide which of the following services?

   a. Translation

   b. IP addressing

   c. Name resolution services

   d. all of the above

3. Which of the following is true about the address range offered by ICS to hosts on the internal network?

   a. It is fixed and cannot be configured.

   b. It is configurable but with limited options.

   c. It is fully configurable with a wide range of options.

   d. none of the above

4. Which of the following represents the IP address of the adapter configured for ICS?

   a. 192.168.0.1

   b. 169.254.0.1

   c. 192.168.1.1

   d. none of the above

5. What is the default gateway for client computers on a network that has ICS enabled?

   a. 192.168.0.1

   b. 169.254.0.1

   c. 192.168.1.1

   d. none of the above

4

PLANNING, CONFIGURING, AND TROUBLESHOOTING DHCP

Labs included in this chapter:

♦ Lab 5.1 Installing and Authorizing Windows Server 2003 DHCP Server

♦ Lab 5.2 Configuring Scopes on a DHCP server

♦ Lab 5.3 DHCP and the Remote Access Service

♦ Lab 5.4 Installing a Standalone DHCP Server

♦ Lab 5.5 Superscopes

Microsoft MCSE Exam #70-293 Objectives	
Objective	Lab
Diagnose and resolve issues related to client computer configuration.	5.1, 5.2, 5.5
Diagnose and resolve issues related to DHCP server address assignment.	5.1, 5.2, 5.3, 5.4, 5.5

Lab 5.1 Installing and Authorizing Windows Server 2003 DHCP Server

Objectives

The goal of this lab activity is to install and configure the DHCP server service on a Windows Server 2003 member server. Because the server is in an Active Directory domain, you also need to authorize the server in Active Directory.

Materials Required

This lab will require the following:

- Two Windows Server 2003 servers installed and configured according to the instructions at the beginning of this lab manual

Note that all the labs in this chapter assume that one server acts as a DHCP server and the other is the DHCP client. In this first lab, you will install and configure the DHCP server service on the server that will become the DHCP server for the lab activities in this chapter. The other Windows Server 2003 server will act as the DHCP client for the lab activities in this chapter.

Estimated completion time: **10 minutes**

Activity Background

The DHCP (Dynamic Host Configuration Protocol) Server service is one of the networking services that can be installed on a Windows Server 2003 system. Once the service has been installed, you can configure scopes. Scopes contain a range of IP addresses that you can assign to client computers configured to obtain IP addresses automatically.

There are several benefits of using DHCP on your network. One benefit is not having to configure client computers manually. Also, if client computers are moved from one location to another, the system obtains a new IP address configuration once restarted on the new subnet.

Before beginning this lab activity, designate one server to be the DHCP server and another to be the DHCP client.

Lab 5-1 should be completed only by the student whose server will act as the DHCP server. If time permits, after completing all labs in this chapter, you can switch roles. If you do not have a partner, you must still have a second Windows Server 2003 server in order to test the functionality of both the DHCP server and the DHCP client.

Activity

Partner One only (the DHCP server):

1. Log on as **Administrator** of the Arctic.local domain with a password of **Password!**.

2. Click **Start**, point to **Control Panel**, and double-click **Network Connections**.

3. In the Network Connections window, right-click **Private** and click **Properties**.

4. In the Private Properties dialog box, click **Internet Protocol (TCP/IP)** and click **Properties**.

5. In the Internet Protocol (TCP/IP) Properties dialog box, click **Use the following IP address**, type **192.168.1XX.1XX** (where *XX* is your assigned student number) in the IP address field, type **255.255.255.0** in the Subnet Mask field, and then click **OK**.

6. Click **Close** to close the Private Properties dialog box, and then close the Network Connections window.

7. Click **Start**, click **Control Panel**, and click **Add or Remove Programs**.

8. In the Add or Remove Programs window, click **Add/Remove Windows Components**.

9. On the Windows Components page, scroll through the list of components until Networking Services is visible. Click **Networking Services** and click **Details**.

10. In the Networking Services dialog box, click the **Dynamic Host Configuration Protocol (DHCP)** check box in the Subcomponents of Networking Services list (as shown in Figure 5-1) and click **OK**.

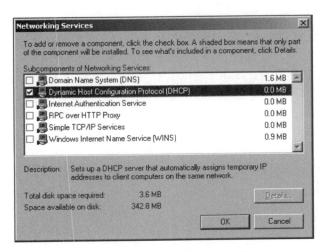

Figure 5-1   Selecting to install the DHCP service

11. On the Windows Components page, click **Next**.

12. On the Completing the Windows Components Wizard page, click **Finish**.

13. Close the Add or Remove Programs window.

14. Click **Start**, point to **Administrative Tools**, and then click **DHCP**. The DHCP console opens.

15. Double-click **studentXX.arctic.local** (where *XX* is your assigned student number). The details pane of the console now displays the text "Configure the DHCP server." If you are unfamiliar with the Windows Server 2003 DHCP service, online Help is available. Press the **F1** key. A Microsoft Management Console window opens displaying help for DHCP. Close the Microsoft Management Console window.

16. In the DHCP window, a red arrow appears next to your server name, indicating that the server has not been authorized in Active Directory. Right-click **DHCP** and click **Manage authorized servers**.

17. In the Manage Authorized Servers dialog box, shown in Figure 5-2, click **Authorize**.

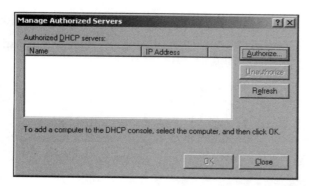

Figure 5-2   The Manage Authorized Servers dialog box

18. In the Authorize DHCP server dialog box, type **192.168.1XX.1XX** (where *XX* is your assigned student number), and then click **OK**.

19. In the Confirm Authorization dialog box, your IP address has been resolved to your server name (as shown in Figure 5-3). Click **OK** to close the Confirm Authorization dialog box.

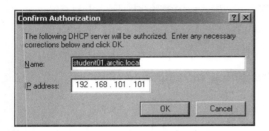

Figure 5-3   The Confirm Authorization dialog box

20. In the Manage Authorized Servers dialog box, student*XX*.arctic.local (where *XX* is your assigned student number) now appears in the list of Authorized DHCP servers, as shown in Figure 5-4. Click **Close** to close the Manage Authorized Servers dialog box.

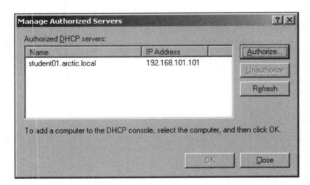

Figure 5-4   Student*XX* appears on the Authorized DHCP servers list

21. In the DHCP window, click **Action** on the menu bar, and click **Refresh**. There is now a green arrow next to the name of your server, indicating that it has been authorized in Active Directory.

22. Close the DHCP window.

Certification Objectives

Objectives for Microsoft Exam #70-293: Planning a Microsoft Windows Server 2003 Network:

- Diagnose and resolve issues related to client computer configuration.

- Diagnose and resolve issues related to DHCP server address assignment.

REVIEW QUESTIONS

1. Which of the following are benefits of using DHCP?

   a. avoids configuration errors caused by manu__

   b. prevents address conflicts between __

   c. decreases time spent confi__ __rs on the network

   d. all of the above

2. Which of __ __tic Private IP addressing.

   a. Windows

   b. Windows __

   c. Windows 20__

   d. Windows XP

3. What type of message __ __ents send when trying to obtain an IP address?

   a. unicast

   b. multicast

   c. broadcast

   d. none of the above

4. How often do DHCP clients attempt to contact a DHCP server after being issued an automatic private IP address?

   a. every 30 seconds

   b. every 60 seconds

   c. every 2 minutes

   d. every 5 minutes

5. Members of the DHCP Administrators group have rights to which of the following?

   a. the local computer only

   b. all DHCP servers in the domain

   c. all servers in the domain

   d. all of the above

LAB 5.2 CONFIGURING SCOPES ON A DHCP SERVER

Objectives

The goal of this lab activity is to create a scope and to configure scope options. You will also create a client reservation for your partner's Private connection.

Materials Required

This lab will require the following:

- Two Windows Server 2003 servers installed and configured according to the instructions at the beginning of this lab manual

- A lab partner; If you are working alone, you must perform the steps for both partners using the two Windows Server 2003 systems

Estimated completion time: **30 minutes**

Activity Background

A DHCP scope is a range of IP addresses that can be assigned to client computers on your Windows Server 2003 network. When creating a scope, you need to configure:

- A range of IP addresses that will be assigned to client computers and an associated subnet mask.

- Exclusions, which are individual IP addresses or a range of IP addresses that will not be assigned to client computers. Examples of IP addresses that you might want to exclude are servers, printers, or any host on your TCP/IP network having a static IP address falling in the range of your scope. Exclusion ranges are optional.

- A scope name.

- A lease duration or amount of time that clients are able to use the IP address they have been assigned.

- Additional options, such as the IP address of a router, DNS server, or WINS server, which are optional.

Client reservations map an IP address to the MAC address of the network adapter card. You can configure client reservations for the systems on your network that always need to receive the same IP address configuration from the DHCP server.

Activity

Partner One only (the DHCP server):

1. If necessary, log on as **Administrator** for the Arctic.local domain with a password of **Password!**.

2. Click **Start**, point to **Administrative Tools**, and click **DHCP**.

3. In the DHCP window, double-click **studentXX.Arctic.local** (where *XX* is your assigned student number).

4. Click **Server Options**. Review the text in the details pane of the DHCP window. Server options are additional parameters that can be assigned to DHCP clients. Server options are the defaults for all scopes and can be overridden by Scope Options.

5. Right-click **studentXX.Arctic.local** (where *XX* is your assigned student number) and click **New Scope**.

6. On the Welcome to the New Scope Wizard page, click **Next**.

7. On the Scope Name page, type **1XX** (where *XX* is your assigned student number). For example, if your server is Student01, your scope name is 101, as shown in Figure 5-5. Click **Next**.

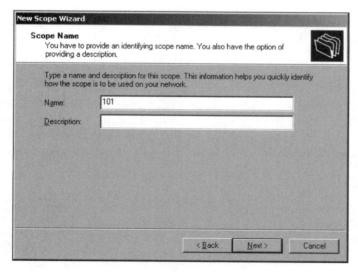

Figure 5-5   Creating a new scope

8. On the IP Address Range page in the Start IP address field, type
192.168.1XX.1, (where *XX* is your assigned student number). In the End IP
address field, type **192.168.1XX.254** (where *XX* is your assigned student
number). The Length field changes from 8 to 24. This number refers to the
number of 1's in the binary representation of the subnet mask, as shown in
Figure 5-6. Click **Next**.

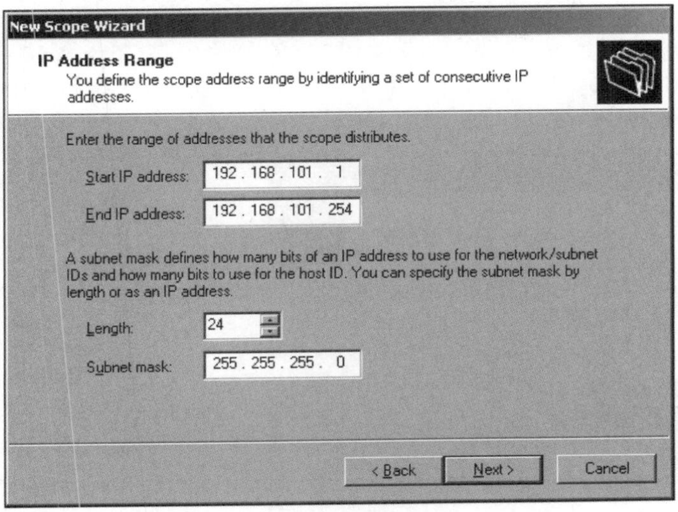

Figure 5-6   Configuring the IP address range

9. On the Add Exclusions page, you need to configure addresses that will not be assigned by your DHCP server. Typically, IP addresses that you would want to exclude are those of hosts (such as computers, printers, router interfaces, and so on) that have static IP addresses that fall within the configured range of your scope. By configuring exclusions, you ensure that the DHCP server does not assign an IP address that is already in use on your network. In the Start IP address field, type **192.168.1XX.1XX** (where *XX* is your assigned student number). For example, for the Student01 server that has a Private connection IP address of 192.168.101.101, you would type "192.168.101.101." Click **Add**. The new IP address appears in the Excluded address range dialog box, as shown in Figure 5-7. Click **Next**.

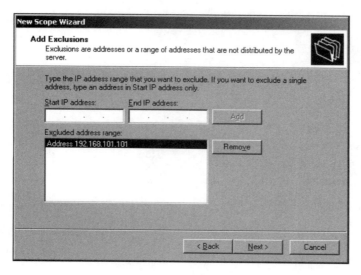

Figure 5-7   Configuring an exclusion range

10. On the Lease Duration page, read the information provided with regards to lease durations, and then click **Next** to accept the default lease duration of eight days.

11. On the Configure DHCP Options page, click the **Yes, I want to configure these options now** option button, and click **Next**.

12. On the Router (Default Gateway) page, type **192.168.1XX.1** (where *XX* is your assigned student number), click **Add**, and then click **Next**.

13. On the Domain Name and DNS Servers page, tab down to the Parent domain field, and then type **Arctic.local**. In the IP address field, type **192.168.1XX.2** (where *XX* is your assigned student number), and then click **Add**. Click **Next**.

14. On the WINS Servers page, type **192.168.1XX.3** (where *XX* is your assigned student number) in the IP address field, and click **Add**. Click **Next**.

15. On the Activate Scope page, click the **No, I will activate this scope later** option button, and then click **Next**.

16. On the Completing the New Scope Wizard page, click **Finish**.

17. In the DHCP window, student*XX*.arctic.local (where *XX* is your assigned student number) appears with a green arrow beside it, whereas the new scope that you have just configured appears with a red arrow beside it, as shown in Figure 5-8. Before you activate this scope you are going to modify the scope properties. Double-click **Scope [192.168.1XX.0] 1XX** (where *XX* is your assigned student number) to expand it, if necessary.

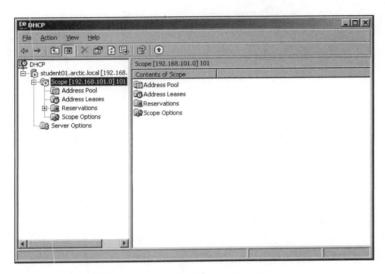

Figure 5-8   The new scope before activation

5

18. Click **Address Pool**. The range of addresses you assigned appears with the description "Address range for distribution." The excluded IP address is marked with a red X and its description reads "IP Addresses excluded from distribution." See Figure 5-9. In this exclusion range, the IP addresses of the DNS and WINS servers on this subnet were not taken into consideration. You will now add an exclusion range that includes the omitted servers.

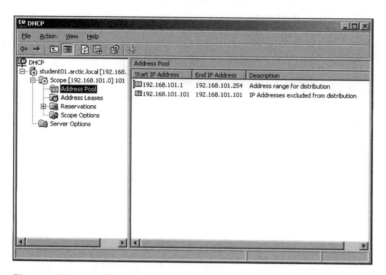

Figure 5-9   Excluding the IP address of the DHCP server from the address pool

19. Right-click **Address Pool** and click **New Exclusion Range**. In the Start IP address field, type **192.168.1XX.1** (where *XX* is your assigned student number). In the End IP address field, type **192.168.1XX.15** (where *XX* is your assigned student number), click **Add**, and then click **Close**. The exclusion range now appears in the address pool along with the original exclusion range you created for the DHCP server.

20. Click **Scope Options**. The options you configured in the wizard appear, as shown in Figure 5-10.

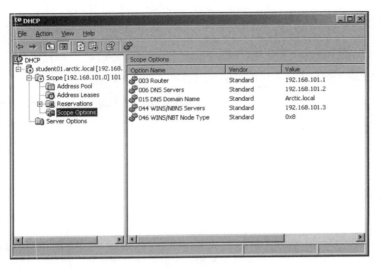

Figure 5-10 The original scope options

21. Right-click **Scope Options** and click **Configure Options**.

22. In the Scope Options dialog box, scroll through the list of available options, and then click **006 DNS Servers**. The Data entry field now becomes available. In the IP Address field, type **192.168.1XX.4** (where *XX* is your assigned student number), and click **Add**.

23. Scroll through the list of available options, and then click **044 WINS/NBNS Servers**. In the IP Address field, type **192.168.1XX.5** (where *XX* is your assigned student number), and then click **Add**.

24. Click **OK** to close the Scope Options dialog box. The changes you made to scope options now appear in the details pane of the DHCP window.

25. Right-click the scope you just created, and click **Activate**. The red arrow disappears.

Partner Two only (the DHCP client computer):

1. If necessary, log on as **Administrator** for the Arctic.local domain with a password of **Password!**.

2. Click **Start**, point to **Control Panel**, and then double-click **Network Connections**.

3. In the Network Connections window, right-click **Private** and click **Properties**.

4. In the Private Properties dialog box, click **Internet Protocol (TCP/IP)** and click **Properties**.

5. In the Internet Protocol (TCP/IP) Properties dialog box, click **Use the following IP address**. In the IP address field, type **192.168.1XX.10** (where XX is your partner's assigned student number), and then type **255.255.255.0** in the Subnet mask field.

6. Click **OK** to close the Internet Protocol (TCP/IP) Properties dialog box, and then click **Close** to close the Private Properties dialog box.

7. Click **Start**, click **Run**, type **cmd**, and then click **OK**.

8. In the command prompt window, type **ipconfig /all** and press **Enter**. Take note of the physical address of your Private connection. Next, your partner is going to use the arp command to obtain the physical address of your partner connection remotely. Leave the command prompt window open for comparison purposes while your partner completes the next step.

Partner One only (the DHCP server):

1. Click **Start**, click **Run**, type **cmd**, and then click **OK**.

2. Next you will ping your partner's Private connection. In the command prompt window, type **ping 192.168.1XX.10** (where XX is your assigned student number) and press **Enter**. You should receive four replies.

3. In the command prompt window, type **arp –a** and press **Enter**. An entry for the 192.168.1XX.10 IP address mapping to the physical address (MAC address) of the network card appears, as shown in Figure 5-11. Write down the physical address of the 192.168.1XX.10 IP address. This is the physical address of your partner's Private connection. You are going to use this information in the next part of this exercise.

Figure 5-11   Viewing the ARP cache

4. In the DHCP window, click **Reservations**. Right-click **Reservations** and click **New Reservation**.

5. In the New Reservation dialog box, type **Lab Partner** in the Reservation name field, type **192.168.1XX.11** (where *XX* is your assigned student number) in the IP address field, and type the value that you wrote down in Step 3 for the physical address of your partner's network card in the MAC address field. See Figure 5-12.

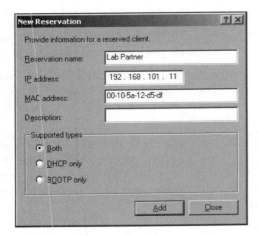

Figure 5-12   Creating the Lab Partner reservation

6. Click **Add** to create the Lab Partner reservation, and then click **Close** to close the New Reservation dialog box.

7. In the DHCP console, double-click **Reservations**.

8. Right-click the new reservation in the details pane and click **Properties**.

9. Under the MAC address field, the hyphens you added in the previous step have been removed. Click **OK**.

Partner Two only (the DHCP client computer):

1. In the Network Connections window, right-click **Private** and click **Properties**.

2. In the Private Properties dialog box, click **Internet Protocol (TCP/IP)** and click **Properties**.

3. In the Internet Protocol (TCP/IP) Properties dialog box, click **Obtain an IP address automatically**, and then click **OK**.

4. Click **Close** to exit the Private Properties dialog box.

5. In the command prompt window, type **ipconfig /all** and press **Enter**. The IP address assigned to the Private connection is the same IP address that was configured in the reservation. The scope options have also been assigned to the Private connection. Also note that the lease expires eight days from now.

Partner One only (the DHCP server):

1. In the DHCP window, right-click the reservation you created for your partner's Private connection, and click **Configure Options**. You will configure the reserved client options in much the same way that you configured the scope options previously.

2. In the Reservation Options dialog box, check the **003 Router** option check box. Under the Data entry field, type **192.168.1XX.6** (where *XX* is your assigned student number) in the IP address field, and then click **Add**.

3. Scroll through the list of available options, and check the **006 DNS Servers** check box. In the IP address field, type **192.168.1XX.7** (where *XX* is your assigned student number), and then click **Add**. Click **OK** to close the Reservation Options dialog box.

4. In the DHCP window, under Reservations, click **192.168.1XX.11 Lab Partner**. In the details pane, the reserved client options appear with a different icon than the other previously configured options. The previously configured router option has been replaced with the reserved client level router option you have just added, as shown in Figure 5-13.

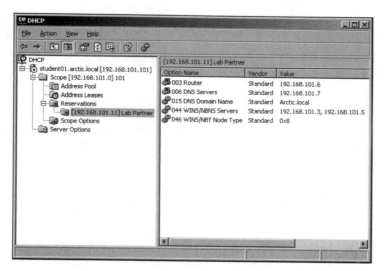

Figure 5-13   Lab Partner reservation options

5. Close the DHCP window.

Partner Two only (the DHCP client computer):

1. In the command prompt window, type **ipconfig /release** and press **Enter**.

2. In the command prompt window, type **ipconfig /renew** and press **Enter**.

3. In the command prompt window, type **ipconfig /all** and press **Enter**. View the IP configuration information for the private connection. The reserved client level options have now overridden the scope options that were initially configured. When there were no conflicting settings, the scope options were inherited by the reserved client.

4. Close the command prompt window, and then close the Network Connections window.

Certification Objectives

Objectives for Microsoft Exam #70-293: Planning a Microsoft Windows Server 2003 Network:

- Diagnose and resolve issues related to client computer configuration.

- Diagnose and resolve issues related to DHCP server address assignment.

REVIEW QUESTIONS

1. Which of the following are required when creating a DHCP scope? (Choose all that apply.)

   a. scope name

   b. subnet mask

   c. range of IP addresses

   d. lease duration

2. Which of the following cannot be modified after a scope has been created?

   a. address range

   b. exclusion range

   c. subnet mask

   d. lease duration

3. Which of the following is not true with regards to scopes?

   a. You should use exclusions for DHCP enabled devices on your network such as print servers.

   b. You should use reservations for devices that are statically configured and that fall within the scope range.

   c. The default lease duration is eight days.

   d. all of the above

4. If server options, scope options, and reservation options are all configured for a particular client, which one will override the others?

   a. server options

   b. scope options

   c. reserved client options

   d. none of the above

5. Which of the following is true with regards to DHCP?

   a. By default, scope options apply to all clients of a DHCP server unless otherwise overridden.

   b. Only properties configured manually at a client computer will override reserved client level options.

   c. Only clients that indicate class membership during leasing activity are configured with class-assigned option values.

   d. all of the above

Lab 5.3 DHCP and the Routing and Remote Access Service

Objectives

The goal of this lab activity is to observe how the Routing and Remote Access service works along with the DHCP Server service in assigning IP addresses to clients connecting remotely to the network.

Materials Required

This lab will require the following:

- Two Windows Server 2003 servers installed and configured according to the instructions at the beginning of this lab manual

- A partner (if available); if this is not possible, you will need to perform the steps for both partners using both Windows Server 2003 systems

Estimated completion time: **20 minutes**

Activity Background

Clients dialing up to a Routing and Remote Access server require an IP address in order to access resources on the internal network. Your DHCP server has the capability of assigning IP addresses to remote access clients through the Routing and Remote Access server. When the DHCP Server service is available on a network, the Routing and Remote

Access server requests IP addresses in blocks of 10 from the DHCP server to be used for remote access connections. When the Routing and Remote Access service is stopped, the addresses are returned to the address pool.

Activity

Partner One only (the DHCP server):

1. If necessary, log on as **Administrator** for the Arctic.local domain with a password of **Password!**.

2. Click **Start**, point to **Administrative Tools**, and click **DHCP**. The DHCP window opens.

3. Double-click **studentXX.arctic.local** (where *XX* is your assigned student number). Double-click **Scope [192.168.1XX.0] 101**.

4. Double-click **Reservations**. Right-click the reservation you configured in Lab 5-2, and click **Delete**. When asked if you are sure you want to delete the reservation, click **Yes**.

5. Click **Scope [192.168.1XX.0] 1XX** (where *XX* is your assigned student number).

6. Click **Address Leases**. At this time no leases have been assigned. Next, you are going to enable and configure Routing and Remote Access on the DHCP server.

7. Click **Start**, point to **Administrative Tools**, and click **Routing and Remote Access**.

8. In the Routing and Remote Access window, right-click **STUDENTXX (local)** (where *XX* is your assigned student number), and click **Configure and Enable Routing and Remote Access**.

9. On the Welcome to the Routing and Remote Access Server Setup Wizard page, click **Next**.

10. On the Configuration page, click **Custom configuration** and click **Next**.

11. On the Custom Configuration page, click **VPN access** and click **Next**.

12. On the Completing the Routing and Remote Access Server Setup Wizard page, click **Finish**.

13. A message appears, indicating that the Routing and Remote Access service has now been installed. Click **Yes** to indicate that you want to start the service.

14. Right-click **STUDENTXX (local)** (where *XX* is your assigned student number) and click **Properties**.

15. In the STUDENT*XX* (local) Properties dialog box, click the **IP** tab. The default for IP address assignment is to assign IP addresses using DHCP. On the bottom of the IP tab, the default setting is to allow RAS to select the adapter. Click the **Adapter** drop-down arrow, and click **Private**, as shown in Figure 5-14.

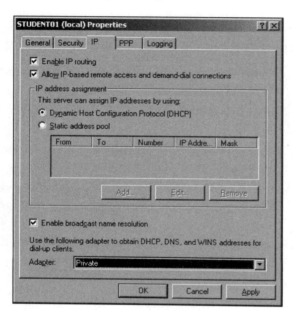

Figure 5-14   Configuring DHCP settings on the Remote Access server

16. Click **OK** to close the STUDENT*XX* (local) Properties dialog box (where *XX* is your assigned student number).

17. Switch to the DHCP window. Press the **F5** key to refresh the display. An additional 10 leases have been obtained. (If you only see a few, wait a few minutes—not all 10 may appear immediately.) The Routing and Remote Access service has requested these addresses from the DHCP server to assign to dial-up clients. See Figure 5-15.

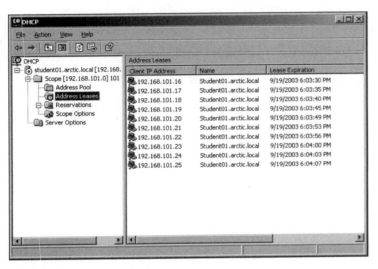

Figure 5-15   Ten IP addresses assigned to the Remote Access server

18. Next, you will create a VPN connection from the client computer and test the IP addressing options that are assigned to the VPN connection. However, first you are going to enable an account for VPN access. Click **Start**, right-click **My Computer**, and click **Manage**.

19. In the Computer Management window, double-click **Local Users and Groups**.

20. Right-click **Users** and click **New User**.

21. In the New User dialog box, type **DhcpVpnTest** in the User name field. Type **Password!** in the Password field and then in the Confirm password field. Uncheck the **User must change password at next logon** check box. Click the **User cannot change password** option button to select it, and then click **Create**. Click **Close** to close the New User dialog box.

22. Click the **Users** container, if necessary. Right-click **DhcpVpnTest** and click **Properties**. Click the **Dial-in** tab. Under Remote Access Permission (Dial-in or VPN), click the **Allow access** option button, and then click **OK** to close the DhcpVpnTest Properties dialog box.

23. Close the Computer Management window, and then close the DHCP window.

Partner Two only (the DHCP client computer):

1. Click **Start**, point to **Control Panel**, and then double-click **Network Connections**. In the Network Connections window, double-click the **New Connection Wizard**.

2. On the Welcome to the New Connection Wizard page, click **Next**.

3. On the Network Connection Type page, click **Connect to the network at my workplace** option and click **Next**.

4. When asked how you want to connect to the network at your workplace, click **Virtual Private Network connection** and click **Next**.

5. On the Connection Name page, type **StudentXX DHCP Test** (where *XX* is your partner's assigned student number) and click **Next**. On the Public Network page, click the **Do Not dial the initial connection** option, and then click **Next**.

6. On the VPN Server Selection page, type **192.168.1XX.101** (where *XX* is your partner's assigned student number), and click **Next**.

7. On the Connection Availability page, verify that the default option is set to **My use only**. Click **Next**.

8. On the Completing the New Connection Wizard page, click **Finish**.

9. In the Connect Student*XX* DHCP Test dialog box (where *XX* is your partner's assigned student number), type **DhcpVpnTest** in the User name field, and then type **Password!** in the Password field. Click **Connect**. If a dialog box appears as shown in Figure 5-16, verify that **DhcpVpnTest** appears in the User name field and **STUDENTXX** (where *XX* is your partner's assigned student number) appears in the Domain field. Click **OK** to close the dialog box.

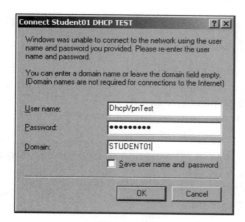

Figure 5-16   Verifying credentials provided for VPN access

10. Once the VPN connection is made, the StudentXX DHCP Test (where XX is your partner's assigned student number) virtual private network connection icon appears as Connected in the Network Connections window. Next you are going to verify the IP address that has been assigned to your VPN connection. Click **Start**, click **Run**, type **cmd**, and then click **OK**.

11. In the command prompt window, type **ipconfig /all** and press **Enter**. Look for the PPP adapter StudentXX DHCP Test (where XX is your partner's assigned student number). The IP address that has been assigned to the virtual private network connection is one of the IP addresses assigned to the Remote Access server for remote access clients.

12. Close the command prompt window, and then close the Network Connections window.

Certification Objectives

Objectives for Microsoft Exam #70-293: Planning a Microsoft Windows server 2003 Network:

- Diagnose and resolve issues related to DHCP server address assignment.

REVIEW QUESTIONS

1. Which of the following is true of user classes?

   a. The ipconfig /setclassid command can be used to set the DHCP class identifier.

   b. The class identifying data set at both DHCP server and member client computers must be identical binary or ASCII data.

   c. Each client computer can be identified only as a member of a single user class at the DHCP server.

   d. all of the above

2. Which of the following is true when a Routing and Remote Access server is configured to use DHCP to assign IP addresses to remote access clients?

   a. The RRAS service obtains 10 IP addresses from the DHCP server.

   b. When the RRAS service is stopped, all addresses obtained through DHCP are released.

   c. RRAS can provide a lease to remote access clients only if options have been predefined using the Default Routing and Remote Access Users class options.

   d. all of the above

3. What happens when all 10 IP addresses assigned from the DHCP server to the Routing and Remote Access server have been leased to clients?

   a. No new clients can   leases one of the IP addresses.

   b. The remote access se

   c. The remote access s

   d. none of the above

4. Which of the followir   Access server when obtaining   apply.)

   a. the IP address of t

   b. the client's leased

   c. when the lease w

   d. the lease duration

5. Which of the follov   he IP configuration obtai

   a. Ping

   b. Ipconfig

   c. Netsh

   d. Arp

LAB 5.4 INSTALLING A STANDALONE DHCP SERVER

Objectives

The goal of this lab activity is to observe what happens when a standalone DHCP server is added to the same subnet as a DHCP server that is a member server in a Windows Server 2003 Active Directory environment.

Materials Required

This lab will require the following:

- Two Windows Server 2003 servers installed and configured according to the instructions at the beginning of this lab manual

Estimated completion time: **20 minutes**

Activity Background

In some networks it is possible for unauthorized DHCP servers to be configured that may assign incorrect IP address configuration information to client computers, causing them not to be able to communicate with domain controllers and domain resources. In order to avoid this happening on Windows 2000 and Windows Server 2003 networks, Microsoft has modified how the DHCP server service operates. Windows 2000 and Windows Server 2003 DHCP servers must be authorized in Active Directory before they can assign addresses to client computers.

On a subnet that hosts an Active Directory network, all DHCP servers must belong to the domain and be authorized by the domain. If a standalone DHCP server is introduced to this subnet, it will not be able to assign addresses to clients.

ACTIVITY

Activity

Partner Two only (the DHCP client computer):

1. Log on as **Administrator** to the Arctic.local domain with a password of **Password!**.

2. Click **Start**, right-click **My Computer**, and click **Properties**.

3. Click the **Computer Name** tab and click **Change**.

4. In the Computer Name Changes dialog box, click the **Workgroup** option button, type **Workgroup**, and then click **OK**.

5. In the Computer Name Changes dialog box, type **Administrator** in the User name field, type Password! in the **Password** field, and then click **OK**.

6. At the Welcome to the WORKGROUP Workgroup message, click **OK**.

7. Click **OK** to the message that tells you that you must restart your computer before the changes will take effect. Click **OK** to close the System Properties dialog box. In the System Settings Change dialog box, click **Yes** to restart your computer now.

8. Log on as **Administrator** to the Student*XX* (where *XX* is your assigned student number) computer with a password of **Password!**. Next, you will install the DHCP server.

9. Click **Start**, point to **Control Panel**, and click **Add or Remove Programs**.

10. In the Add or Remove Programs window, click **Add/Remove Windows Components**.

11. On the Windows Components page, scroll down through the list of available components, click **Networking Services**, and click **Details**.

12. In the Networking Services dialog box, check the **Dynamic Host Configuration Protocol (DHCP)** check box, and click **OK**.

13. Click **Next** on the Windows Components page.

14. On the Completing the Windows Components Wizard page, click **Finish**.

15. Close the Add or Remove Programs window.

16. Click **Start**, point to **Administrative Tools**, and click **DHCP**.

17. Double-click **StudentXX.Arctic.local** (where *XX* is your assigned student number). Your server name appears with a red arrow next to it. Close the DHCP console window.

18. Unplug the network cable to both network adapter cards on the back of your computer.

19. Click **Start**, point to **Administrative Tools**, and click **DHCP.** A green arrow appears next to the name of your server.

20. Leave the DHCP window open. Plug in both network cables again.

21. Right-click **StudentXX** in the DHCP window, and click **Refresh**. A red arrow appears next to your server name once again. In the details pane the status appears as Not Authorized.

22. Click **Start**, right-click **My Computer**, and click **Manage**.

23. In the Computer Management window, double-click **Event Viewer**.

24. Right-click **System** and click **Properties**.

25. In the System Properties dialog box, click the **Filter** tab.

26. Click the **Event source** drop-down arrow, and click **DHCPServer**. In the Event ID field, type **1045**, as shown in Figure 5-17. Click **OK** to close the System Properties dialog box.

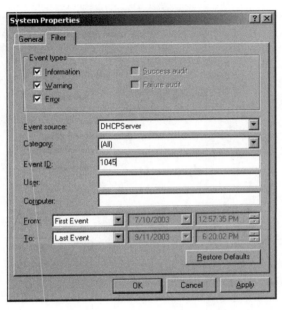

Figure 5-17   Filtering the System Log for DHCP events

27. Verify that System is selected and then double-click the first error event in the details pane. Your screen should resemble Figure 5-18. The DHCP/BINL service on the local computer determined that it was not authorized to start, and it has stopped servicing clients. This computer belongs to a workgroup and has encountered a DHCP server belonging to an Active Directory domain on the same network. Click **OK** to close the Event Properties dialog box, and then close the Event Viewer window.

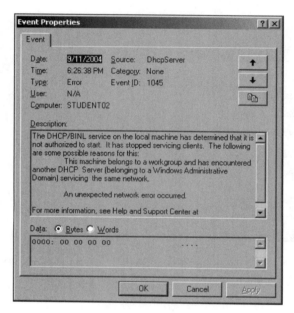

Figure 5-18   Event ID 1045

28. Close the Computer Management console. You are now going to join the Student*XX* (where *XX* is your assigned student number) computer back to the Arctic.local domain.

29. Click **Start**, right-click **My Computer**, and click **Properties**.

30. In the System Properties dialog box, click the **Computer Name** tab.

31. On the Computer Name tab, click **Change**.

32. In the Computer Name Changes dialog box, click **Domain** in the Member of field, type **Arctic.local**, and then click **OK**.

33. When asked to provide credentials of a user who has permission to join the domain, type **Administrator** in the User name field, and type **Password!** in the Password field. Click **OK**.

34. At the Welcome to the Arctic.local domain message, click **OK**.

35. Click **OK** to the message that tells you that you must restart your computer before the changes will take effect.

36. Click **OK** to close the System Properties dialog box.

37. In the System Settings Change dialog box, click **Yes** to restart your computer now.

38. Log on as **Administrator** to the Arctic.local domain with a password of **Password!**.

39. Click **Start**, point to **Control Panel**, and click **Add or Remove Programs**.

40. In the Add or Remove Programs window, click **Add/Remove Windows Components**.

41. Scroll through the list of components, uncheck the **Networking Services** check box, and click **Next**.

42. On the Completing the Windows Components Wizard page, click **Finish**.

43. Close the Add or Remove Programs window.

Certification Objectives

Objectives for Microsoft Exam #70–293: Planning a Microsoft Windows Server 2003 Network:

- Diagnose and resolve issues related to DHCP server address assignment.

REVIEW QUESTIONS

1. How often do unauthorized DHCP servers repeat the detection process by default?

   a. every 5 minutes

   b. every 10 minutes

   c. every 15 minutes

   d. every 60 minutes

2. Which of the following broadcast messages is sent by DHCP servers when trying to verify whether they are authorized to start?

   a. DHCPDISCOVER

   b. DHCPOFFER

   c. DHCPREQUEST

   d. DHCPINFORM

3. How often do authorized DHCP servers repeat the detection process by default?

   a. every 5 minutes

   b. every 10 minutes

   c. every 15 minutes

   d. every 60 minutes

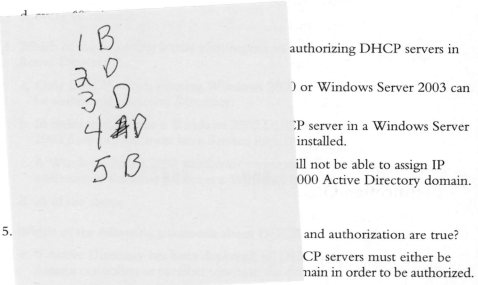

4. What _____ is true with regard to authorizing DHCP servers in Active Directory?

   a. Only a DHCP server running Windows 2000 or Windows Server 2003 can be authorized in Active Directory.

   b. In order to authorize a DHCP server, the DHCP server in a Windows Server 2003 network must have Service Pack 1 installed.

   c. A Windows 2000 DHCP server that is not authorized will not be able to assign IP addresses to clients if it belongs to a Windows 2000 Active Directory domain.

   d. all of the above

5. Which of the following statements about DHCP _____ and authorization are true?

   a. If Active Directory has been deployed, all DHCP servers must either be domain controllers or member servers in the domain in order to be authorized.

   b. If a standalone DHCP server detects an authorized server on the same subnet, it will automatically stop leasing IP addresses to clients.

   c. When installed in a multiple forest environment, DHCP servers seek authorization from within their forest only. However, once the server is authorized, it can lease IP addresses to clients from other forests if routers have DHCP/BOOTP forwarding enabled.

   d. all of the above

LAB 5.5 SUPERSCOPES

Objectives

The goal of this lab activity will be to create a superscope, which is a new feature on Windows 2000 and Windows Server 2003 DHCP servers, that enables you to group multiple scopes into one large scope.

Materials Required

This lab will require the following:

- Two Windows 2003 Servers installed and configured according to the instructions at the beginning of this lab manual

■ A lab partner (if available); if this is not possible, you will need to perform the steps for both partners using both Windows Server 2003 systems

Estimated completion time: **30 minutes**

Activity Background

You will also disable one of the member scopes and force a client computer to obtain an IP address from a particular member scope in the superscope. You will then investigate what happens to the member scopes after a superscope has been deleted.

Superscopes may be useful when your existing address pool does not contain enough IP addresses to assign to clients on your network due to network expansion, or if you want to migrate your clients toward a new address range.

ACTIVITY

Activity

Partner One only (the DHCP server):

1. If necessary, log on as **Administrator** to the Arctic.local domain with a password of **Password!**.

2. Click **Start**, point to **Administrative Tools**, and click **DHCP**.

3. In the DHCP window, double-click **studentXX.arctic.local** (where *XX* is your assigned student number), right-click **studentXX.arctic.local**, and then click **New Superscope**.

4. On the Welcome to the New Superscope Wizard page, click **Next**.

5. On the Superscope Name page, type **1XX** (where *XX* is your assigned student number). Click **Next**.

6. On the Select Scopes page, click the **[192.168.1XX.0] 1XX** (where *XX* is your assigned student number) scope you created in Lab 5-1. Click **Next**.

7. On the Completing the New Superscope Wizard page, click **Finish**.

8. Double-click **Superscope 1XX** (where *XX* is your assigned student number). At this time the superscope only contains the member scope you created in Lab 5-1. Next, you are going to create another member scope.

9. Right-click **Superscope 1XX** (where *XX* is your assigned student number) and click **New Scope**.

10. In the Welcome to the New Scope Wizard page, click **Next**.

11. On the Scope Name page, type **2XX** (where *XX* is your assigned student number). For example, if you are sitting at the Student01 computer your assigned student number is 01; therefore, you would type 201 as your Scope Name. Click **Next**.

12. On the IP Address Range page, type **192.168.2XX.1** (where *XX* is your assigned student number) in the Start IP address field, type **192.168.2XX.254** (where *XX* is your assigned student number) in the End IP address field. The Length and Subnet mask fields are filled in as you type the Start IP address. See Figure 5-19. Click **Next**.

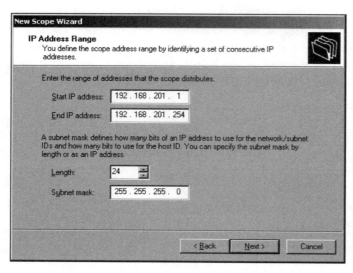

Figure 5-19   Configuring the member scope IP address range

13. Click **Next** on the Add Exclusions page, and then click **Next** to accept the default Lease Duration.

14. On the Configure DHCP Options page, click the **No, I will configure these options later** option button, and then click **Next**.

15. On the Completing the New Scope Wizard page, click **Finish**.

16. In the DHCP window, right-click **Scope [192.168.2XX.0] 2XX** (where *XX* is your assigned student number), and click **Activate**.

17. Double-click **Scope [192.168.1XX.0] 1XX** (where *XX* is your assigned student number), and then click **Address Pool**.

18. To delete the exclusion ranges you created in Lab 5-2, right-click each exclusion range, click **Delete**, and when asked if you're sure you want to delete each range, click **Yes**. Perform this step for each exclusion range so that there are no exclusion ranges configured for this scope.

19. Rather than deactivate the scope you created in Lab 5-2, you will set up an exclusion range for the range of IP addresses currently in the pool. Under Scope [192.168.1*XX*.0] 1*XX* (where *XX* is your assigned student number), right-click **Address Pool** and click **New Exclusion Range**. In the Add Exclusion dialog box, type **192.168.1XX.1** (where *XX* is your assigned student number) in the Start IP address field. In the End IP address field, type **192.168.1XX.254** (where *XX* is your assigned student number), and click **Add**. Click **Close** to close the Add Exclusion dialog box The start and end IP addresses for the address range and the excluded address range should be identical. As shown in Figure 5-20, the blue exclamation mark now appears next to both the student*XX*.arctic.local (where *XX* is your assigned student number) and the initial scope you created in Lab 5-2.

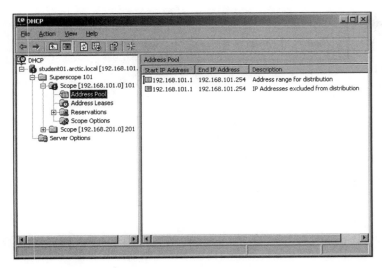

Figure 5-20   Excluding all addresses in the range

Partner Two only (the DHCP client computer):

1. Click **Start**, click **Run**, type **cmd**, and click **OK**.

2. In the command prompt window, type **ipconfig /release** and press **Enter**.

3. In the command prompt window, type **ipconfig /renew** and press **Enter**. The IP address for the private connection now displays an address from the second member scope that was added to the DHCP server.

Partner One only (the DHCP server):

1. Expand **Scope [192.168.1XX.0] 1XX** (where *XX* is your assigned student number), and then click **Address Pool**. Right-click the excluded address range, and click then **Delete**. When asked if you're sure, click **Yes**. The blue exclamation marks disappear.

2. Right-click **Superscope 1XX** (where *XX* is your assigned student number), and click **Delete**. To the resulting message that appears (as shown in Figure 5–21), click **Yes**. The two scopes you created in this chapter remain in the DHCP console window, as shown in Figure 5–22.

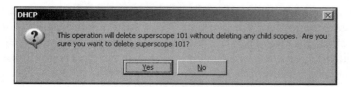

Figure 5-21   Message indicating that child scopes will remain when superscope is deleted

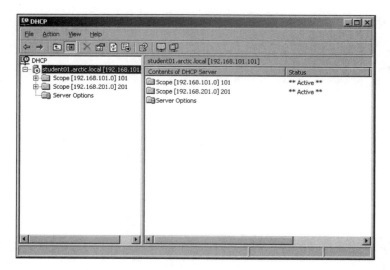

Figure 5-22   The remaining member scopes

Partner Two only (the DHCP client computer):

1. In the command prompt window, type **ipconfig /release** and press **Enter**.

2. In the command prompt window, type **ipconfig /renew** and press **Enter**. You received an IP address from the scope your partner created in Lab 5-2. When both scopes exist within the superscope, client computers can be assigned IP addresses from either of the member scopes (as long as one of the scopes matches the network address of the network adapter assigning IP addresses to clients). When you delete the superscope, leaving two individual scopes, the DHCP server assigns IP addresses based on the network address of its network adapter cards. Therefore, in this lab, you received an IP address from the original scope as its address range is on the same subnet as the DHCP server's Private connection IP address.

Partner One only (the DHCP server):

1. You will now uninstall the DHCP service. Close the DHCP console window, and then click **Start** and click **Manage Your Server**.

2. In the Manage Your Server window, click **Add or remove a role**.

3. On the Preliminary Steps page, click **Next**.

4. On the Server Role page, click **Remote access/VPN server** and click **Next**.

5. On the Role Removal Confirmation page, check the **Remove the remote access/VPN server role** check box, and click **Next**.

6. A message appears, indicating that you are disabling the router and removing its configuration and asking if you want to reconfigure the router and continue. Click **Yes**.

7. On the Remote Access/VPN Server Role Removed page, click **Finish**.

8. In the Manage Your Server window, click **Add or remove a role**.

9. On the Preliminary Steps page, click **Next**.

10. On the Server Role page, click **DHCP server** and click **Next**.

11. On the Role Removal Confirmation page, check the **Remove the DHCP server role** check box, and click **Next**.

12. On the DHCP server Role Removed page, click **Finish**.

13. Close the Manage Your Server window.

14. Click **Start**, point to **Control Panel**, and double-click **Network Connections**.

15. In the Network Connections window, right-click **Private** and click **Properties**.

16. In the Private Properties dialog box, click **Internet Protocol (TCP/IP)** and click **Properties**.

17. In the Internet Protocol (TCP/IP) Properties dialog box, click the **Obtain an IP address automatically** option button to select, click the **Obtain DNS server address automatically** option button to select, and then click **OK** to close the dialog box.

18. Click **Close** to close the Private Properties dialog box.

19. Close the Network Connections window and log off.

Partner Two only (the DHCP client):

1. You need to release the lease that was obtained from the DHCP server in this lab activity. In the command prompt window, type **ipconfig /release** and press **Enter**.

2. In the command prompt window, type **ipconfig /renew** and press **Enter**.

3. Close the command prompt window and log off.

Certification Objectives

Objectives for Microsoft Exam #70-293: Planning a Microsoft Windows Server 2003 Network:

- Diagnose and resolve issues related to client computer configuration.

- Diagnose and resolve issues related to DHCP server address assignment.

REVIEW QUESTIONS

1. In which of the following situations would you implement a superscope?

   a. when the available address pool is nearly depleted and you need to add another range of IP addresses to extend the amount of addresses available on that physical network segment

   b. when clients must be migrated to a new scope eventually

   c. when two DHCP servers are required on the same physical network to manage separate logical IP networks

   d. all of the above

2. When a superscope is deleted, what happens to the member scopes?

   a. They are deactivated.

   b. They are deleted as well.

   c. They remain as invidividual scopes.

   d. none of the above

3. Which of the following can be implemented when removing old scopes without disrupting DHCP service to clients on the subnet?

   a. activating a replacement scope on the subnet before the old scope is deactivated

   b. deactivating the old scope and forcing clients to seek new leases from other available DHCP servers before removing the old scope

   c. using superscopes, reservations, and exclusion ranges to provide a smooth transition for clients from one scope to another

   d. all of the above

4. When creating a superscope, how many scopes must be available on the server?

   a. none

   b. one

   c. two or more

   d. only three

5. Which of the following is a method that can ensure that clients will be able to acquire an IP address on a subnet?

   a. configuring more than one DHCP server per subnet for fault tolerance

   b. using routers capable of forwarding BOOTP and DHCP traffic

   c. using DHCP relay agents on each routed subnet

   d. all of the above

5

PLANNING, CONFIGURING, AND TROUBLESHOOTING WINS

Labs included in this chapter:

- ◆ Lab 6.1 The lmhosts file
- ◆ Lab 6.2 Installing and Configuring a WINS Server
- ◆ Lab 6.3 Creating Static Mappings in the WINS Database
- ◆ Lab 6.4 Configuring WINS Replication
- ◆ Lab 6.5 Backing Up and Restoring the WINS Database

Microsoft MCSE Exam #70-293 Objectives	
Objective	**Lab**
Plan a NetBIOS name resolution strategy.	6.1, 6.2, 6.3, 6.4, 6.5
Plan a WINS replication strategy.	6.2, 6.4
Plan NetBIOS name resolution by using the Lmhosts file.	6.1

LAB 6.1 THE LMHOSTS FILE

Objectives

The goal of this lab activity is to investigate the function of the lmhosts file.

Materials Required

This lab will require the following:

- Windows Server 2003 installed and configured according to the instructions at the beginning of this lab manual

Estimated completion time: **30 minutes**

Activity Background

The lmhosts file is a static file that can be configured to enable a system to locally resolve NetBIOS names to IP addresses. Although systems are able to resolve the NetBIOS names of computers on the same subnet, these broadcasts will not pass through the router. On these networks, some type of NetBIOS name resolution method is required. By using an lmhosts file, you can enter the IP address to computer name mappings entries in the lmhosts file in order to resolve names of computers on remote subnets.

In this lab, you will modify the lmhosts file using a text editor. Additionally, you will also investigate the nbtstat command-line utility and how it can be used when troubleshooting problems with name resolution.

ACTIVITY

Activity

1. If necessary, log on as **Administrator** of the Arctic.local domain with a password of **Password!**.

2. Right-click **Start** and click **Explore**.

3. In Windows Explorer, navigate to the C:\Windows\system32\drivers\etc directory.

4. Right-click the **lmhosts.sam** file and click **Copy**.

5. Right-click in the details pane and click **Paste**. A file called Copy of lmhosts.sam appears in the C:\Windows\System32\drivers\etc directory.

6. In the details pane, right-click **lmhosts.sam** and click **Rename**. Type **lmhosts** and press **Enter**. If prompted, click **Yes** to confirm that the file will not have an extension. Note that if you have already renamed the lmhosts.sam file "lmhosts" (with no file extension), this step will not be necessary.

7. Double-click **lmhosts**.

8. In the Open With dialog box, under Programs, click **Notepad** and click **OK**.

9. Maximize the lmhosts – Notepad window. Scroll down to the bottom of the file. Note the comment that mentions that it is not advisable to just add lmhost entries to the bottom of this file as the entire file is parsed on each lookup, including the comments. For the purposes of this lab, you are going to add your entries onto the bottom of this file. In a production environment, this would not be considered good practice.

10. Move your insertion point to the end of the last line of the lmhosts file and press **Enter**. You are now going to add your own entries into this lmhosts file.

11. First you will add an entry for the Instructor computer. Remember that the IP address of the Instructor computer is 192.168.1.10. As your system is configured to use DNS at this point, when you attempt to communicate with the Instructor computer, you will use the right IP address, but the wrong NetBIOS name. Type **192.168.1.10**, press the **spacebar**, and type **trainer**.

12. Click **File** on the menu bar, and click **Save**.

13. Click **Start**, click **Run**, type **cmd**, and click **OK**.

14. In the command prompt window, type **ping trainer** and press **Enter**. You should receive four replies. Leave the command prompt window open as you will be switching back to it shortly.

15. Switch back to Notepad. Place your cursor just before the entry you made for 192.168.1.10 trainer, and press **Enter**. You are going to put an entry into the lmhosts file that is not a valid IP address on this subnet. Type **192.168.1.253**, press the **spacebar**, type **trainer**, and then press **Enter**. (If there is a computer on your subnet with this IP address, ask your instructor to provide an IP address that is not configured on any host on your network). You now have two separate entries in your lmhosts file for trainer. The file will be parsed from top to bottom. Next, you are going to see what happens when incorrect entries are placed in the lmhosts file.

16. Click **File** on the menu bar, and click **Save**. You were able to communicate with the Instructor computer when you used a different NetBIOS name, but the correct IP address. This time you are using an incorrect IP address. In this activity you are not using the Instructor NetBIOS name, as the DNS server would be able to resolve it to the correct IP address.

17. Before attempting to ping the trainer computer again, you will first use the Nbtstat command-line utility to view the contents of the local NetBIOS name cache on your computer. In the command prompt window, type **nbtstat /?** and press **Enter**. The syntax for the command appears. This utility can be used to display protocol statistics and current TCP/IP connections using NBT (NetBIOS over TCP/IP).

18. The first parameter that you will use with the nbtstat command is -c, which will show the NetBIOS name cache on the local computer. Type **nbtstat -c** and press **Enter**. A mapping appears under the Classroom adapter's NetBIOS Remote Cache Name Table for Trainer mapping the name trainer to the IP address 192.168.1.10.

19. Scroll up in the command prompt window. The -R switch can be used to purge and reload the remote cache name table. Type **nbtstat -R** and press **Enter**. The message "Successful purge and preload of the NBT Remote Cache Name Table" appears.

20. Type **ping trainer** and press **Enter**. The name trainer is resolved to the IP address 192.168.1.253. However, the request times out as there is no computer with this IP address on your network. In your lmhosts file you have two entries for trainer. The lmhosts file is parsed in order. Once a name has been resolved to an IP address, the system will not read the remainder of the lmhosts file. It is very important that you be careful when creating entries in the lmhosts file.

21. Switch to Notepad, and then delete **192.168.1.253 trainer**. Click **File** on the menu, and click **Save**.

22. Next, you will examine the effect of using different parameters in the lmhosts file. The first parameter that you will look at is the #PRE tag. The #PRE tag causes entries to be preloaded into the name cache. In the command prompt window, type **nbtstat -R** and press **Enter**. The message 'Successful purge and preload of the NBT Remote Cache Name Table' appears.

23. Type **nbtstat -c** and press **Enter**. There is no mapping in the local NetBIOS Remote Cache Name Table for the trainer entry.

24. Next, you are going to modify the 192.168.1.10 trainer entry so that it will be preloaded into the NetBIOS Remote Cache Name Table. Modify the entry so that it now reads "192.168.1.10 trainer #PRE." Click **File** on the menu bar, and click **Save**.

25. In the command prompt window, type **nbtstat -R** and press **Enter**. The message 'Successful purge and preload of the NBT Remote Cache Name Table' appears. Three mappings now appear in the NetBIOS Remote Cache Name Table for TRAINER.

26. Next you will use the #BEGIN_ALTERNATE, #END_ALTERNATE, and #INCLUDE tags. In Notepad, modify the entries in your lmhosts file to appear as follows:

192.168.1.10 instructor #PRE

#BEGIN_ALTERNATE

#INCLUDE \\instructor\student*XX*\lmhosts

#END_ALTERNATE

(where *XX* is your assigned student number). Your lmhosts file should now appear as shown in Figure 6-1.

Figure 6-1   Using the #INCLUDE tag in an lmhosts file

27. Click **File** on the menu bar, and click **Save**. You have now configured your local lmhosts file to point to a central lmhosts file on the server. The system that contains the centralized lmhosts file must have an entry in the local lmhosts file with the #PRE tag. This information is provided in the lmhosts.sam file. If you scroll through the document you will be able to read the instructions for using the tags appropriately.

28. Close **Notepad**.

29. Click **Start**, point to **Administrative Tools**, and click **Computer Management**.

30. In the Computer Management console, right-click **Computer Management (Local)** and click **Connect to another computer**.

31. In the Select Computer window, type **instructor** and click **OK**.

32. In the Computer Management (INSTRUCTOR) console, double-click **System Tools**, double-click **Shared Folders**, and then click **Shares**. The shares on the Instructor computer appear in the details pane.

33. Right-click **Shares** and click **New Share**.

34. On the Welcome to the Share a Folder Wizard page, click **Next**.

35. On the Folder Path page, click **Browse**.

36. In the Browse For Folder dialog box, click **C$** and then click **Make New Folder**. Type **StudentXX** (where *XX* is your assigned student number) and click **OK**.

37. On the Folder Path page, click **Next**.

38. On the Name, Description, and Settings page, click **Next**.

39. On the Permissions page, click the **Administrators have full access; other users have read-only access** option button to select it, and then click **Finish**.

40. On the Sharing was Successful page, click **Close**, and then close the Computer Management console.

41. In Windows Explorer, right-click **Copy of lmhosts.sam** in the C:\Windows\System32\drivers\etc folder, and click **Copy**.

42. Click **Start**, click **Run**, type **\\Instructor\StudentXX** (where *XX* is your assigned student number) and click **OK**.

43. Right-click in the \\Instructor\StudentXX window, and click **Paste**. The Copy of lmhosts.sam file appears.

44. Right-click **Copy of lmhosts.sam** and click **Rename**. Type **lmhosts** and press **Enter**. Click **Yes** to confirm the change, if necessary.

45. Double-click **lmhosts** in the \\Instructor\StudentXX window.

46. In the Open With dialog box, click **Notepad** and click **OK**.

47. Scroll down to the bottom of the lmhosts file, type **192.168.1.99 include**, and press **Enter**. Click **File** on the menu bar, and click **Save**.

48. Close **Notepad**. Close the \\Instructor\StudentXX window (where *XX* is your assigned student number). You are now going to ping the system entry that you created in the centralized lmhosts file on the server.

49. In the command prompt window, type **nbtstat –R** and press **Enter**. The message "Successful purge and preload of the NBT Remote Cache Name Table" appears.

50. In the command prompt window, type **ping include**, shown in Figure 6-2, and press **Enter**. The name include will be resolved to the IP address 192.168.1.99. However, you will receive four Request timed out messages. This is because there is no computer on your network at the present time that has the IP address 192.168.1.99. However, you know that your local lmhosts file referred to the centralized lmhosts file to resolve the name include, as that entry was not made in your local lmhosts file. Close the command prompt window.

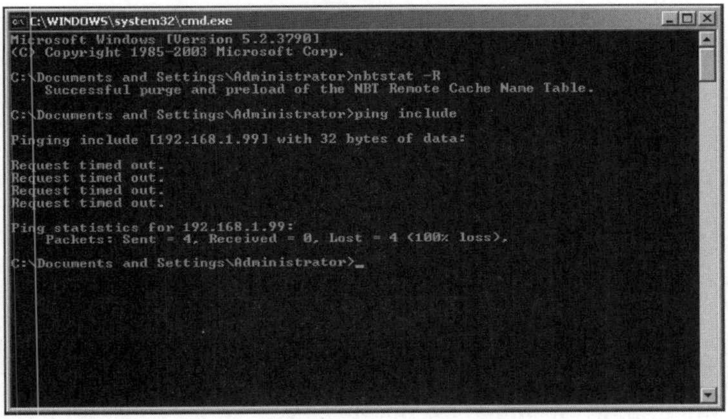

Figure 6-2   Name resolved using a centralized lmhosts file

51. In Windows Explorer, right-click the **lmhosts** file and click **Delete**. When asked if you are sure you want to send lmhosts to the Recycle Bin, click **Yes**.

52. Right-click **Copy of lmhosts.sam** and click **Rename**. Type **lmhosts.sam** and press **Enter**.

53. Close Windows Explorer.

54. In the command prompt window, type **nbtstat –R** and press **Enter**. The message "Successful purge and preload of the NBT Remote Cache Name Table" appears.

55. Type **ping include** and press **Enter**. You are unable to resolve the name to an IP address.

56. Close the command prompt window and the Computer Management console.

Certification Objectives

Objectives for Microsoft Exam #70-293: Planning a Microsoft Windows Server 2003 Network:

- Plan a NetBIOS name resolution strategy.

- Plan NetBIOS name resolution by using the Lmhosts file.

REVIEW QUESTIONS

1. Where is the lmhosts file located?

    a. %systemroot%\system32

    b. %systemroot%\system32\drivers

    c. %systemroot%\system32\drivers\etc

    d. none of the above

2. What is the name of the sample lmhosts file on a Windows Server 2003 system?

    a. lmhosts.txt

    b. lmhosts.sam

    c. lmhosts

    d. none of the above

3. Which of the following is a necessary component when using a centralized lmhosts file to resolve NetBIOS names?

    a. the provision of a mapping for the IP address of the server on which the centralized lmhosts file is located prior to the #INCLUDE statement

    b. the mapping of the server on which the centralized lmhosts file is located must use the #PRE tag.

    c. the specification of the # symbol before the BEGIN_ALTERNATE, END_ALTERNATE and #INCLUDE statements.

    d. all of the above

4. Which switch would you use with the Nbtstat command-line utility to purge and reload the remote cache name table?

    a. –C

    b. –N

    c. –r

    d. –R

5. Which switch would you use with the Nbtstat command-line utility to list the cache of remote names and their IP addresses?

   a. –C

   b. –N

   c. –r

   d. –R

Lab 6.2 Installing and Configuring a WINS Server

6

Objectives

The goal of this lab activity is to install and configure a WINS server using the Manage Your Server window.

Materials Required

This lab will require the following:

- A Windows Server 2003 server installed and configured according to the instructions at the beginning of this lab manual

Estimated completion time: **10 minutes**

Activity Background

WINS is a service that maintains a dynamic mapping of NetBIOS names to IP addresses. If you are running earlier versions of Windows, the WINS service is required in order to resolve and locate computers and resources on your network.

ACTIVITY

Activity

1. Click **Start**, point to **Control Panel**, and double-click **Network Connections**.

2. In the Network Connections window, right-click **Private** and click **Disable**.

3. Click **Start** and click **Manage Your Server**.

4. In the Manage Your Server window, click **Add or remove a role**.

5. On the Preliminary Steps page, review the requirements, and click **Next**.

6. On the Server Role page, under Server Role, click **WINS server** and click **Next**.

7. On the Summary of Selections page, click **Next**.

8. If prompted to insert the Windows Server 2003 CD, click **OK**.

9. In the Files Needed dialog box, click **Browse**. In the Locate File dialog box, click the **Look in** drop-down arrow, and click the **C:\i386** directory (if necessary). Then click the **WINSCTRS.DL_** file and click **Open**.

10. In the Files Needed dialog box, the Copy files from field now displays C:\i386. Click **OK**.

11. On the This Server is Now a WINS Server page, click **Finish**.

12. In the Manage Your Server window, under WINS Server, click **Review the next steps for this role**. Help appears. Note that if you are unsure about configuring a WINS server, help is available on your system. Close the Configure Your Server window.

13. Close the Manage Your Server window.

14. In the Network Connections window, right-click **Classroom** and click **Properties**.

15. In the Classroom Properties dialog box, click **Internet Protocol (TCP/IP)** and click **Properties**.

16. In the Internet Protocol (TCP/IP) Properties dialog box, click **Advanced**.

17. In the Advanced TCP/IP Settings dialog box, click the **WINS** tab.

18. On the WINS tab, under WINS addresses, in order of use, click **Add**.

19. In the TCP/IP WINS Server dialog box, type **192.168.1.1XX** (where *XX* is your assigned student number) and click **Add**. You have just configured the WINS server to be a client of itself. When services are starting up on this computer, they will register themselves in the WINS database on this server.

20. Under NetBIOS Setting, click the **Enable NetBIOS over TCP/IP** option button to select (as shown in Figure 6-3). Click **OK** to close the Advanced TCP/IP Settings dialog box.

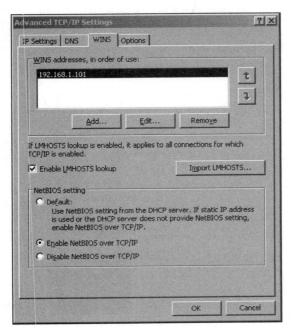

Figure 6-3   Configuring the WINS server as a client of itself

21. Click **OK** to close the Internet Protocol (TCP/IP) Properties dialog box.

22. Click **Close** to close the Classroom Properties dialog box and then close the Network Connections window.

Certification Objectives

Objectives for Microsoft Exam #70-293: Planning a Microsoft Windows Server 2003 Network:

- Plan a NetBIOS name resolution strategy.

- Plan a WINS replication strategy.

REVIEW QUESTIONS

1. Which of the following is a recommendation when implementing WINS servers on your network?

    a. having at least two WINS servers for fault tolerance purposes

    b. configuring clients with the IP address of more than one WINS server

    c. configuring the TCP/IP properties of each WINS server to point to itself as a WINS server

    d. all of the above

2. For security reasons, which of the following steps should be taken?

    a. Restrict physical or wireless access to network.

    b. Disable burst handling.

    c. Use Network Monitor to capture packets to determine if the WINS Server is under attack.

    d. all of the above

3. When a computer running Windows server 2003 is configured with the IP address of a WINS server, which of the following node types does it use?

    a. P node

    b. B node

    c. hybrid node

    d. mixed node

4. What is the default renewal interval for entries in the WINS database?

    a. eight days

    b. six days

    c. four days

    d. three days

5. Which of the following is a benefit of using WINS on your network?

   a. WINS is a dynamic database that registers and resolves NetBIOS names on your network.

   b. It eliminates the need to maintain lmhosts files.

   c. It provides a reduction in NetBIOS-based traffic on the network because clients can query WINS servers for name resolution and registration requests.

   d. all of the above

LAB 6.3 CREATING STATIC MAPPINGS IN THE WINS DATABASE

6

Objectives

The goal of this lab activity is to create static mappings in the WINS database.

Materials Required

This lab will require the following:

- Windows Server 2003 installed and configured according to the instructions at the beginning of this lab manual

Estimated completion time: **10 minutes**

Activity Background

Computer name to IP address mappings, for the most part, are added to the WINS server database when clients contact the WINS server to register, release or renew their NetBIOS names. However, you may also want to manually enter mappings in the WINS database as well. For systems that are not WINS clients and that will not register themselves in the WINS database, you can create static mappings for these systems in the WINS database to enable your WINS clients to locate these computers on our network. Static mappings remain in the WINS database indefinitely.

ACTIVITY

Activity

1. If necessary, log on as **Administrator** of the Arctic.local domain with a password of **Password!**.

2. Click **Start**, point to **Administrative Tools**, and click **WINS**. The WINS console opens.

3. If necessary, double-click **Student**xx **[192.168.1.1XX]** (where XX is your assigned student number).

4. Right-click **Active Registrations** and click **New Static Mapping**.

5. In the New Static Mapping dialog box, type **Student#** (where **#** is the word for the number in your server name; for example, for Student01 you type STUDENTONE) in the Computer name field. In the IP address field, type **192.168.1.1XX** (where *XX* is your assigned student number). You are going to create a unique static mapping. There are several types of mappings that can be created in the WINS database. Unique mappings are used to associate a computer name to a single IP address. Group mappings are used to specify the workgroup to which your computer belongs. Domain Name mappings are used to create mappings for domain controllers in the WINS database. Internet Group mappings are used for administrative purposes to organize how resources (such as file and print servers) appear to users browsing the network. Multihomed mappings are used for systems that have more than one IP address. This type of mapping would apply to systems that had one network adapter card configured to use multiple IP addresses, and also to systems having multiple network adapter cards. Click **OK** to close the New Static Mapping dialog box.

6. Expand STUDENT01 [192.168.1.1*XX*], if necessary, and then right-click **Active Registrations** and click **Display Records**.

7. In the Display Records dialog box, click the **Record Mapping** tab, if necessary. Check the **Filter records matching this Name pattern** check box. Tab down to the field and type **s*** (as shown in Figure 6-4). Click **Find Now**. Both the static and dynamic mappings appear in the Active Registrations window.

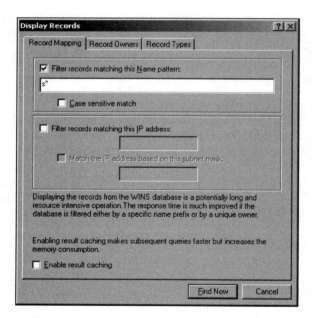

Figure 6-4   Filtering records matching the s* name pattern

8. Click **Active Registrations**. The static mappings you created should appear in the details pane. Static mappings are denoted by an x in the Static column. You should now see mappings for STUDENT01 and also for STUDENTONE (as shown in Figure 6-5).

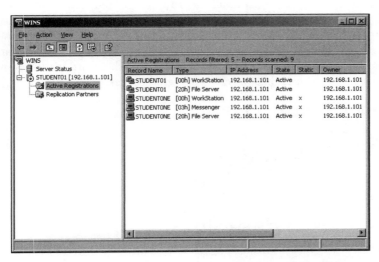

Figure 6-5   Static mappings are denoted by an x in the Static column

9. Right-click **Active Registrations** and click **Display Records**. Click the **Record Mapping** tab and then uncheck the **Filter records matching this Name pattern** check box. Click the **Record Owners** tab. You can also filter by the WINS server on which the record was created. Click the **Record Types** tab. By default, all record types are selected. Click **Clear All**. Check the **[00h] WorkStation** check box (as shown in Figure 6-6) to select it, and then click **Find Now**. Three records display: one for the domain Arctic, one for your Student*XX* server (where *XX* is your assigned student number), and another created for the Student# (where # is the word for the number in your server name) static mapping you created earlier.

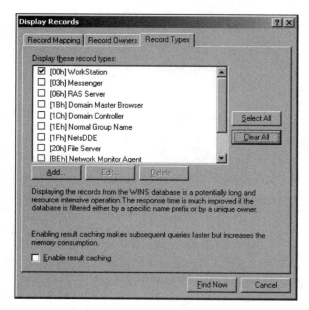

Figure 6-6   Filtering by record types

10. Close the WINS console.

Certification Objectives

Objectives for Microsoft Exam #70-293: Planning a Microsoft Windows Server 2003 Network:

- Plan a NetBIOS name resolution strategy.

REVIEW QUESTIONS

1. Which of the following is a method by which name to address mappings can be added to the WINS server database?

   a. dynamically, by clients contacting a WINS server

   b. by Static entries made by an administrator

   c. by importing an lmhosts file

   d. all of the above

2. By default, if WINS has both a static and a dynamic entry for the same name, what action is taken?

   a. The static entry is preserved.

   b. The dynamic entry is preserved.

   c. The administrator will receive an error message and be prompted to choose which mapping to retain in the database.

   d. none of the above

3. Which of the following types of deletions is supported on WINS?

   a. deleting multiple records in the database at one time

   b. deleting database records stored on a single server

   c. deleting database records that have replicated to databases on other WINS servers

   d. all of the above

4. What appears in the State field after a database record has been deleted?

   a. deleted

   b. extinct

   c. tombstoned

   d. none of the above

6

5. After records have been marked as tombstoned, _____.

    a. they are treated as inactive and released from use

    b. the owner WINS server will not respond to or resolve queries for those names unless registered again by the client

    c. after the Extinction interval has elapsed, the records will expire and be removed with scavenging

    d. all of the above

LAB 6.4 CONFIGURING WINS REPLICATION

Objectives

The goal of this lab is to demonstrate how to configure WINS replication partners.

Materials Required

This lab will require the following:

- Two Windows Server 2003 servers installed and configured according to the instructions at the beginning of this lab manual

- A lab partner (if available)

Estimated completion time: **15 minutes**

Activity Background

When multiple WINS servers are operating on your network, it is essential that they be configured to replicate the records in their databases to the other WINS servers on the network. This ensures that regardless of which WINS server a client registers with or query, all NetBIOS names in use on the network can be resolved to IP addresses.

ACTIVITY

Activity

1. If necessary, log on as **Administrator** for the Arctic.local domain with a password of **Password!**.

2. Click **Start**, and click **Manage Your Server**.

3. In the Manage Your Server window, under WINS Server, click **Manage this WINS server**.

4. Double-click **StudentXX [192.168.1.1XX]** (where *XX* is your assigned student number), if necessary.

5. Click **Replication Partners**. Review the explanation of the function of a Replication Partner displayed in the details pane of the WINS console.

6. Right-click **Replication Partners**, then click **New Replication Partner**.

7. In the New Replication Partner dialog box, type **192.168.1.1XX** (where *XX* is your partner's assigned student number). Click **OK**. Your partner's computer now appears in the details pane for Replication Partners. The IP address has been resolved to the name of your partner's server. The default configuration of a replication partner is Push/Pull, as indicated in the Type field.

8. Right-click **Replication Partners** and click **Properties**. The default setting on the General tab is the Replicate only with partners option, as shown in Figure 6-7.

6

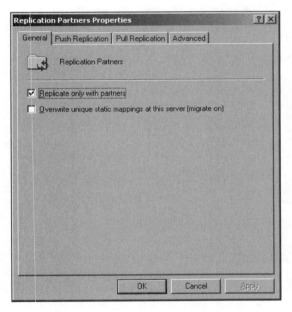

Figure 6-7   Replication Partners Properties dialog box

9. Click the **Push Replication** tab, as shown in Figure 6-8. By default, the At service startup option is not selected. This would enable your WINS server to notify its partners of the status of its database when the service initializes. By default the When address changes option is also not selected. This would enable your WINS server to inform its partners whenever an address changes in a mapping record. The Use persistent connections for push replication partners option has been selected. This will increase replication speed, as the server will maintain the connection and will not have to reestablish it every time it needs to share updated information in the database with its partners. This is not recommended on WAN links.

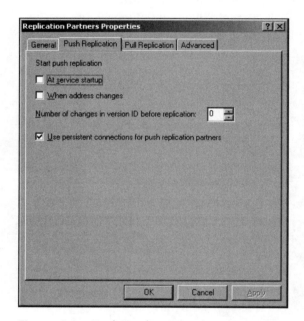

Figure 6-8   Push Replication tab

10. Click the **Pull Replication** tab, as shown in Figure 6-9. You can configure a time for when replication can start. If no time is specified, automatic pull replication will not occur. Once automatic replication has occurred, the replication interval is every 30 minutes by default. The Number of retries field specifies how many attempts should be made to retry the connection should a connection fail during replication. The Start pull replication at service startup and the Use persistent connections for pull replication partners options are also selected by default.

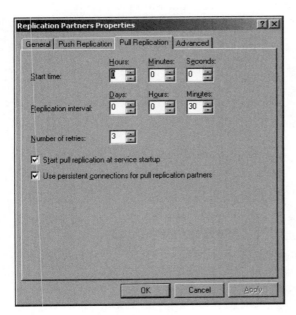

Figure 6-9   Pull Replication tab

6

11. Click the **Advanced** tab, as shown in Figure 6-10. You have the capability of only accepting records from certain WINS servers or blocking records from certain WINS servers. You can enable automatic partner configuration. If this is enabled, a WINS server will send out multicast announcements to announce its presence on the network. Any WINS servers discovered through these multicast announcements will be added as push/pull replication partners. Additionally they will replicate to one another every two hours. When the WINS server shuts down, any partners discovered through these multicast announcements will be removed as a replication partner. It is recommended that you choose this option only if your network has three or less WINS servers.

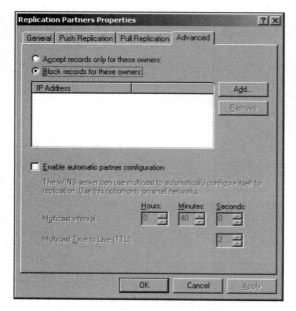

Figure 6-10   Advanced tab

12. Click **Cancel** to close the Replication Partners Properties dialog box. You are not going to modify these properties at this time.

13. You have just looked at the replication partner properties for all replication partners of this WINS Server. Next, you will look at the configuration options for individual replication partners. Right-click **Student***XX* (where *XX* is your partner's assigned student number) and click **Properties**.

14. Click the **Advanced** tab. Click the **Replication partner type** drop-down arrow. There are three options: Push/Pull (the default), Push, and Pull. Click **Push**. The Pull replication options are no longer available. The only configurable option for a Push partner is the Number of changes in version ID before replication option. Click the Replication partner type drop-down arrow, and click **Pull**. The Push replication options are no longer available. Pull partners rely on a schedule and replicate at intervals. Click the **Replication partner type** drop-down arrow, and click **Push/Pull**. This is the recommended option for WINS server replication partners. Click **Cancel**. You are now going to force replication between the WINS servers.

15. Right-click **Replication Partners** and click **Replicate Now**. A message appears, asking if you are sure you want to start replication now. Click **Yes**. A message appears, indicating that the replication request has been queued on the server and to check the event log for status on when this operation is completed. Click **OK**.

16. Right-click **Active Registrations** and click **Display Records**. In the Display Records dialog box, click the **Record Owners** tab. Click **Select All** and then click **Find Now**. You will now see the mappings from your partner's WINS server. Scroll over to the Owner field. Records from your server are denoted by your IP address. Records created on your partner's WINS server are denoted by the IP address of your partner's server.

17. Click the first static mapping for your partner's WINS server under Active Registrations, press and hold down the **Shift** key on your keyboard, and click the last static mapping entry for your partner's WINS server (as shown in Figure 6-11). Press **Delete**.

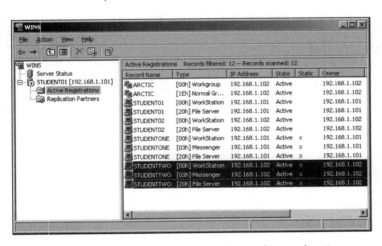

Figure 6-11   Viewing WINS registrations after replication

18. The Delete Multiple Records dialog box appears, asking whether you are deleting the record on this WINS server only or if you want it to replicate to other WINS servers as having been deleted. Click the **Replicate deletion of these records to other servers (tombstone)** option button (as shown in Figure 6-12). Click **OK**.

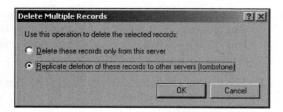

Figure 6-12   Selecting to tombstone records in the WINS database

19. A dialog box appears, informing you that tombstoning replica records will cause this WINS server to take ownership of the record and asking if you want to continue. Click **Yes**. The state of the static entries for your partner's server has now been flagged as "Tombstoned."

20. Close the WINS console and the Manage Your Server window.

Certification Objectives

Objectives for Microsoft Exam #70-293: Planning a Microsoft Windows Server 2003 Network:

- Plan a NetBIOS name resolution strategy.

- Plan a WINS replication strategy.

REVIEW QUESTIONS

1. What is the recommended configuration for WINS replication partners?

a. push

b. pull

c. push/pull

d. none of the above

2. Which of the following are options that can be configured on a WINS server to initiate a Pull partner to request replication with its partners? (Choose all that apply.)

   a. when the WINS service starts

   b. after a certain period of time has passed

   c. after an IP address change occurs for a mapping in the database

   d. when a particular number of changes in version ID have occurred in the database

3. Which of the following are options that can be configured on a WINS server to initiate a Push partner to notify other WINS servers of changes to their database? (Choose all that apply.)

   a. when the WINS service starts

   b. after a certain period of time has passed

   c. after an IP address change occurs for a mapping in the database

   d. after a certain number of version ID changes to the database

4. Which of the following are true with regards to WINS replication?

   a. Convergence time is the amount of time required for a WINS entry to replicate from the owner WINS server to all other WINS servers on the network.

   b. The hub and spoke model is the recommended model for WINS replication.

   c. According to Microsoft, it is recommended to have one WINS server and a backup server for every 10,000 computers on the network.

   d. all of the above

5. What type of announcements is made by automatic partner configuration?

   a. unicast

   b. multicast

   c. broadcast

   d. none of the above

LAB 6.5 BACKING UP AND RESTORING THE WINS DATABASE

Objectives

The goal of this lab activity is to backup and restore the WINS database.

Materials Required

This lab will require the following:

- Two Windows Server 2003 servers installed and configured according to the instructions at the beginning of this lab manual

- A lab partner (if available)

Estimated completion time: 15 minutes

Activity Background

The WINS console provides methods by which you can both back up and restore the WINS database file. The WINS server can be configured to back up the database when the service is stopped or if the server is shutdown. Additionally, the database can also be backed up manually through the WINS console. Should the WINS database become corrupted, this feature will prove to be valuable to you. In this lab, you will back up the WINS database and then restore it.

Activity

1. Click **Start**, point to **Administrative Tools**, and click **WINS**.

2. In the WINS console, right-click **StudentXX [192.168.1. XX]** (where *XX* is your assigned student number) and click **Back Up Database**.

3. In the Browse For Folder dialog box, click **Local Disk (C:)**. Click **Make New Folder**. Type **WINS Backup** and press **Enter**. Click **OK** to close the Browse For Folder dialog box.

4. When the database backup is completed successfully, the message shown in Figure 6-13 appears. Click **OK**.

Figure 6-13   Backing up the WINS database

5. Right-click **StudentXX [192.168.1.1XX]**, click **All Tasks**, and click **Stop**. Your server name now appears with a red X in the WINS console window. The details pane of the window displays the status "Cannot find the WINS Server." Close the WINS console window.

6. Right-click **Start** and click **Explore**. Navigate to the C:\Windows\system32\wins directory. There are several files in that directory: j50, j50.chk, j5000001, res1, res2, wins, and wins.pat. Right-click **wins.mdb** (the WINS database file) and click **Delete**. When asked if you are sure you want to send 'wins.mdb' to the Recycle Bin, click **Yes**.

7. Navigate to the C:\WINS Backup\wins_bak\new directory. There are three files in this directory: j5000001.log, wins.mdb, and wins.pat.

8. Click **Start**, point to **Administrative Tools**, and click **WINS**.

9. In the WINS console, right-click **StudentXX [192.168.1.1XX]** (where *XX* is your assigned student number), click **All Tasks**, and then click **Start**.

10. Right-click **Active Registrations** and click **Display Records**. Click the **Record Owners** tab and click **Find Now**. The static entries that you had made in the database are missing, as are the records that were replicated from your partner's WINS server. Close the WINS console window.

11. In Windows Explorer, navigate to the C:\Windows\system32\wins directory. Note that the wins.mdb file is now there. There is now a file called winstmp.mdb in that directory that was not there before either. However, this is not the WINS database that holds your mappings.

12. Click **Start**, point to **Administrative Tools**, and click **WINS**.

13. In the WINS console, right-click **StudentXX [192.168.1.1XX]** (where *XX* is your assigned student number), click **All Tasks**, and click **Stop**.

14. Right-click **StudentXX [192.168.1.1XX]** (where *XX* is your assigned student number), and click **Restore Database**.

15. In the Browse For Folder dialog box, click **Local Disk (C:)**, click **WINS Backup**, and click **OK**. A message appears, indicating that the database restore was completed successfully (as shown in Figure 6-14). Click **OK**.

Figure 6-14   Restoring the WINS database

16. Right-click **Active Registrations** and click **Display Records**. Click the **Record Owners** tab. Both your WINS server and your partner's WINS server appear. Make sure both check boxes are checked; if not, click **Select All** and then click **Find Now**. Your WINS database has been restored.

17. Close the WINS console.

18. Click **Start** and click **Manage Your Server**.

19. In the Manage Your Server window, click **Add or remove a role**.

20. On the Preliminary Steps page, click **Next**.

21. On the Server Role page, click **WINS server** and then click **Next**.

22. On the Role Removal Confirmation page, check the **Remove the WINS server role** check box, and click **Next**.

23. On the WINS Server Role Removed page, click **Finish**.

24. Close the Manage Your Server window.

25. Click **Start**, point to **Control Panel**, and double-click **Network Connections**.

26. In the Network Connections window, right-click **Classroom** and click **Properties**.

27. In the Classroom Properties dialog box, click **Internet Protocol (TCP/IP)** and click **Properties**.

28. In the Internet Protocol (TCP/IP) Properties dialog box, click **Advanced**.

29. In the Advanced TCP/IP Settings dialog box, click the **WINS** tab.

30. Click your WINS server's IP address under WINS addresses in order of use, and click **Remove**. Under NetBIOS setting, click **Default**. Click **OK** to close the Advanced TCP/IP Settings dialog box.

31. Click **OK** to close the Internet Protocol (TCP/IP) Properties dialog box.

32. Click **Close** to close the Classroom Properties dialog box.

33. Right-click **Private** and click **Enable**.

34. Close the Network Connections window and Windows Explorer, and then log off.

Certification Objectives

Objectives for Microsoft Exam #70-293: Planning a Microsoft Windows Server 2003 Network:

- Plan a NetBIOS name resolution strategy.

REVIEW QUESTIONS

1. After you specify the backup directory for the WINS database, how often does WINS perform complete database backups by default?

   a. every 3 hours

   b. every 6 hours

   c. every 12 hours

   d. every 24 hours

2. Which of the following types of backups are not supported by WINS?

   a. manual backups of the database

   b. automatic backups of the database

   c. backing up to a remote drive

   d. all of the above

3. What is the default location for the WINS database path?

   a. %systemroot%

   b. %systemroot%\system32

   c. %systemroot%\system32\wins

   d. none of the above

6

4. Which of the following is a recommended practice when maintaining WINS servers on your network?

   a. Periodically back up registry entries for the WINS server.

   b. Before decommissioning WINS servers, reconfigure clients to point to other WINS servers as their primary and secondary WINS servers.

   c. Store the WINS database and backup files on computers that are physically secure from unauthorized access.

   d. all of the above

5. Which of the following is true about WINS and security?

   a. The default location of the WINS database and log files provides the best NTFS security.

   b. You should create static WINS entries for critical servers to ensure that the name isn't registered by another server during maintenance procedures.

   c. Restrict membership of the WINS Users group to minimize the number of users that can administer the WINS server.

   d. all of the above

PLANNING A DNS STRATEGY

Labs included in this chapter:

♦ Lab 7.1 Installing and Configuring a Windows Server 2003 DNS Server

♦ Lab 7.2 Integrating DNS and DHCP

♦ Lab 7.3 Integrating DNS and WINS

♦ Lab 7.4 Creating a Standard Secondary Forward Lookup Zone Using the Dnscmd Command-Line Utility

♦ Lab 7.5 Using the Dnscmd Command-Line Utility

Microsoft MCSE Exam #70-293 Objectives	
Objective	Lab
Plan a DNS namespace design.	7.1, 7.4, 7.5
Plan zone replication requirements.	7.4
Plan for DNS security.	7.4
Examine the interoperability of DNS with third-party DNS solutions.	7.3
Diagnose and resolve issues related to DNS services.	7.1, 7.2, 7.3
Diagnose and resolve issues related to client computer configuration.	7.1, 7.2, 7.3

LAB 7.1 INSTALLING AND CONFIGURING A WINDOWS SERVER 2003 DNS SERVER

Objectives

The goal of this lab is to investigate creating zones and using dynamic updates.

Materials Required:

This lab will require the following:

- Two Windows Server 2003 systems installed and configured according to the instructions at the beginning of this lab manual

- A lab partner; if no partner is available, you will need to designate one system to be the DNS server and the other to be the DNS client. Complete the steps on both systems in sequence

Estimated completion time: **45 minutes**

Activity Background

The DNS (Domain Name System) is a fundamental service on a Windows Server 2003 network. When accessing resources on other computers, users find that it is easier to remember computer names than IP addresses. DNS is the service that resolves, or maps, computer names to IP addresses. Users only have to remember the name of a computer and the DNS service translates this into an IP address before the packets are sent onto the network. There are several new features in the Windows Server 2003 implementation of DNS.

Activity

This lab activity requires two Windows Server 2003 systems. You will need to designate one system to be the DNS server and the other to be the DNS client. These steps must be completed in the order that they appear, otherwise the expected results will not occur.

Both partners:

1. If necessary, log on as **Administrator** to the Arctic.local domain with a password of **Password!**.

2. First, you are going to remove your system from the Arctic.local domain. Click **Start**, right-click **My Computer**, and click **Properties**.

3. In the System Properties dialog box, click the **Computer Name** tab. At this time your server is a member of the Arctic.local domain. Click **Change**.

4. In the Computer Name Changes dialog box, under the Member of section, click **Workgroup**. Type **WORKGROUP** and click **OK**.

5. The Computer Name Changes dialog box appears. In order to remove your computer from the domain, you need to provide credentials. In the User name field, type **Administrator**. In the Password field, type **Password!**. Click **OK**.

6. The Welcome to the WORKGROUP workgroup message appears. Click **OK**.

7. A message appears, indicating that you must restart this computer for the changes to take effect. Click **OK**.

8. Click **OK** to close the System Properties dialog box.

9. A message appears, indicating that you must restart this computer for the changes to take effect and asking if you want to restart your computer now. Click **No**.

On the DNS server only:

1. Click **Start**, right-click **My Computer**, and click **Properties**.

2. Click the **Computer Name** tab and click **Change**.

3. In the Computer Name Changes dialog box, click **More**.

4. In the DNS Suffix and NetBIOS Computer Name dialog box, under Primary DNS Suffix of this computer, type **Partner01.local**, as shown in Figure 7-1. Click **OK**.

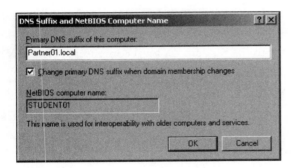

Figure 7-1 DNS Suffix and NetBIOS Computer Name dialog box on the DNS server

5. In the Computer Name Changes dialog box, the Full computer name field displays StudentXX.Partner01.local (where XX is your assigned student number). See Figure 7-2. Click **OK** to close the Computer Name Changes dialog box.

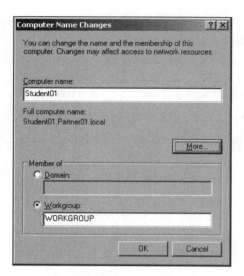

Figure 7-2   Full computer name

6. The Computer Name Changes message box appears, indicating that you must restart this computer for the changes to take effect. Click **OK**.

7. Click **OK** to close the System Properties dialog box.

8. The Computer Name Changes message box appears, indicating that you must restart this computer for the changes to take effect and asking if you want to restart your computer now. Click **Yes**.

9. Log on as **Administrator** to the Student*XX* local computer (where *XX* is your assigned student number) with a password of **Password!**.

10. Click **Start**, point to **Control Panel**, and double-click **Network Connections**.

11. In the Network Connections window, right-click **Classroom** and click **Disable**.

12. Right-click **Private** and click **Properties**.

13. In the Private Properties dialog box, click **Internet Protocol (TCP/IP)** and click **Properties**.

14. On the General tab, click the **Use the following IP address** option button to select it. In the IP address field, type **192.168.1XX.1XX** (where *XX* is your assigned student number). For example, if you are at Student01 you would type 192.168.101.101. The Subnet mask field is filled in for you with 255.255.255.0 as your subnet mask. In the Preferred DNS server field, type **192.168.1XX.1XX** (where *XX* is your assigned student number). You have just configured your Private connection IP address settings to refer to your local DNS server, as shown in Figure 7-3.

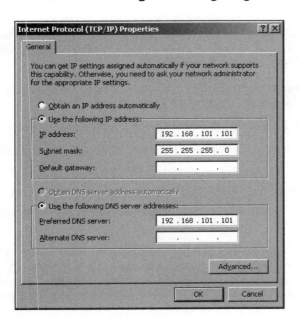

Figure 7-3   Internet Protocol (TCP/IP) Properties dialog box on the DNS server

15. Click **OK** to close the Internet Protocol (TCP/IP) Properties dialog box.

16. Click **OK** to close the Private Properties dialog box.

17. Close the Network Connections window.

On the DNS client only:

1. Click **Start**, right-click **My Computer**, and click **Properties**.

2. Click the **Computer Name** tab and click **Change**.

3. In the Computer Name Changes dialog box, click **More**.

4. In the DNS Suffix and NetBIOS Computer Name dialog box, under Primary suffix of this computer, type **Partner02.local** and then click **OK**.

5. In the Computer Name Changes dialog box, the Full computer name field displays Student*XX*.Partner02.local (where *XX* is your assigned student number). Click **OK** to close the Computer Name Changes dialog box.

6. The Computer Name Changes message box appears, indicating that you must restart this computer for the changes to take effect. Click **OK**.

7. Click **OK** to close the System Properties dialog box.

8. The Computer Name Changes message box appears, indicating that you must restart this computer for the changes to take effect and asking if you want to restart your computer now. Click **Yes**.

9. Log on as **Administrator** to the Student*XX* local computer (where *XX* is your assigned student number) with a password of **Password!**.

10. Click **Start**, point to **Control Panel**, and double-click **Network Connections**.

11. In the Network Connections window, right-click **Classroom** and click **Disable**.

12. Right-click **Private** and click **Properties**.

13. In the Private Properties dialog box, click **Internet Protocol (TCP/IP)** and click **Properties**.

14. On the General tab, click the **Use the following IP address** option button to select it. In the IP address field, type **192.168.1XX.1YY** (where *XX* is your partner's assigned student number and where *YY* is your assigned student number). For example if you are at Student02 the IP address of your partner's assigned student number (the DNS server), would be 01 and your assigned student number (the DNS client) is 02. Therefore you would type 192.168.101.102. The Subnet mask field is filled in for you with 255.255.255.0 as your subnet mask. In the Preferred DNS server field, type **192.168.1XX.1XX** (where *XX* is your partner's assigned student number). Again if you are at Student02, you would type 192.168.101.101. You have now configured your partner's computer to be your DNS server, as shown in Figure 7-4.

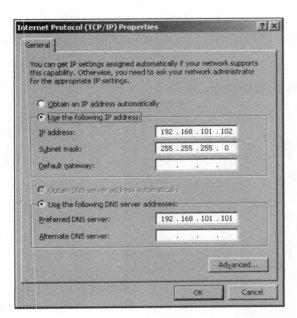

Figure 7-4   Internet Protocol (TCP/IP) Properties dialog box on the DNS client

15. Click **OK** to close the Internet Protocol (TCP/IP) Properties dialog box.

16. Click **OK** to close the Private Properties dialog box.

17. Close the Network Connections window.

DNS server only:

1. Click **Start** and click **Manage Your Server**.

2. In the Manage Your Server window, click **Add or remove a role**. The Configure Your Server Wizard starts.

3. On the Preliminary Steps page, click **Next**.

4. On the Server Role page, under Server Role, click **DNS server** and click **Next**.

5. On the Summary of Selections page, note that the Configure Your Server Wizard is going to install the DNS server and then run the Configure a DNS Server Wizard to configure DNS. Click **Next**.

6. The Welcome to the Configure a DNS Server Wizard page appears. Click **DNS Checklists**. A Microsoft Management Console opens. Review the options under Checklist: Configuring a DNS server. If you are unsure of what steps must be taken when installing and configuring your DNS server, you can refer to this checklist, which is available through Help. Close the Microsoft Management Console.

7. On the Welcome to the Configure a DNS Server Wizard page, click **Next**.

8. On the Select Configuration Action page, review the available options, and click the **Create a forward lookup zone (recommended for small networks)** option button, as shown in Figure 7-5. Click **Next**.

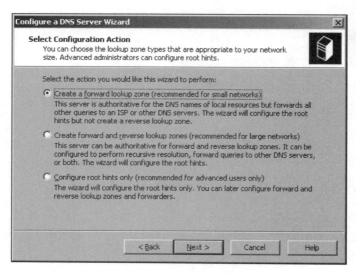

Figure 7-5   Creating a forward lookup zone

9. On the Primary Server Location page, click the **This server maintains the zone** option button, as shown in Figure 7-6. Click **Next**.

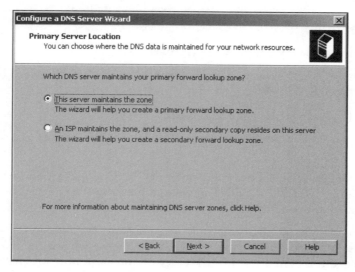

Figure 7-6   Primary Server Location page

10. On the Zone Name page, type **Partner01.local**, as shown in Figure 7-7. Click **Next**.

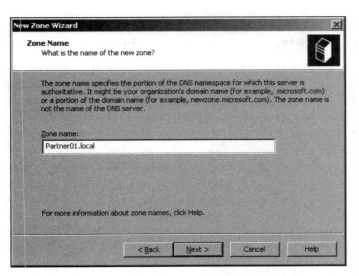

Figure 7-7   Creating the Partner01.local forward lookup zone

11. On the Zone File page, note that the default setting in the Create a new file with this file name field is **Partner01.local.dns**. Click **Next**.

12. On the Dynamic Update page, note that the Allow only secure dynamic updates (recommended for Active Directory) option is not available. This option is available only for Active Directory integrated zones. Your server is not a domain controller, and, therefore, this is not an available option at this time. Click the **Allow both nonsecure and secure dynamic updates** option button to select it. This option is considered to be a significant security vulnerability because updates can be accepted from untrusted sources. However, at this time, your Classroom connection is disabled, so the only computer that your system is connected to is your partner's server. The other available option on this page is the Do not allow dynamic updates option. With this option selected, dynamic updates of resource records are not accepted by this zone, and resource records must be updated manually. Later on in this lab activity, you will observe the effect of this setting on another zone file. Click **Next**.

13. On the Forwarders page, click the **No, it should not forward queries** option button. If connected to the Internet, your DNS server would still be able to resolve names using the root name servers. Click **Next**.

14. On the Completing the Configure a DNS Server Wizard page, click **Finish**. A DNS message box may appear with the following text: "The Configure a DNS Server Wizard could not configure root hints. To configure root hints manually or copy them from another server, in the server properties, select the Root Hints tab." Click **OK** to close the message box.

15. When the This Server is Now a DNS Server page appears, click **Finish**.

16. In the Manage Your Server window, under DNS Server, click **Manage this DNS server**.

17. The DNS console opens. Click **Student*XX*** (where *XX* is your assigned student number). Event Viewer is available from within this console. Double-click **Event Viewer**. The only event log available from this console is DNS Events.

18. Maximize the DNS console, if necessary. Double-click **DNS Events**. Looking under the Event column, double-click the first entry that displays **3150**. Under the Description field, note that Event Viewer has tracked the creation of version 1 of the zone Partner01.local.dns, as shown in Figure 7-8. Click **OK**.

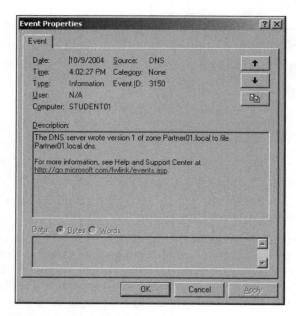

Figure 7-8   Event ID 3150

19. Double-click **Forward Lookup Zones**.

20. Click **Partner01.local** under Forward Lookup Zone. There are three resource records in the zone: the Start of Authority (SOA) record, a Name Server (NS) record, and a Host (A) record, as shown in Figure 7-9.

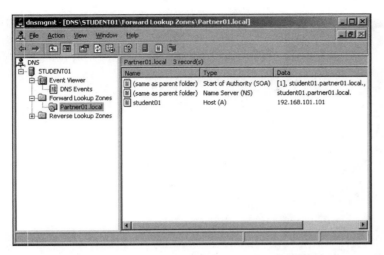

Figure 7-9   Resource records in the Partner01.local forward lookup zone

7

21. Right-click **Partner01.local** and click **Properties**.

22. In the Partner01.local Properties dialog box, note that the Dynamic updates option is configured to Nonsecure and secure. Click **Cancel** to close the Partner01.local Properties dialog box.

23. Right-click **Forward Lookup Zones** and click **New Zone**.

24. On the Welcome to the New Zone Wizard page, click **Next**.

25. On the Zone Type page, verify that Primary zone is selected, and then click **Next**.

26. On the Zone Name page, type **Partner02.local** and then click **Next**.

27. On the Zone File page, verify that Partner02.local.dns appears in the Create a new file with this file name field. Click **Next**.

28. On the Dynamic Update page, verify that the Do not allow dynamic updates option is selected, as shown in Figure 7-10, and then click **Next**.

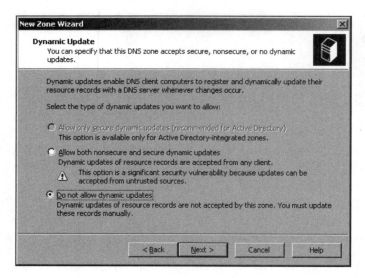

Figure 7-10   The Do not allow dynamic updates option selected

29. On the Completing the New Zone Wizard page, review the selections you have made for this forward lookup zone, and then click **Finish**.

30. You now have two forward lookup zones. Double-click **Partner02.local**. There are two resource records in this zone: a Start of Authority (SOA) record and a Name Server (NS) record.

31. Click **Reverse Lookup Zones**. Review the information provided in the details pane of the window.

32. Right-click **Reverse Lookup Zones** and click **New Zone**.

33. On the Welcome to the New Zone Wizard page, click **Next**.

34. On the Zone Type page, verify that **Primary zone** is selected, and click **Next**.

35. On the Reverse Lookup Zone Name page, click in the Network ID field, and then type **192.168.1XX** (where *XX* is your assigned student number). For example, if you are sitting at Student01 you would type 192.168.101 in the Network ID field. Once you have completed entering this information, the Reverse lookup zone name field displays 1*XX*.168.192.in-addr.arpa (where *XX* is your assigned student number). See Figure 7-11. Click **Next**.

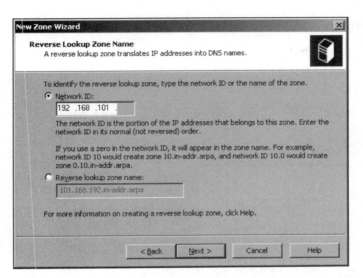

Figure 7-11   Creating the XX.168.192.in-addr.arpa reverse lookup zone

36. On the Zone File page, the Create a new file with this file name field now displays 1*XX*.168.192.in-addr.arpa.dns (where *XX* is your assigned student number. Click **Next**.

37. On the Dynamic Update page, click the **Allow both nonsecure and secure dynamic updates** option button to select it. Click **Next**.

38. On the Completing the New Zone Wizard page, review the settings you have configured for this reverse lookup zone, and click **Finish**. The reverse lookup zone appears in the DNS console.

On the DNS client only:

1. Click **Start**, click **Run**, type **cmd**, and click **OK**.

2. In the command prompt window, type **ipconfig /registerdns** and press **Enter**. The message, "Registration of the DNS resource records for all adapters of this computer has been initiated. Any errors will be reported in the Event Viewer in 15 minutes" appears. You have just registered the DNS records for your network adapters with the DNS service running on your partner's server. (Recall that you configured this in your Private connection's Internet Protocol (TCP/IP) Properties dialog box.)

On the DNS server only:

1. In the DNS console, right-click **Partner02.local** and click **Refresh**. No resource record has been added for the DNS client in the zone file. This is because when you created the forward lookup zone you configured the zone properties to not allow dynamic updates.

2. Right-click **Partner02.local** and click **Properties**.

3. In the Partner02.local Properties dialog box, under Dynamic updates, click the drop-down arrow and click **Nonsecure and secure**. Click **OK** to close the Partner02.local Properties dialog box.

On the DNS client only:

1. In the command prompt window, type **ipconfig /registerdns** and press **Enter**. Again, you are attempting to register the DNS records for all your network adapters with the DNS server.

2. Close the command prompt window.

On the DNS server only:

1. In the DNS console, right-click **Partner02.local** and click **Refresh**. A Host (A) record has been added for the DNS client computer. See Figure 7-12.

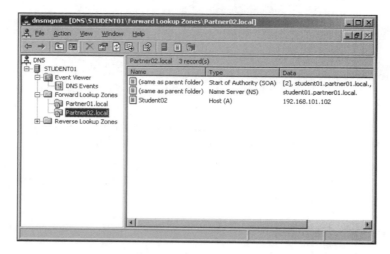

Figure 7-12   DNS client Host (A) record has been added to the Partner02.local forward lookup zone

2. Close the DNS console.

3. Close the Manage Your Server window.

Certification Objectives

Objectives for Microsoft Exam #70-293: Planning a Microsoft Windows Server 2003 Network:

- Plan a DNS namespace design.

- Diagnose and resolve issues related to DNS services.

- Diagnose and resolve issues related to client computer configuration.

REVIEW QUESTIONS

1. What is the default type of zone created on a member server?

   a. standard primary

   b. standard secondary

   c. Active Directory integrated

   d. stub zone

2. What is the default type of zone created on a domain controller?

   a. standard primary

   b. standard secondary

   c. Active Directory integrated

   d. stub zone

3. If you install Windows Server 2003 and do not configure forward or reverse lookup zones, what is this configuration called?

   a. a forwarder

   b. a caching only server

   c. a stub zone

   d. none of the above

4. Which of the following type of records is used to resolve one hostname to another hostname?

   a. A record

   b. MX record

   c. CNAME record

   d. PTR record

5. Which of the following is the default setting for dynamic updates when creating a Standard Primary forward lookup zone?

   a. Do not allow dynamic updates

   b. Allow both nonsecure and secure dynamic updates

   c. Allow only secure dynamic updates (recommended for Active Directory)

   d. none of the above

7

Lab 7.2 Integrating DNS and DHCP

Objectives

The goal of this lab is to configure the DNS and DHCP service, as well as the client configuration settings in order to take advantage of this feature.

Materials Required

This lab will require the following:

- Two Windows Server 2003 systems installed and configured according to the instructions at the beginning of this lab manual

- A lab partner; if no partner is available, you will need to designate one system to be the DNS server and the other to be the DNS client. Complete the steps on both systems in sequence

Estimated completion time: **30 minutes**

Activity Background

Windows Server 2003 DNS service offers the ability to integrate the DNS and DHCP services for registering client name to IP address mappings in the DNS database. By default Windows 2000 and Windows XP clients will automatically update their own host (A) records on the DNS server and will request that the DHCP server updates the associated Pointer (PTR) records for them. There are also additional settings available on zone properties to update both these records for other clients that are unable to update their own records in the DNS database.

ACTIVITY

Activity

On the DNS client only:

1. If necessary, log on as **Administrator** of the Student*XX* local computer (where *XX* is your assigned student number) with a password of **Password!**.

2. Click **Start**, right-click **My Computer**, and click **Properties**.

3. In the System Properties dialog box, click the **Computer Name** tab and then click **Change**.

4. In the Computer Name Changes dialog box, click **More**.

5. In the DNS Suffix and NetBIOS Computer Name dialog box, press **Delete** to delete Partner02.local. The field should now be empty. Click **OK**.

6. In the Computer Name Changes dialog box, the Full computer name field now displays Student*XX* (where *XX* is your assigned student number). Click **OK** to close the Computer Name Changes dialog box.

7. The Computer Name Changes message box appears, indicating that you must restart this computer for the changes to take effect. Click **OK**.

8. Click **OK** to close the System Properties dialog box.

9. The Computer Name Changes message box appears, indicating that you must restart this computer before the new settings will take effect and asking you want to restart your computer now. Click **Yes**.

On the DNS server only:

1. If necessary, log on as **Administrator** of the Student*XX* local computer (where *XX* is your assigned student number) with a password of **Password!**.

2. Click **Start** and click **Manage Your Server**.

3. In the Manage Your Server window, click **Add or remove a role**.

4. On the Preliminary Steps page, click **Next**.

5. On the Server Role page, click **DHCP server** to select it, and click **Next**.

6. On the Summary of Selections page, click **Next**.

7. On the Welcome to the New Scope Wizard page, click **Next**.

8. On the Scope Name page, type **1*XX*** (where *XX* is your assigned student number). Click **Next**.

9. On the IP Address Range page, in the Start IP address field, type **192.168.1*XX*.1** (where *XX* is your assigned student number. In the End IP address field, type **192.168.1*XX*.100** (where *XX* is your assigned student number). In the Subnet Mask field, type **255.255.255.0**, as shown in Figure 7-13. Click **Next**.

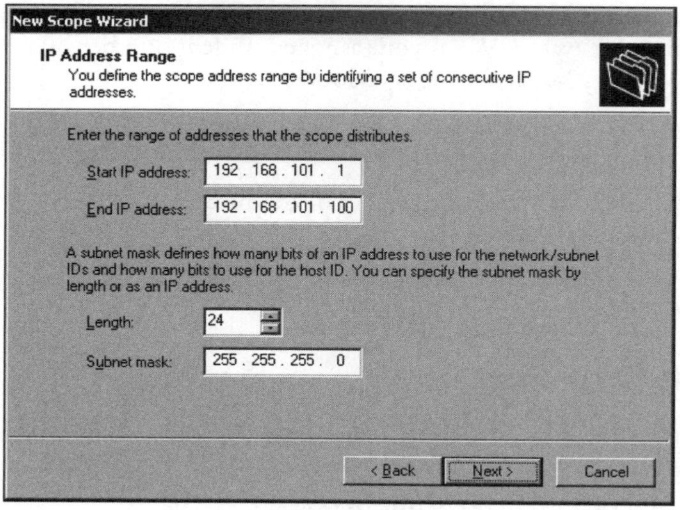

Figure 7-13   Configuring the IP address range

10. On the Add Exclusions page, click **Next**.

11. On the Lease Duration page, click **Next**.

12. On the Configure DHCP Options page, verify that the **Yes, I want to configure these options now** option button is selected. Click **Next**.

13. On the Router (Default Gateway) page, click **Next**.

14. On the Domain Name and DNS Servers page, type **Partner01.local** in the Parent domain field. In the Server name field, type **Student*XX*** (where *XX* is your assigned student number), and click **Resolve**. The IP address of your server should appear in the IP address field. Click **Add**. See Figure 7-14. Click **Next**.

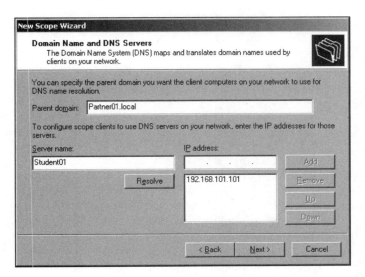

Figure 7-14   Configuring the Parent domain and Server name options

15. On the WINS Servers page, click **Next**.

16. On the Activate Scope page, verify that the **Yes, I want to activate this scope now** option button is selected, and click **Next**.

17. On the Completing the New Scope Wizard page, click **Finish**.

18. On the This Server is now a DHCP Server page, click **Finish**.

19. In the Manage Your Server window, under the DHCP Server section, click **Manage this DHCP server**.

20. In the DHCP console, double-click **studentXX.partner01.local [192.168.1XX.1XX]** (where XX is your assigned student number). A green arrow should appear next to your server name. Recall that in Lab 7-1 you disabled your Classroom connection. If your Classroom connection were enabled, your DHCP server would detect the Arctic.local Active Directory domain. Also, the following activity would not work because your DHCP server would not start because it is not authorized in Active Directory. If you see a red arrow next to your server name, disable your Classroom connection.

21. Double-click **Scope [192.168.1XX.0] 1XX** (where XX is your assigned student number). Double-click **Address Leases**. There are currently no leases.

22. Right-click **StudentXX.partner01.local [192.168.1XX.1XX]** (where XX is your assigned student number), and click **Properties**. Click the **DNS** tab. The default setting is to dynamically update DNS A and PTR records only if requested by the DHCP clients, as shown in Figure 7-15. Click **OK** to close the studentXX.partner01.local [192.168.1XX.1XX] Properties dialog box.

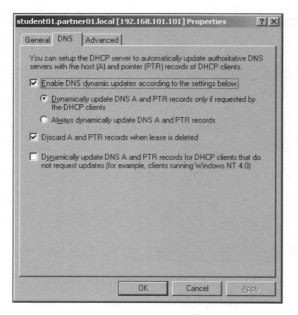

Figure 7-15   Dynamic update options on the DHCP server

On the DNS client only:

1. Log on as **Administrator** of the Student*XX* local computer (where *XX* is your assigned student number) with a password of **Password!**.

2. Click **Start**, point to **Control Panel**, and double-click **Network Connections**.

3. Right-click **Private** and click **Properties**.

4. In the Private Properties dialog box, click **Internet Protocol (TCP/IP)** and click **Properties**.

5. In the Internet Protocol (TCP/IP) Properties dialog box, click the **Obtain an IP address automatically** option button to select it. Click the **Obtain DNS server address automatically** option button to select it. Click **OK** to close the Internet Protocol (TCP/IP) Properties dialog box.

6. Click **Close** to close the Private Properties dialog box.

7. Close the Network Connections window.

8. Click **Start**, click **Run**, type **cmd**, and click **OK**.

9. In the command prompt window, type **ipconfig /all** and press **Enter**. The Connection-specific DNS Suffix field displays Partner01.local, which was configured in the scope properties of your partner's DHCP server. The IP address you have obtained is within the IP address range configured on your partner's DHCP server. The DHCP Server and DNS Server fields both point to the IP address of your partner's server. See Figure 7-16.

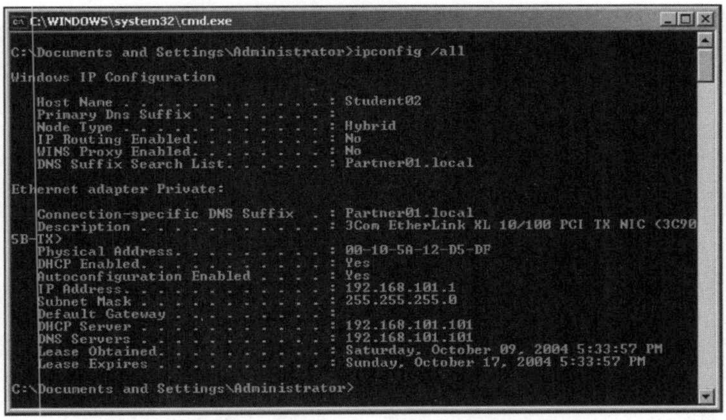

```
C:\WINDOWS\system32\cmd.exe                                    _ □ X

C:\Documents and Settings\Administrator>ipconfig /all

Windows IP Configuration

    Host Name . . . . . . . . . . . : Student02
    Primary Dns Suffix  . . . . . . :
    Node Type . . . . . . . . . . . : Hybrid
    IP Routing Enabled. . . . . . . : No
    WINS Proxy Enabled. . . . . . . : No
    DNS Suffix Search List. . . . . : Partner01.local

Ethernet adapter Private:

    Connection-specific DNS Suffix  . : Partner01.local
    Description . . . . . . . . . . : 3Com EtherLink XL 10/100 PCI TX NIC (3C90
5B-TX)
    Physical Address. . . . . . . . : 00-10-5A-12-D5-DF
    DHCP Enabled. . . . . . . . . . : Yes
    Autoconfiguration Enabled . . . : Yes
    IP Address. . . . . . . . . . . : 192.168.101.1
    Subnet Mask . . . . . . . . . . : 255.255.255.0
    Default Gateway . . . . . . . . :
    DHCP Server . . . . . . . . . . : 192.168.101.101
    DNS Servers . . . . . . . . . . : 192.168.101.101
    Lease Obtained. . . . . . . . . : Saturday, October 09, 2004 5:33:57 PM
    Lease Expires . . . . . . . . . : Sunday, October 17, 2004 5:33:57 PM

C:\Documents and Settings\Administrator>
```

Figure 7-16   Using ipconfig /all to view IP configuration settings

On the DNS server only:

1. In the DHCP console, right-click **Address Leases** and click **Refresh**. The lease obtained from your partner's server appears.

2. Close the DHCP console.

3. In the Manage Your Server window, click **Manage this DNS server**. The DNS console opens.

4. Double-click **Forward Lookup Zones**. Double-click **Partner01.local**. The Host (A) record for your partner's server does not appear. Right-click **Partner01.local** and click **Properties**. On the General tab, note that the Dynamic updates field is configured to Nonsecure and secure. The zone is configured to allow dynamic updates. Next, you will look at the configuration settings on the DNS client computer. Click **Cancel** to close the Partner01.local Properties dialog box.

5. Click **Reverse Lookup Zones**. Click **192.168.1XX.x Subnet** (where *XX* is your assigned student number and where x is an x). There is a pointer (PTR) record for the DHCP (and DNS) client computer. The IP address has been registered on the DNS server. However, the connection-specific DNS name of the client computer has not been registered. The connection-specific DNS name of the client computer will be the first label of the full computer name on the Computer Name tab in the System Properties dialog box along with the DNS suffix of this connection. See Figure 7-17.

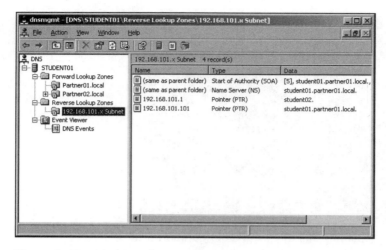

Figure 7-17   Viewing the pointer (PTR) record for the client computer in the reverse lookup zone

On the DNS client only:

1. Click **Start**, right-click **My Computer**, and click **Properties**.

2. Click the **Computer Name** tab. The Full computer name field displays **StudentXX** (where *XX* is your assigned student number). Click **Cancel** to close the System Properties dialog box.

3. Click **Start**, point to **Control Panel**, and double-click **Network Connections**.

4. Right-click **Private** and click **Properties**.

5. In the Private Properties dialog box, click **Internet Protocol (TCP/IP)** and click **Properties**.

6. In the Internet Protocol (TCP/IP) Properties dialog box, click **Advanced**.

7. In the Advanced TCP/IP Settings dialog box, click the **DNS** tab.

8. Click the **Use this connection's DNS suffix in DNS registration** check box to select it, as shown in Figure 7-18. The connection-specific DNS suffix will now be appended to the computer name in DNS registration. Click **OK** to close the Advanced TCP/IP Settings dialog box.

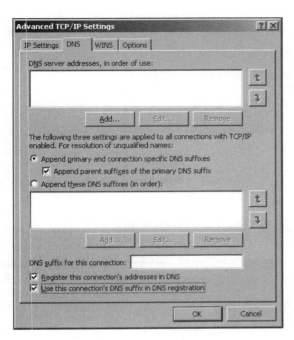

Figure 7-18   The Register this connection's DNS suffix in DNS registration check box

9. Click **OK** to close the Internet Protocol (TCP/IP) Properties dialog box.

10. Click **Close** to close the Private Properties dialog box.

11. Close the Network Connections window.

12. You are now going to try to register your computer's full computer name appended to the Parent domain DNS suffix that has been assigned through the DHCP server scope options. In the command prompt window, type **ipconfig /registerdns** and press **Enter**.

13. Close the command prompt window.

On the DNS server only:

1. In the DNS console, right-click **Partner01.local** and click **Refresh**. The Host (A) record for your partner's server appears. See Figure 7-19.

7

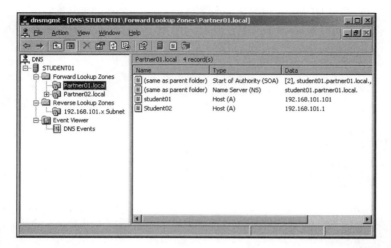

Figure 7-19   The new Host (A) record appears in the Partner01.local forward lookup zone

    2. Close the DNS console.

Certification Objectives

Objectives for Microsoft Exam #70-293: Planning a Microsoft Windows Server 2003 Network:

- Diagnose and resolve issues related to DNS services.

- Diagnose and resolve issues related to client computer configuration.

REVIEW QUESTIONS

    1. What is the default setting on DHCP servers for integration with DNS?

      a. To dynamically update DNS A records only if requested by the DHCP clients

      b. To dynamically update DNS PTR records only if requested by the DHCP clients

      c. To dynamically update DNS A and PTR records only if requested by the DHCP clients

      d. none of the above

2. For which clients will a Windows Server 2003 DHCP server update DNS records by default (if requested)? (Choose all that apply.)

   a. Windows 98

   b. Windows NT Workstation 4.0

   c. Windows 2000

   d. Windows XP

3. Which option would you configure if you wanted the DHCP server to be responsible for updating A and PTR records for your Windows 2000 and Windows XP clients?

   a. Dynamically update DNS A and PTR records only if requested by the DHCP clients

   b. Always dynamically update DNS A and PTR records

   c. Dynamically update DNS A and PTR records for DHCP clients that do not request updates

   d. none of the above

4. Which clients request that the DHCP serve update the PTR record but update their own A records? (Choose all that apply.)

   a. Windows 98

   b. Windows NT Workstation 4.0

   c. Windows 2000

   d. Windows XP

5. Which option might be preferable to select if both DHCP and DNS were running on the same server and you wanted to reduce network traffic?

   a. Dynamically update DNS A and PTR records only if requested by the DHCP clients

   b. Always dynamically update DNS A and PTR records

   c. Dynamically update DNS A and PTR records for DHCP clients that do not request updates

   d. none of the above

7

LAB 7.3 INTEGRATING DNS AND WINS

Objectives

The goal of this lab is to investigate different methods of integrating DNS and WINS Lookups.

Materials Required

This lab will require the following:

- Two Windows Server 2003 systems installed and configured according to the instructions at the beginning of this lab manual

Estimated completion time:**30 minutes**

Activity Background

The DNS service can be integrated with WINS lookup. When a client queries a DNS server and the requested name is not found in the DNS database, the DNS server can be configured to query a WINS server in order to resolve the name. By configuring WINS lookup on a DNS zone, systems that are not WINS-enabled (for example, UNIX) can indirectly access mappings stored in the WINS database. WINS lookup is not supported by non-Microsoft DNS servers. If your zone file is stored on non-Microsoft DNS servers you can choose to not replicate the WINS lookup records in zone transfers.

ACTIVITY

Activity

On the DNS server only:

1. If necessary, log on as **Administrator** of the Student*XX* local computer (where *XX* is your assigned student number) with a password of **Password!**.

2. Click **Start** and click **Manage Your Server**.

3. In the Manage Your Server window, click **Add or remove a role**.

4. On the Preliminary Steps page, click **Next**.

5. On the Server Role page, click **WINS server** and click **Next**.

6. On the Summary of Selections page, verify that **Install WINS** appears, and click **Next**.

7. The Insert Disk message box appears. Click **OK**.

8. In the Files Needed dialog box, click **Browse**. The Locate File dialog box displays.

9. In the Locate File dialog box, click **My Computer**. Double-click **Local Disk (C:)** and double-click the **i386** directory. Click the **WINSCTRS.DL_** file and click **Open**.

10. In the Files Needed dialog box, verify that the Cope files from fields displays **C:\i386**. Click **OK**.

11. On the This Server is Now a WINS Server page, click **Finish**.

12. In the Manage Your Server window, click **Manage this WINS server**. (You may need to scroll down in the Manage Your Server window in order to view this option.) The WINS console opens.

13. Next, you are going to add static mappings into the WINS server database. Double-click **STUDENTXX [192.168.1XX.1XX]** (where *XX* is your assigned student number).

14. Right-click **Active Registrations** and click **New Static Mapping**. In the New Static Mapping dialog box, type **COMPUTERA** in the Computer name field. In the IP address field, type **192.168.1XX.201** (where *XX* is your assigned student number). Click **Apply**.

15. In the New Static Mapping dialog box, type **COMPUTERB** in the Computer name field. In the IP address field, type **192.168.1XX.202** (where *XX* is your assigned student number). Click **Apply**.

16. In the Computer name field in the New Static Mapping dialog box, type **COMPUTERC**. In the IP address field, type **192.168.1XX.203** (where *XX* is your assigned student number). Click **OK**.

17. Close the WINS console.

18. In the Manage Your Server window, click **Manage this DHCP server**. The DHCP console opens.

19. Next, you are going to modify the properties of the scope to assign the IP address of the WINS server to resolve NetBIOS names on your network. In the DHCP console, double-click **studentXX.partner01.local [192.168.1XX.1XX]** (where *XX* is your assigned student number). Click **Scope [192.168.1XX.0] 1XX** (where *XX* is your assigned student number).

20. Right-click **Scope Options** and click **Configure Options**.

21. In the Scope Options dialog box, scroll down through the list of available options, and click **044 WINS/NBNS Servers**. In the Server name field, type **StudentXX** (where *XX* is your assigned student number). Click **Resolve**. The IP address of your server appears in the IP address fields. Click **Add**.

7

22. Under Available options, check the **046 WINS/NBT Node Type** check box to select it. Place your insertion point at the end of the content of the Byte field, press the **Backspace** key, and then type **8**. The Byte field should now display 0x8. There are four node types available: B, P, M, and H. B node indicates a broadcast. Clients configured with this node type use a broadcast to resolve NetBIOS names to IP addresses. Clients configured as P node query a NetBIOS Name Server in order to resolve NetBIOS names to IP addresses. M node clients use broadcasts first and then query a WINS server to resolve NetBIOS names. H node clients query a NetBIOS Name Server first and then use a broadcast to resolve NetBIOS names.

23. Click **OK** to close the Scope Options dialog box.

On the DNS client only:

1. If necessary, log on as **Administrator** of the Student*XX* local computer (where *XX* is your assigned student number) with a password of **Password!**.

2. Click **Start**, click **Run**, type **cmd**, and click **OK**.

3. In the command prompt window, type **ipconfig /release** and press **Enter**.

4. In the command prompt window, type **ipconfig /renew** and press **Enter**.

5. In the command prompt window, type **ipconfig /all** and press **Enter**. The Primary WINS Server field should now display the IP address of the WINS server. This option was just configured in the Scope Options dialog box for the DHCP server.

6. In the command prompt window, type **ping computera** and press **Enter**. The name computera is resolved to the IP address 192.168.1*XX*.201 (where *XX* is your partner's assigned student number). The request times out because there is no computer with that IP address on your subnet. However, your computer was able to successfully query the WINS server to resolve the name to the correct IP address.

On the DNS server only:

1. In the DHCP console, click **Scope Options**. In the details pane, right-click **044 WINS/NBNS Servers** and click **Delete**. When asked if you are sure you want to delete this item, click **Yes**.

2. Right-click **046 WINS/NBT Node Type** and click **Delete**. When asked if you are sure you want to delete this item, click **Yes**.

3. Another way to use WINS to resolve names to IP addresses involves configuring the properties of a DNS zone to use WINS lookup. In the Manage Your Server window, under DNS Server, click **Manage this DNS server**. The DNS console opens.

4. Double-click **Student*XX*** (where *XX* is your assigned student number) to expand it, and then double-click **Forward Lookup Zones**. Click **Partner01.local**, and then right-click **Partner01.local** and click **Properties**.

5. Click the **WINS** tab and click the **Use WINS forward lookup** option button to select it. Non-Microsoft DNS servers do not support WINS lookup records. If this zone were being replicated to non-Microsoft DNS servers, you would also need to select the Do not replicate this record check box. Because you are using only Microsoft DNS servers in this lab activity, you do not need to select this option.

6. In the IP address field, type the IP address of your Private connection, and then click **Add**. See Figure 7-20.

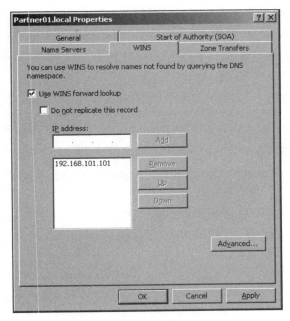

Figure 7-20   Configuring the Partner01.local zone to use WINS forward lookup

7. Click **OK** to close the Partner01.local Properties dialog box.

On the DNS client only:

1. You will now use the Ipconfig utility to release the WINS options that were obtained in your previous lease from the DHCP server. In the command prompt window, type **ipconfig /release** and press **Enter**.

2. Type **ipconfig /renew** and press **Enter**.

3. Type **ipconfig /all** and press **Enter**. The Primary WINS Server option no longer appears in the configuration settings you have received from the DHCP server.

4. Type **ping computerb** and press **Enter**. The name computerb is resolved to computerb.Partner01.local with an IP address 192.168.1.*XX*.202 (where *XX* is your partner's assigned student number). The request times out because there is no computer with that IP address on your subnet. However, your system was able to resolve the name computerb by querying the Partner01.local forward lookup zone. When this name was not found in the zone file, the DNS server used WINS forward lookup to query the WINS database on your partner's server.

On the DNS server only:

1. In the DNS console, right-click **Partner01.local** and click **Properties**.

2. On the WINS tab, click the **Use WINS forward lookup** option button to deselect it, and then click **OK**.

3. Non-Microsoft DNS servers do not support WINS lookup records; therefore, you might prefer to use another method for configuring WINS lookups. In the DNS console, right-click **Forward Lookup Zones** and then click **New Zone**.

4. On the Welcome to the New Zone Wizard page, click **Next**.

5. On the Zone Type page, accept the default setting of **Primary zone** and click **Next**.

6. On the Zone Name page, type **Wins** and click **Next**.

7. On the Zone File page, verify that the default setting is to create a file called Wins.dns. Click **Next**.

8. On the Dynamic Update page, verify that the setting is configured not to allow dynamic updates. Click **Next**.

9. On the Completing the New Zone Wizard page, click **Finish**. The Wins forward lookup zone now appears in the DNS console.

10. Double-click **WINS** to select this forward lookup zone.

11. Right-click **WINS** and click **Properties**.

12. Click the **WINS** tab, and click the **Use WINS forward lookup** option button to select. In the IP address field, type the IP address of your server's private connection. Click **Add**. Click **OK** to close the WINS Properties dialog box. In the DNS console, a WINS lookup record appears under the Type column for the Wins forward lookup zone. See Figure 7-21. (This record would also have appeared in the Partner01.local zone when it was configured to use WINS forward lookups.)

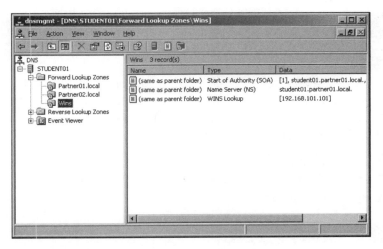

Figure 7-21   WINS lookup record

13. Close the DHCP and DNS consoles.

On the DNS client only:

1. Click **Start**, point to **Control Panel**, and double-click **Network Connections**.

2. In the Network Connections window, right-click **Private** and click **Properties**.

3. In the Private Properties dialog box, click **Internet Protocol (TCP/IP)** and click **Properties**.

4. In the Internet Protocol (TCP/IP) Properties dialog box, click **Advanced**.

5. In the Advanced TCP/IP Settings dialog box, click the **DNS** tab.

6. Click the **Append these DNS suffixes (in order)** option button to select it. Click **Add**. In the TCP/IP Domain Suffix dialog box, type **Partner01.local** and click **Add**.

7. Click **Add**. In the TCP/IP Domain Suffix dialog box, type **Wins** and click **Add**. The Advanced TCP/IP Settings dialog box appears, as shown in Figure 7-22.

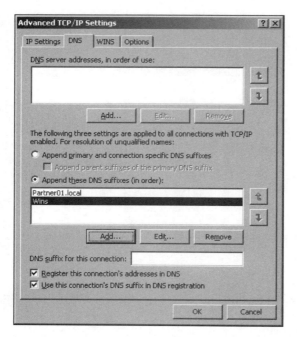

Figure 7-22   Append these DNS suffixes (in order)

8. Click **OK** to close the Advanced TCP/IP Settings dialog box.

9. Click **OK** to close the Internet Protocol (TCP/IP) Properties dialog box.

10. Click **OK** to close the Private Properties dialog box.

11. In the command prompt window, type **ping computerc** and press **Enter**. The name computerc is resolved to computerc.Wins with the IP address 192.168.1XX.203 (where XX is your partner's assigned student number) that was assigned in the static record.

12. Close the command prompt window.

13. In the Network Connections window, right-click **Private** and click **Properties**.

14. In the Private Properties dialog box, click **Internet Protocol (TCP/IP)** and click **Properties**.

15. In the Internet Protocol (TCP/IP) Properties dialog box, click **Advanced**.

16. In the Advanced TCP/IP Settings dialog box, click the **DNS** tab. Click the **Append primary and connection specific DNS suffixes** option button to select it. Check the **Append parent suffixes of the primary DNS suffix** check box. Click **OK** to close the Advanced TCP/IP Settings dialog box.

17. Click **OK** to close the Internet Protocol (TCP/IP) Properties dialog box.

18. Click **OK** to close the Private Properties dialog box.

19. Close the Network Connections window.

On the DNS server only:

1. In the DNS console, right-click **Wins** and click **Delete**. When asked if you want to delete the zone Wins from the server, click **Yes**. Close the DNS console.

2. Close the DHCP console.

Certification Objectives

Objectives for Microsoft Exam #70-293: Planning a Microsoft Windows Server 2003 Network:

- Examine the interoperability of DNS with third-party DNS solutions.

- Diagnose and resolve issues related to DNS services.

- Diagnose and resolve issues related to client computer configuration.

REVIEW QUESTIONS

1. What is the fastest way to configure WINS forward lookups if all of your DNS servers are running Windows Server 2003?

   a. Do nothing. WINS forward lookups are configured by default.

   b. Configure the properties of the forward lookup zone to use WINS forward lookups.

   c. Configure a new empty forward lookup zone. Configure the properties of the zone to use WINS forward lookups.

   d. none of the above

2. If your network also has non–Microsoft DNS servers in addition to Windows Server 2003 DNS servers, how do you configure WINS forward lookups on the DNS server?

   a. Do nothing. WINS forward lookups are configured by default.

   b. Configure the properties of the forward lookup zone to use WINS forward lookups.

   c. Configure a new empty forward lookup zone. Configure the properties of the zone to use WINS forward lookups

   d. none of the above

3. Which of the following are methods by which you can configure a client to use WINS forward lookups?

   a. through DHCP options

   b. on the properties of the forward lookup zone

   c. through the DNS tab in the Advanced TCP/IP Settings dialog box of the network connection.

   d. all of the above

4. What is the default setting for the Cache time-out setting on WINS lookup records?

   a. 5 minutes

   b. 10 minutes

   c. 15 minutes

   d. depends on the TTL of the record on the WINS server

5. What is the default value for the lookup time-out interval?

   a. 1 second

   b. 2 seconds

   c. 5 seconds

   d. none of the above

LAB 7.4 USING THE DNSCMD COMMAND-LINE UTILITY

Objectives

The goal of this lab is to create a standard secondary lookup zone using the Dnscmd command-line utility to create zones, create records in the zones and to view resource records in a zone.

Materials Required

This lab will require the following:

■ Two Windows Server 2003 systems installed and configured according to the instructions at the beginning of this lab manual

Estimated completion time: **30 minutes**

Activity Background

To ensure that clients are able to resolve names to IP addresses, it is recommended that you have at least two DNS servers that host each zone. Secondary servers can also be used to load balance an existing server for that DNS namespace. Another recommendation for better performance is to place secondary servers on the same side of a WAN link as clients in order to ensure name resolution services should the link fail. Secondary servers receive a copy of the zone file through a process called Zone Transfer.

Activity

On both the DNS client and the DNS server:

1. If necessary, log on as **Administrator** of the Student*XX* local computer (where *XX* is your assigned student number) with a password of **Password!**.

2. Insert your Windows Server 2003 Enterprise Edition CD.

3. Right-click **Start** and click **Explore**. Click your CD-ROM drive.

4. Click **SUPPORT** and then click **TOOLS**.

5. Double-click **SUPTOOLS.MSI**.

6. On the Welcome to the Windows Support Tools Setup Wizard page, click **Next**.

7. On the End User License Agreement page, click the **I Agree** option button to select it, and click **Next**.

8. On the User Information page, click **Next**.

9. On the Destination Directory page, click **Install Now**.

10. On the Completing the Windows Support Tools Setup Wizard page, click **Finish**.

11. Close Windows Explorer.

On the first (original) DNS server created in this chapter only:

1. If necessary, log on as **Administrator** to the Student*XX* local computer (where *XX* is your assigned student number) with a password of **Password!**.

2. Click **Start**, click **Run**, type **cmd**, and click **OK**.

3. In the command prompt window, type **dnscmd /?** and press **Enter**. The available parameters for the Dnscmd command-line utility appear. Review the available options.

4. Type **dnscmd /zoneprint partner02.local** and press **Enter**. The resource records for the partner02.local zone are displayed. The only Name Server (NS) record listed is for this server, as shown in Figure 7-23.

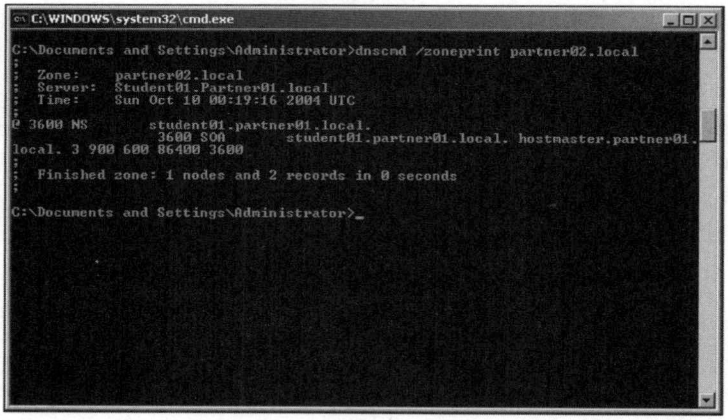

Figure 7-23   Using dnscmd /zoneprint to view resource records in the Partner02.local zone

5. Type **dnscmd student*XX* /recordadd partner02.local student*YY* a 192.168.1*XX*.1*YY*** (where *XX* is the your assigned student number (the original DNS server's assigned student number, and where *YY* is your partner's assigned student number (the DNS client's assigned student number) and press **Enter**. The "Add a Record for Student*YY*.partner02.local at partner02.local Command completed successfully" message appears, as shown in Figure 7-24.

Figure 7-24   Using dnscmd /recordadd to create new records in the partner02.local zone

7

6. Type **dnscmd student*XX* /recordadd partner02.local @ /openacl ns student*YY*.partner02.local** (where *XX* is your assigned student number [the original DNS server's assigned student number], and where *YY* is your partner's assigned student number [the DNS client's assigned student number]) and press **Enter**. The message "Add NS Record for partner02.local at partner02.local Command completed successfully" appears, as shown in Figure 7-25.

Figure 7-25   Using dnscmd /recordadd to add a Name Server (NS) record for the partner02.local zone

7. In the command prompt window, type **dnscmd /zoneprint partner02.local** and press **Enter**. The resource records for the partner02.local zone are displayed. Both computers are now name servers for this zone. See Figure 7-26.

Figure 7-26   Using dnscmd /zoneprint to view additions to the partner02.local zone

8. Close the command prompt window.

9. Click **Start**, point to **Administrative Tools**, and click **DNS**.

10. In the DNS console, double-click **Partner02.local**. There are two Name Server (NS) records for this zone, as shown in Figure 7-27. Close the DNS console.

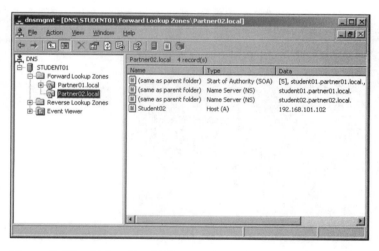

Figure 7-27   Using the DNS console to view records in the partner02.local zone

On the DNS client only:

1. Click **Start**, point to **Control Panel**, and double-click **Network Connections**.

2. Right-click **Private** and click **Properties**.

3. In the Private Properties dialog box, click **Internet Protocol (TCP/IP)** and click **Properties**.

4. In the Internet Protocol (TCP/IP) Properties dialog box, click the **Use the following IP address** option, and then make the following changes:

IP Address dent	192.168.1XX.1YY (where XX is your partner's assigned student number and where YY is the your assigned student number)
Subnet mask	255.255.255.0

5. Click **Use the following DNS server addresses**. After completing this step, the Internet Protocol (TCP/IP) Properties dialog box should appear, as shown in Figure 7-28. Then, type the IP address of your partner's Private connection as the preferred DNS server.

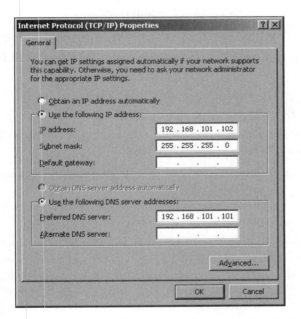

7

Figure 7-28 Modifying the Internet Protocol (TCP/IP) properties of the second DNS server

6. Click **OK** to close the Internet Protocol (TCP/IP) Properties dialog box.

7. Click **Close** to close the Private Properties dialog box.

8. Close the Network Connections window.

9. Click **Start**, right-click **My Computer**, and click **Properties**.

10. In the System Properties dialog box, click the **Computer Name** tab and then click **Change**.

11. In the Computer Name Changes dialog box, click **More**.

12. In the DNS Suffix and NetBIOS Computer Name dialog box, type **Partner02.local** and click **OK**.

13. In the Computer Name Changes dialog box, the Full computer name field now appears as Student*XX*.Partner02.local (where *XX* is your assigned student number). Click **OK** to close the Computer Name Changes dialog box.

14. The Computer Name Changes message box appears, indicating that you must restart this computer for the changes to take effect. Click **OK**.

15. Click **OK** to close the System Properties dialog box.

16. The Computer Name Changes message box appears, indicating that you must restart this computer before the new settings will take effect and asking if you want to restart your computer now. Click **Yes**.

17. Log on as **Administrator** to the Student*XX* local computer (where *XX* is your assigned student number) with a password of **Password!**.

18. Click **Start**, point to **Control Panel**, and click **Add or Remove Programs**.

19. In the Add or Remove Programs window, click **Add/Remove Windows Components**.

20. On the Windows Components page, scroll through the components listed, click **Networking Services**, and then click **Details**.

21. In the Networking Services dialog box, check the **Domain Name System (DNS)** check box, click **OK**, and then click **Next**.

22. On the Completing the Windows Components Wizard page, click **Finish**.

23. Close the Add or Remove Programs window.

24. Click **Start**, click **Run**, type **cmd**, and click **OK**.

25. In the command prompt window, type **dnscmd studentXX /zoneadd partner02.local /secondary 192.168.1YY.1YY /file partner02.local.dns** (where *XX* is your assigned student number, and where *YY* is your partner's assigned student number), and press **Enter**. The message "DNS Server Student*XX* created zone partner02.local Command completed successfully" appears, as shown in Figure 7-29.

Figure 7-29   Using dnscmd /zoneadd to create a secondary forward lookup zone

26. In the command prompt window, type **dnscmd studentXX /zoneprint partner02.local** (where *XX* is your assigned student number), and press **Enter**. The resource records for the partner02.local zone appear, as shown in Figure 7–30.

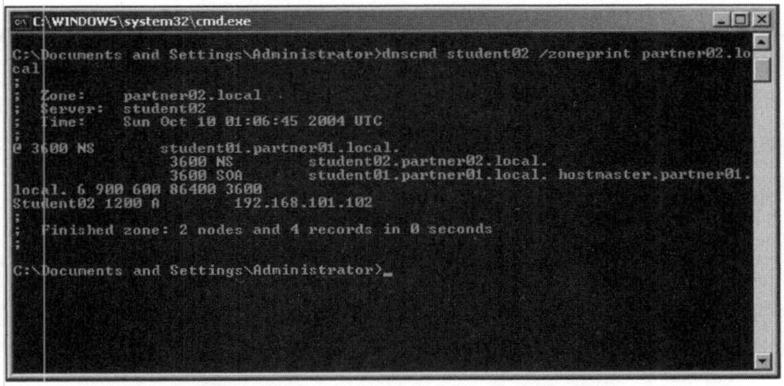

Figure 7-30   Using dnscmd /zoneprint to view the partner02.local zone on the additional DNS server

27. Close the command prompt window.

Certification Objectives

Objectives for Microsoft Exam #70-293: Planning a Microsoft Windows Server 2003 Network:

- Plan a DNS namespace design.

- Plan zone replication requirements.

- Plan for DNS security.

REVIEW QUESTIONS

1. What is the default setting on the Zone Transfers tab?

   a. Allow zone transfers to any server

   b. Allow zone transfers only to servers listed on the Name Servers tab

   c. Allow zone transfers only to the following servers

   d. none of the above

2. Which of the following types of zones can be updated directly? (Choose all that apply.)

   a. Active Directory integrated

   b. standard primary

   c. standard secondary

   d. stub

3. Which of the following zone types is not available on a member server?

   a. Active Directory integrated

   b. standard primary

   c. standard secondary

   d. stub

4. Which zone type contains a security mechanism to control which users are allowed to update DNS records?

   a. Active Directory integrated

   b. standard primary

   c. standard secondary

   d. stub

5. Which of the following zone types offers multimaster replication?

   a. Active Directory integrated

   b. standard primary

   c. standard secondary

   d. stub

LAB 7.5 USING THE DNSCMD COMMAND-LINE UTILITY

Objectives

The goal of this lab is to create a stub zone using the Dnscmd command-line utility and the /zoneadd parameter.

Materials Required

This lab will require the following:

- Two Windows Server 2003 systems installed and configured according to the instructions at the beginning of this lab manual

7

Estimated completion time: **15 minutes**

Activity Background

Stub zones can be used for various reasons such as to keep delegated zone information current, improve name resolution, and simplify DNS administration. However, stub zones are not authoritative for that zone. They contain resource records that allow them to direct queries for that namespace to the servers that are authoritative for that zone.

ACTIVITY

Activity

On the second DNS server:

1. If necessary, log on as **Administrator** to the Student*XX* local computer (where *XX* is your assigned student number) with a password of **Password!**.

2. Click **Start**, click **Run**, type **cmd**, and click **OK**.

3. In the command prompt window, type **dnscmd student*XX* /zoneadd partner01.local /stub 192.168.1*YY*.1*YY* /file partner01.local.dns** (where *XX* is your assigned student number, and where *YY* is your partner's assigned student number) and press **Enter**. (For example, if you were sitting at student02, you would type "dnscmd student02 /zoneadd partner01.local /stub 192.168.101.101 /file partner01.local.dns" and then press Enter.) The message "DNS server student*XX* created zone partner01.local: Command completed successfully" appears, as shown in Figure 7–31.

Figure 7-31   Using dnscmd /zoneadd to add a stub zone for the partner01.local zone

4. In the command prompt window, type **dnscmd student*XX* /zoneprint partner01.local** and press **Enter**. The resource records for the zone appear, as shown in Figure 7-32.

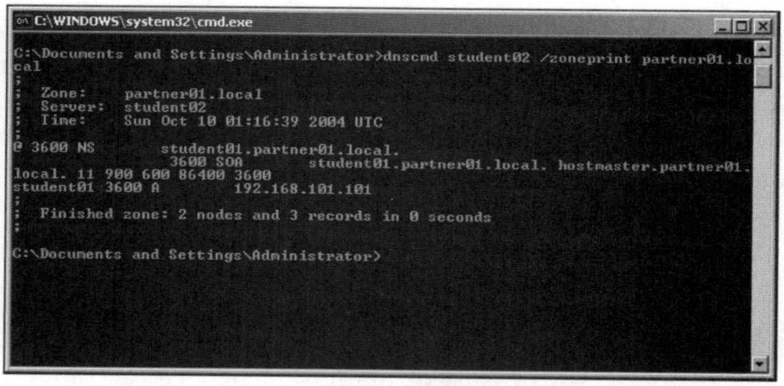

Figure 7-32   Using dnscmd /zoneprint to view the records in the partner01.local zone

On the original DNS server:

1. If necessary, log on as **Administrator** to the Student*XX* local computer (where *XX* is your assigned student number) with a password of **Password!**.

2. Click **Start**, click **Run**, type **cmd**, and click **OK**.

3. In the command prompt window, type **dnscmd student*XX* /recordadd partner01.local computerd a 192.168.1*XX*.204** (where *XX* is your assigned student number), and press **Enter**. The message "Add a Record for computerd.partner01.local at partner01.local Command completed successfully" appears, as shown in Figure 7-33.

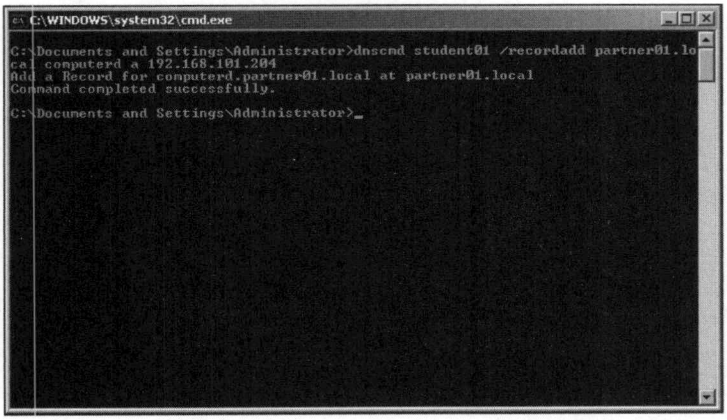

Figure 7-33   Using dnscmd /recordadd to add a Host (A) record to the partner01.local zone

4. Type **dnscmd student*XX* /zoneprint partner01.local** (where *XX* is your assigned student number), and press **Enter**. (For example, if you were sitting at student01, you would type "dnscmd student01 /zoneprint partner01.local" and then press Enter.) The zone records appear, as shown in Figure 7–34.

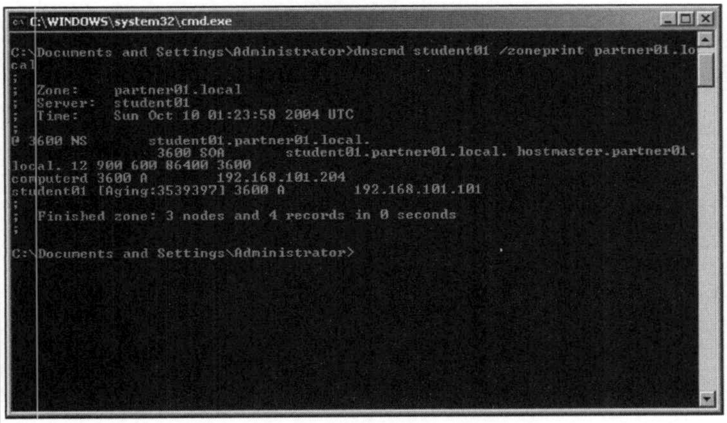

Figure 7-34   Using dnscmd /zoneprint to view additions to the partner01.local zone

5. Close the command prompt window.

6. Click **Start**, point to **Administrative Tools**, and click **DNS**.

7. In the DNS console, click **Student*XX*** (where *XX* is your assigned student number). Double-click **Forward Lookup Zones**. Double-click **Partner01.local**. The new host record for computerd appears. Close the DNS console.

On the second DNS server:

1. In the command prompt window, type **dnscmd studentXX /zoneprint partner01.local** (where *XX* is your assigned student number), and press **Enter**. The record that has just been added at the Primary zone does not appear. This is because your server contains a stub zone. Stub zones only contain the Start of Authority, Name Server, and glue records, and, therefore, the new record will not appear in the stub zone.

2. Close the command prompt window.

3. Click **Start**, point to **Administrative Tools**, and click **DNS**.

4. In the DNS console, click **StudentXX** (where *XX* is your assigned student number). Double-click **Forward Lookup Zones**. In the Type column, the Partner01.local zone is listed as Stub.

5. Double-click **Partner01.local** and view the records listed. The DNS server that contains a stub zone will forward name resolution queries to the servers listed as Name Servers for the Partner01.local zone. Because this server is not listed as a Name Server for the Partner01.local zone, it will simply forward name resolution requests to the Name Servers listed in its stub zone.

6. Close the DNS console.

On the original DNS server only:

1. Click **Start** and click **Manage Your Server**.

2. In the Manage Your Server window, click **Add or remove a role**.

3. On the Preliminary Steps page, click **Next**.

4. On the Server Role page, click **DHCP server** and click **Next**.

5. On the Role Removal Confirmation page, check the **Remove the DHCP server role** check box, and click **Next**.

6. On the DHCP Server Role removed page, click **Finish**.

7. In the Manage Your Server window, click **Add or remove a role**.

8. On the Preliminary Steps page, click **Next**.

9. On the Server Role page, click **WINS server** and click **Next**.

10. On the Role Removal Confirmation page, check the **Remove the WINS server role** check box, and click **Next**.

11. On the WINS server Role removed page, click **Finish**.

12. Close the Manage Your Server window.

On both servers:

1. Click **Start**, point to **Control Panel**, and double-click **Network Connections**.

2. In the Network Connections window, right-click **Classroom** and click **Enable**.

3. Close the Network Connections window.

Certification Objectives

Objectives for Microsoft Exam #70-293: Planning a Microsoft Windows Server 2003 Network:

■ Plan a DNS namespace design.

REVIEW QUESTIONS

7

1. Which of the following zone types contains copies of the primary zone information?

    a. Active Directory integrated zones

    b. secondary zones

    c. stub zones

    d. none of the above

2. Which of the following zone files have .dns file extension? (Choose all that apply.).

    a. primary zones

    b. secondary zones

    c. stub zones

    d. Active Directory integrated zones

3. Which type of zone involves specifying a Master DNS Server? (Choose all that apply.)

    a. Active Directory integrated

    b. standard primary

    c. standard secondary

    d. stub

4. Which type of record might be found on a stub zone?

   a. SOA

   b. NS

   c. Glue

   d. all of the above

5. Which of the following zone types are not authoritative for a zone? (Choose all that apply.)

   a. Active Directory integrated

   b. standard primary

   c. standard secondary

   d. stub

8

Managing and Troubleshooting DNS

Labs included in this chapter:

♦ Lab 8.1 Logging and Monitoring DNS

♦ Lab 8.2 Testing a Caching-only DNS Server with DNSLint

♦ Lab 8.3 Testing a Forwarding-only DNS Server with DNSLint

♦ Lab 8.4 Monitoring Zone Transfers

♦ Lab 8.5 Confirming DNS Server Records with NSLookup

Microsoft MCSE Exam #70-293 Objectives	
Objective	Lab
Diagnose and resolve issues related to DNS services.	8.1. 8.2, 8.3, 8.4, 8.5
Plan network traffic monitoring. Tools might include Network Monitor and System Monitor.	8.1
Diagnose and resolve issues related to name resolution cache information.	8.2, 8.3, 8.4
Plan a forwarding configuration.	8.3
Plan zone replication requirements.	8.4

LAB 8.1 LOGGING AND MONITORING DNS

Objectives

The goal of this lab activity is to learn about the DNS event log, DNS debug logging, and DNS counters in the Performance Monitor.

Materials Required:

This lab will require the following:

- A Windows Server 2003 system installed and configured according to the instructions at the beginning of this lab manual

Estimated completion time: **30 minutes**

Activity Background

To optimize DNS services, you must be able to monitor your DNS server performance. Windows Server 2003 offers sufficient built-in tools to meet this need and provide detailed service information to troubleshoot as well.

Activity

1. If necessary, log on as **Administrator** to the Arctic.local domain with a password of **Password!**.

2. You need to remove your system from the Arctic.local domain. Click **Start**, right-click **My Computer**, and click **Properties**.

3. In the System Properties dialog box, click the **Computer Name** tab. Note that your server is a member of the Arctic.local domain. Click **Change**.

4. In the Computer Name Changes dialog box, click the **Workgroup** option button in the Member of section, type **Workgroup**, and then click **OK**.

5. You need to provide credentials to remove your computer from the domain. In the User name text box, type **Administrator**, and then in the Password text box, type **Password!**. Click **OK**.

6. A welcome message appears. Click **OK**.

7. A message appears, indicating that you must restart your computer for the changes to take effect. Click **OK**.

8. Click the **Computer Name** tab, and click **Change**.

9. In the Computer Name Changes dialog box, click **More**.

10. In the DNS Suffix and NetBIOS Computer Name dialog box, under Primary DNS Suffix of this computer, type **PartnerXX.local** (where *XX* is your assigned student number). For example, if Student01 is the DNS server in this lab activity, your primary DNS suffix would be Partner01.local. Click **OK**.

11. Click **OK** to close the Computer Name Changes dialog box.

12. Click **OK** to the message that indicates that you must restart your computer for the changes to take effect.

13. Click **OK** to close the System Properties dialog box.

14. A message appears, indicating that you must restart your computer for the changes to take effect. Click **Yes**.

15. Log on as **Administrator** with a password of **Password!**.

16. You need to confirm your IP settings. Click **Start**, right-click **My Computer**, and click **Explore**.

17. In the left pane, click the **+ (plus sign)** next to Control Panel and then click **Network Connections**.

18. Hold down the **Alt** key and double-click the **Classroom** connection to access its Properties page.

19. On the General tab, click **Internet Protocol (TCP/IP)** and click **Properties**.

8

20. If necessary, click the **Use the following IP address** option button, and then set the following IP information (as shown in Figure 8-1):

IP address: **192.168.1.1XX** (where *XX* is your student number)

Subnet mask: **255.255.255.0**

Default gateway: **192.168.1.10**

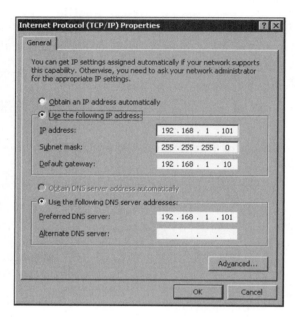

Figure 8-1   Classroom connection IP settings

21. If necessary, click the **Use the following DNS server addresses** option button, and set the following DNS information:

Preferred DNS server: **192.168.1.1XX** (where *XX* is your student number)

Alternate DNS server: none (Delete any IP that might appear.)

22. Click **OK** to close the Internet Protocol (TCP/IP) Properties dialog box.

23. Click **Close** to exit the Classroom Properties dialog box.

24. Return to the Network Connections window. Right-click the **Private** connection and click **Disable**.

To reset the DNS server to defaults and clear out the logs:

1. Click **Administrative Tools** in the console tree, and then double-click **DNS** to open the dnsmgmt snap-in.

2. Double-click your DNS server **StudentXX** (where *XX* is your student number) to expand it, if necessary.

3. In the right pane, double-click **Forward Lookup Zones**.

4. You need to delete each of the forward lookup zones. In the right pane, right-click a zone and click **Delete**. Click **Yes** to confirm the deletion. Repeat for each forward lookup zone to be deleted.

5. In the left pane, click **Reverse Lookup Zones**. In the right pane, delete each zone using the same method provided in Step 4.

6. In the left pane, double-click **Event Viewer**, right-click **DNS Events**, and then click **Clear all Events**. A dialog box appears, asking if you want to save your events before clearing. Click **No**.

7. Right-click your DNS server **StudentXX** (where *XX* is your student number), and click **Properties**.

8. Click the **Advanced** tab, click the **Reset to Default** option button, and click **Apply**. Note that this resets the options only in the Advanced tab.

9. You need to reset the options and settings for your DNS server manually. Configure the following settings on the tab indicated:

Interfaces tab: Select the **All IP addresses** option.

Forwarders tab: The DNS Domains setting should read **All other DNS domains** and nothing else. The Forwarder selection list should be empty. The value of the Number of seconds before forwarded query times-out option should be **5**. The Do not use recursion option should not be selected.

Root Hints tab: The options here should be fully populated with the 13 root servers—A through M.

Monitoring: Nothing should be selected.

Event Logging: All events should be selected.

Debug Logging: This option should not be selected.

10. Click **OK**. Your DNS server is now configured back to its default settings.

11. You need to confirm that you have no DNS resolution cached. Click **Start**, click **Run**, type **cmd**, and then click **OK**.

8

12. Type **ipconfig /displaydns** and press **Enter**. You should see entries only for 1.0.0.127.in-addr.arpa and localhost, as shown in Figure 8-2. If not, type **ipconfig /flushdns** and press **Enter**. Once you receive the confirmation message that your DNS resolver list has been flushed, type **ipconfig /displaydns** and press **Enter** to confirm. Close the window.

Figure 8-2   ipconfig /displaydns after cache has been cleared

13. Return to your Explorer window. In the Administrative Tools folder, double-click **Performance** to open the Performance Monitor.

14. The monitor starts with three default counters being charted at one-second intervals. Click the first counter in the lower right, and then click **Delete**. Delete the other two counters until nothing is being charted.

15. Above the chart, click the **+ (plus sign)** to add counters. Click the **Performance object** drop-down arrow, and click **DNS**. Click **Explain** to open the Explain text box. Hold down the **Ctrl** key and click the following counters:

    Recursive Queries/sec

    Recursive Query Failure/sec

    TCP Query Received/sec

    Total Query Received/sec

    UDP Query Received/sec

16. Click **Add** to add all of the selected counters to the chart. Click **Close** to close the Add Counters window.

17. Right-click the chart and click **Properties**. Click the **Graph** tab. In the Vertical scale section, set the Maximum value to **10**, and then click **OK**. Figure 8-3 shows a configured Performance Monitor. Minimize the Performance Monitor.

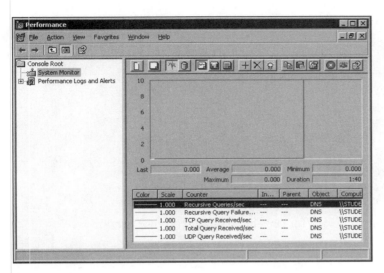

Figure 8-3   Configuring the Performance Monitor

18. Return to the dnsmgmt window. Right-click your DNS server **StudentXX** (where *XX* is your student number), and click **Properties**.

19. Click the **Debug Logging** tab. Check the **Log packets for debugging** check box. Accept all of the defaults. Leave the Log file name text box blank. It will use the default file location C:\WINDOWS\system32\dns\dns.log. Click **OK** to close the window.

20. Click **Start**, click **Run**, type **cmd**, and then click **OK**.

21. Type **cd \windows\system32\dns** and press **Enter**.

22. Type **dir** and press **Enter**. You will see that the file dns.log has been created.

23. In order to improve the readability of the log entries, you can resize the window. Click the upper-left corner of the Command Prompt window, as shown in Figure 8-4, and then click **Properties**. Click the **Layout** tab, click in the **Width** box in the Window Size area, type **150**, and then click **OK**.

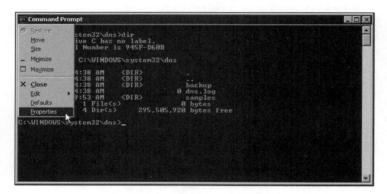

Figure 8-4   Access properties for current command prompt window

24. The Apply Properties dialog box appears. Click **OK** to accept the default value.

25. Type **type dns.log** and press **Enter**. Don't be concerned if there is nothing there yet; you haven't made any queries to log. To check the log periodically throughout the following labs, return to this Command Prompt window and use the **up** arrow key or the **F3** key, and then press **Enter**.

26. Minimize the Command Prompt window. You now have three performance and troubleshooting tools running and configured to log DNS events.

Certification Objectives

Objectives for Microsoft Exam #70-293: Planning a Microsoft Windows Server 2003 Network:

- Diagnose and resolve issues related to DNS services.

- Plan network traffic monitoring. Tools might include Network Monitor and System Monitor.

REVIEW QUESTIONS

1. What is the default location of dns.log?

   a. \Temp\dns.log

   b. \Windows\System32\dns.log

   c. \Windows\System32\Dns\dns.log

   d. \Documents and Settings\Administrator\dns.log

2. Which of the following are checked by default in the Debug Logging tab? (Choose all that apply.)

   a. TCP

   b. Notifications

   c. Requests

   d. Queries/Transfers

3. What can you use to monitor changes in the dns.log? (Choose all that apply.)

   a. Wordpad.exe

   b. dns.log

   c. tail -f dns.log

   d. Notepad.exe

4. When you first open the System Monitor, which of the following are the default counters? (Choose all that apply.)

   a. Pages/sec

   b. % processor time

   c. Current disk queue length

   d. Average disk queue length

5. Which Performance Monitor counter would you add to chart the number of successful zone transfers for your DNS server?

   a. IXFR Success Sent

   b. AXFR Success Sent

   c. Dynamic Update Received

   d. Zone Transfer Success

8

Lab 8.2 Testing a Caching-only DNS Server with DNSLint

Objectives

The goal of this lab activity is to learn about the advantages and disadvantages of using a "caching-only" DNS server.

Materials Required:

This lab will require the following:

- A Windows Server 2003 system installed and configured according to the instructions at the beginning of this lab manual

- Performance Monitor and debug logging configured according to Lab 8.1

- Windows Support Tools installed as instructed in Lab 7.4

Estimated completion time: **15 minutes**

Activity Background

A caching-only DNS server hosts no zones. It can only perform queries, cache the answers, and return the results. It is not authoritative for any domains, and the information that it contains is limited to what has been cached while resolving queries. The advantages of a caching-only configuration are that it reduces network utilization for subsequent queries and there are no zone transfers to utilize bandwidth. The disadvantages are that cached information may be out of date and result in errors; also since the server will only query root servers for domains that are not in its cache, it will not resolve domains that are not registered on the Internet, such as a corporate Intranet site.

DNSLint is a command-line utility that allows you verify correct DNS configuration. It has commands that help you confirm that a zone is correctly configured, or verify records for Active Directory.

ACTIVITY

Activity

1. You should already be logged in as Admnistrator with your performance monitors running. The dns.log should be displayed in the extended Command Prompt window.

2. Click **Start**, click **Run**, type **cmd**, and then click **OK** to open another Command Prompt window. Two Comand Prompt windows should be open.

3. Type **cd ** and press **Enter**.

4. Type **dnslint /ql autocreate** and press **Enter**. This command creates a sample query list document: C:\in-dnslint.txt. See Figure 8-5.

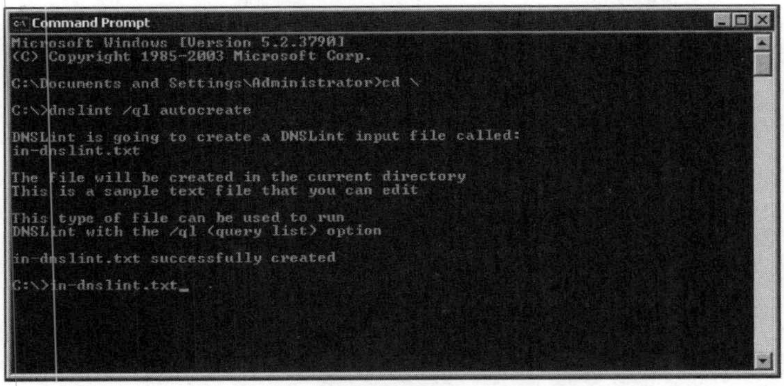

Figure 8-5   Creating DNSLint sample file

5. Type **in-dnslint.txt** and press **Enter**. The file will open in Notepad. Read through the sample file. Lines beginning with a semicolon are comments.

6. Near the bottom of the file, edit the content to read as shown in bold in the following code:

   +This DNS server is called: **StudentXX** (where *XX* is your student number)

   [dns~server] 192.168.1.1XX (where *XX* is your student number)
   ```
   microsoft.com,a,r        ;A record
   207.46.197.100,ptr,r  ;PTR record
   microsoft.com,cname,r ;CNAME record
   microsoft.com,mx,r       ;MX record
   instructor.arctic.local,a,r
   server1.arctic.local,a,r
   server2.arctic.local,a,r
   ```

7. Press the **Alt+F** keys, and then press **A**. Name the file **dnstest1.txt** and save it on drive C:. Close Notepad.

8. Type **dnslint /ql dnstest1.txt** and press **Enter**. In a moment, a report appears in Internet Explorer. Notice that the arctic.local resolutions failed.

9. Check the Performance Monitor. Note the small spike in the chart for recursive queries.

10. Read your dns.log in the Command Prompt window. It can take up to a minute for recent entries to be written to the dns.log. Use the legend in Figure 8-6 to interpret the results.

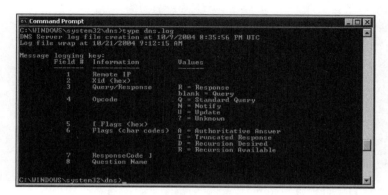

Figure 8-6   DNS debug log legend

11. Close the Internet Explorer window with the DNSLint report.

12. Return to the DNSLint Command Prompt window. Type **dnslint /ql dnstest1.txt /no_open /y** and press **Enter**. This will perform the test again but without opening the results in Internet Explorer.

13. Check the Performance Monitor. The only recursive queries that are left are for those that were unresolved in the last test.

14. Check your dns.log again, and you will see that most queries were resolved without sending a query to another DNS server, meaning they were resolved from cache.

15. You can repeat the test, but you must first clear the cache. If neccessary, click **Start**, click **Administrative Tools**, and then click **DNS** to open the dnsmgmt window. Right-click your DNS server **StudentXX** (where *XX* is your student number), and click **Clear Cache**. See Figure 8-7.

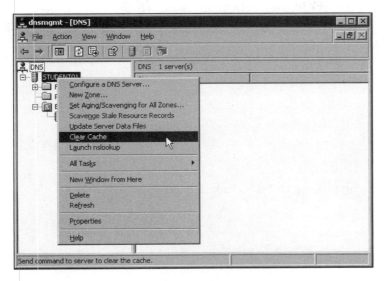

Figure 8-7 Clearing DNS server cache

Certification Objectives

Objectives for Microsoft Exam #70-293: Planning a Microsoft Windows Server 2003 Network:

- Diagnose and resolve issues related to DNS services.

- Diagnose and resolve issues related to name resolution cache information.

REVIEW QUESTIONS

1. Which of the following components are optional in a DNSLint input file? (Choose all that apply.)

   a. DNSLint

   b. lines that begin with + (a plus sign)

   c. lines that begin with [(a square bracket)

   d. lines that begin with ; (a semicolon)

   e. the transport protocol field

2. The following code is a valid DNSLint input file. True or False?

```
DNSLint
[dns~server] 192.168.1.10
server1.arctic.local,a,i
```

3. Which of the following are valid record types in DNSLint? (Choose all that apply.)

   a. mx

   b. svr

   c. ns

   d. cname

   e. srv

4. Which transport protocol do standard queries use?

   a. UDP

   b. TCP

   c. IP

   d. none of the above

5. How can you clear the cache of your DNS server?

   a. Use the ipconfig /dnsflush command.

   b. Use the ipconfig /flushdns command.

   c. Use the dnslint /flushdns command.

   d. Right-click the DNS server in the dnsmgmt window, and then click Clear Cache.

LAB 8.3 TESTING A FORWARDING-ONLY DNS SERVER WITH DNSLINT

Objectives

The goal of this lab activity is to learn about the advantages of using a forwarding-only DNS server.

Materials Required:

This lab will require the following:

- A Windows Server 2003 system installed and configured according to the instructions at the beginning of this lab manual

- Performance Monitor and Debug Logging configured according to Lab 8.1

- Windows Support Tools installed as instructed in Lab 7.4

Estimated completion time: **30 minutes**

Activity Background

A forwarding-only DNS server hosts no zones. It queries its configured forwarders, caches the answers, and returns the results. It is not authoritative for any domains and the information that it contains is limited to what has been cached while resolving queries. However, unlike caching-only servers, forwarding-only DNS servers can be configured to forward requests for internal domains to an internal DNS server capable of resolving hostnames that the Internet root servers could not.

ACTIVITY

Activity

1. You should already be logged in as Admnistrator with your performance monitors running. The dns.log should be displayed in the extended Command Prompt window.

2. If necessary, open your dnsmgmt window. Click **Start**, click **Administrative Tools**, and then click **DNS**.

3. Right-click your server and click **Properties**.

4. Click the **Forwarders** tab.

5. With the All other DNS domains option selected, enter **192.168.1.10** in the Forwarder IP list, and then click **Add**.

8

6. Check the **Do not use recursion for this domain** check box to select it, as shown in Figure 8-8. Click **OK**.

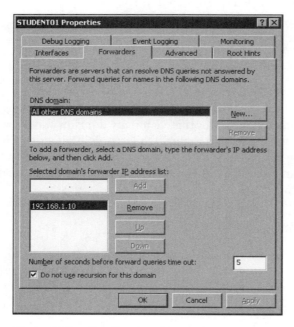

Figure 8-8   Configuring forwarders

7. Return to your dnslist Command Prompt window.

8. Type **cd ** and press **Enter**.

9. Type **dnslint /ql dnstest1.txt** and press **Enter**. Type **y** to overwrite the dnslint.htm file. After a moment, the DNSLint report appears in Internet Explorer. Notice that the arctic.local resolutions succeeded.

10. Check the Performance Monitor. Note the spike in recursive queries. See Figure 8-9.

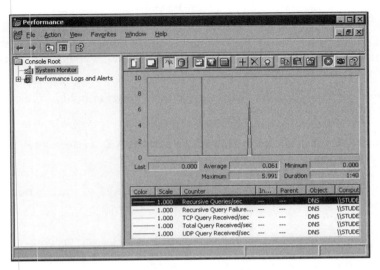

Figure 8-9   Performance Monitor spike in recursive queries chart

11. Read your dns.log (or the following sample code). Note the four-stage resolution process.

```
11:29:16 510 PACKET  UDP Rcv 192.168.1.101    2dfb    Q
[0001   D   NOERROR] (9)microsoft(3)com(0)
11:29:16 510 PACKET  UDP Snd 192.168.1.10     0a3d    Q
[0001   D   NOERROR] (9)microsoft(3)com(0)
11:29:16 510 PACKET  UDP Rcv 192.168.1.10     0a3d R Q
[8081   DR  NOERROR] (9)microsoft(3)com(0)
11:29:16 510 PACKET  UDP Snd 192.168.1.101    2dfb R Q
[8081   DR  NOERROR] (9)microsoft(3)com(0)
```

12. Close Internet Explorer with the DNSLint report.

13. Return to the DNSLint Command Prompt window. Type **dnslint /ql dnstest1.txt /no_open /y** and press **Enter**.

14. Check the Performance Monitor, and note that there were no recursive queries.

15. Check your dns.log (or the following sample code), and notice that resolution of these domains is now a two-stage process as the domains are being resolved in the cache of your local DNS and are no longer forwarded.

```
11:29:58 510 PACKET  UDP Rcv 192.168.1.101    6c9e    Q
[0001   D   NOERROR] (9)microsoft(3)com(0)
11:29:58 510 PACKET  UDP Snd 192.168.1.101    6c9e R Q
[8081   DR  NOERROR] (9)microsoft(3)com(0)
```

16. You can repeat the test, but you must first clear the cache. Return to the dns-mgmt window, right-click your DNS server **StudentXX** (where *XX* is your student number), and then click **Clear Cache**.

17. The default behavior of DNSLint is to perform name resolution queries using the UDP protocol. Modify the configuration to request some TCP queries. Return to the DNSLint Command Prompt window. Type **dnstest1.txt** and press **Enter**. The file will open in Notepad.

18. Edit the content of the file, changing the text shown in bold in the code to read as follows:

```
+This DNS server is called: StudentXX (where XX is your
student number)

[dns~server] 192.168.1.1XX (where XX is your student
number)

microsoft.com,a,r,tcp       ;A record
207.46.197.100,ptr,r,tcp    ;PTR record
microsoft.com,cname,r,tcp   ;CNAME record
microsoft.com,mx,r          ;MX record
instructor.arctic.local,a,r,tcp
server1.arctic.local,a,r
server2.arctic.local,a,r,tcp
```

19. Type **Alt+F** and then press **A**. Name the file **dnstest2.txt** and save it in C:. Close Notepad.

20. Return to your dnsmgmt window. Right-click your DNS server **StudentXX** (where *XX* is your student number), and click **Clear Cache**.

21. Return to the Command Prompt window, type **dnslint /ql dnstest2.txt**, and then press **Enter**. When prompted, type **Y** to overwrite the previous dnslint.htm file. After a moment, the DNSLint report appears in Internet Explorer. Review the report and then close Internet Explorer.

22. Check the Performance Monitor and dns.log for evidence of the TCP DNS requests. Note in the dns.log that your DNS server receives the request and returns an answer to the client with TCP but sends the request to its forwarders in UDP.

23. Return to the DNSLint window and repeat the request. Type **dnslint /ql dnstest2.txt /no_open /y** and press **Enter**.

24. Check the Performance Monitor and dns.log to see that the answers were resolved from the cache.

25. Return to your dnsmgmt window. Right-click your DNS server **StudentXX** (where *XX* is your student number), and click **Properties**.

26. Click the **Monitoring** tab, click the **A simple query against this DNS server** option button, and then click the **Test Now** command button several times rapidly.

27. Check the Performance Monitor for a query spike.

28. Check your dns.log. Interpret the results using the legend in Figure 8-10.

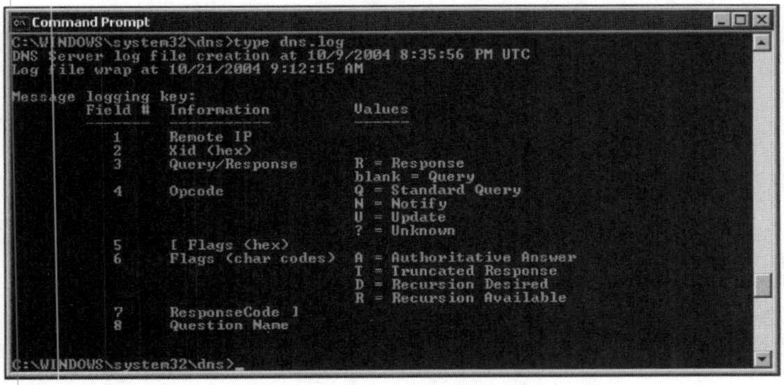

Figure 8-10   DNS debug log legend

29. Return to the Monitoring tab of the STUDENT*XX* Properties dialog box. Click to deselect the **A simple query against this DNS server** option. Click to select the **A recursive query to other DNS servers** option button, and then click **Test Now** several times rapidly.

30. Check the Performance Monitor and dns.log for results.

31. Close your DNS server Properties window by clicking **Cancel**. Close the dnsmgmt window. Close the DNSLint Command Prompt window. Minimize the Performance Monitor and the Command Prompt window so you can continue to check them in the next lab.

Certification Objectives

Objectives for Microsoft Exam #70-293: Planning a Microsoft Windows Server 2003 Network:

- Plan a forwarding configuration.

- Diagnose and resolve issues related to DNS services.

- Diagnose and resolve issues related to name resolution cache information.

REVIEW QUESTIONS

1. Which of these dns.log entries indicates that the query was resolved from a forwarder?

   a. 06:47:11 E40 PACKET UDP Rcv 192.168.1.101 8ac5 Q [0001 D NOERROR] (10)instructor(6)arctic(5)local(0)

   b. 06:47:11 E40 PACKET UDP Snd 192.168.1.101 8ac5 R Q [8081 DR NOERROR] (10)instructor(6)arctic(5)local(0)

   c. 06:47:47 E40 PACKET UDP Rcv 192.168.1.101 335a Q [0001 D NOERROR] (10)instructor(6)arctic(5)local(0)

   d. 06:47:47 E40 PACKET UDP Snd 192.168.1.10 2434 Q [0001 D NOERROR] (10)instructor(6)arctic(5)local(0)

   e. 06:47:47 E40 PACKET UDP Rcv 192.168.1.10 2434 R Q [8085 A DR NOERROR] (10)instructor(6)arctic(5)local(0)

   f. 06:47:47 E40 PACKET UDP Snd 192.168.1.101 335a R Q [8085 A DR NOERROR] (10)instructor(6)arctic(5)local(0)

2. Which of these dns.log entries indicates that the query was resolved from cache?

   a. 06:47:11 E40 PACKET UDP Rcv 192.168.1.101 8ac5 Q [0001 D NOERROR] (10)instructor(6)arctic(5)local(0)

   b. 06:47:11 E40 PACKET UDP Snd 192.168.1.101 8ac5 R Q [8081 DR NOERROR] (10)instructor(6)arctic(5)local(0)

   c. 06:47:47 E40 PACKET UDP Rcv 192.168.1.101 335a Q [0001 D NOERROR] (10)instructor(6)arctic(5)local(0)

   d. 06:47:47 E40 PACKET UDP Snd 192.168.1.10 2434 Q [0001 D NOERROR] (10)instructor(6)arctic(5)local(0)

   e. 06:47:47 E40 PACKET UDP Rcv 192.168.1.10 2434 R Q [8085 A DR NOERROR] (10)instructor(6)arctic(5)local(0)

   f. 06:47:47 E40 PACKET UDP Snd 192.168.1.101 335a R Q [8085 A DR NOERROR] (10)instructor(6)arctic(5)local(0)

3. In your dns.log, which flags indicate that the response was authoritative? (Choose all that apply.)

   a. [8084 A R

   b. [8081 DR

   c. [0001 D

   d. [8385 A DR

4. Provided on the Monitoring tab of a DNS server, which test actually performs a reverse lookup?

   a. simple query

   b. recursive query

   c. both

   d. none of the above

5. If your DNSLint input file includes the instructor.arctic.local,a,i,tcp entry, for what are you querying?

   a. iterative query for a nameserver record

   b. iterative query for a mail exchange record using TCP

   c. iterative query for a host record using TCP

   d. recursive query for a host record using TCP

8

LAB 8.4 MONITORING ZONE TRANSFERS

Objectives

The goal of this lab activity is to demonstrate some of the monitoring tools available to track the performance of your DNS replication strategy when using standard zones.

Materials Required:

This lab will require the following:

- A Windows Server 2003 system installed and configured according to the instructions at the beginning of this lab manual

- A lab partner (if available)

Estimated completion time: **40 minutes**

NOTE

In this lab activity, you will work with a partner. One of you will be the primary DNS server and the other will be the secondary DNS server.

Activity Background

When optimizing DNS, you need to consider the bandwidth utilization of zone transfers. A perfectly fault tolerant DNS architecture would have a DNS server at every location that has a current and complete copy of all the records. However such a system would generate a great deal of network traffic. Monitoring zone transfers is an important step in understanding the effects of your DNS architecture and planning optimizations.

ACTIVITY

Activity

On both servers:

1. You should already be logged in as Admnistrator with your performance monitors running. The dns.log should be displayed in the extended Command Prompt window.

2. In the Performance Monitor, right-click one of the performance counters in the lower-right corner, and then click **Properties**.

3. In the System Monitor Properties window, click the **Data** tab. Click the top counter in the list. Hold down the **Shift** button and click the bottom counter in the list to select all entries. Click **Remove**.

4. Click **Add**. In the Add Counters window, click the **Performance object** list arrow, and click **DNS**. Note that AXFR is a full zone transfer and IXFR is an incremental zone transfer. Press and hold the **Ctrl** key and click the following counters:

   ```
   AXFR Request Received
   AXFR Request Sent
   AXFR Response Received
   AXFR Success Received
   AXFR Success Sent
   IXFR Request Received
   IXFR Request Sent
   IXFR Response Received
   IXFR Success Received
   IXFR Success Sent
   Notify Received
   Notify Sent
   Zone Transfer Failure
   Zone Transfer Request Received
   Zone Transfer SOA Request Sent
   Zone Transfer Success
   ```

5. Click **Add**. Click **Close** to close the Add Counters window. Your screen should resemble Figure 8-11. Click **OK** to close the System Monitor Properties window.

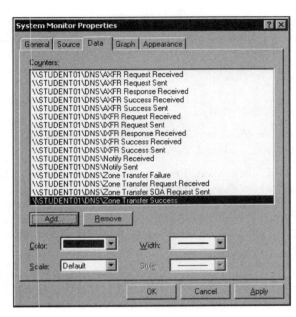

Figure 8-11   Enabling counters to monitor zone transfers

6. With so many counters active, you might find it helpful if highlight is turned on. In the Performance Monitor, click the button with a light bulb icon or press the **Ctrl+H** keys. Now you can select individual counters and have them highlighted in the chart. Minimize the Performance Monitor.

7. Return to Windows Explorer, expand the **Control Panel**, expand **Network Connections**, right-click the **Private** connection, and click **Enable**.

8. To open the dnsmgmt snap-in tool, click **Start**, point to **Administrative Tools**, and then click **DNS**.

9. Click your DNS server **StudentXX** (where *XX* is your student number). In the right pane, double-click **Event Viewer** and then double-click **DNS Events**. Note that there have been no DNS events throughout the previous labs.

10. Right-click your DNS server **StudentXX** (where *XX* is your student number), and click **Properties**. Click the **Interfaces** tab and confirm that your Classroom and Private IP addresses appear and that the All IP addresses option is selected.

11. Click the **Debug Logging** tab. Check the **Notifications** check box. In the Log file section at the bottom of the window, type **Clear** in the File path and name text box, and then click **Apply**. Delete **Clear** from the File path and name text box, so that the box is empty again, and then click **Apply**. This clears the debug log file. You can return to your extended Command Prompt window, and then press **F3** or the **up arrow** key to confirm that the file has been cleared successfully.

12. Click **OK** to close the STUDENT*XX* Properties window.

On the primary DNS server only:

1. In the dnsmgmt window, right-click your DNS server **Student*XX*** (where *XX* is your student number), and click **New Zone**.

2. In the New Zone Wizard, click **Next**. Primary Zone is selected by default. Click **Next**. Forward Lookup Zone is selected by default. Click **Next**. In the Zone name box, type **Partner*XX*.local** (where *XX* is your assigned student number). Click **Next**, and then click **Next** to accept the default file name. The Do not allow dynamic updates option is selected by default. Click **Next**. Click **Finish** to create the zone.

3. In the right pane of the dnsmgmt window, double-click **Forward Lookup Zones**, click the new zone to select it, right-click **Partner*XX*.local** (where *XX* is your assigned student number), and then click **New Host (A)**.

4. In the New Host window, type **student*YY***. In the IP address field, type **192.168.1*XX*.1*YY*** (where *YY* is your partner's assigned student number and *XX* is your student number). Click **Add Host**. Click **OK** to close the success message, and click **Done** to close the Add Host window.

5. Right-click the **Partner*XX*.local** zone and click **Properties**.

6. Click the **Name Servers** tab, and then click **Add**.

7. In the New Resource Record window, type **Student*YY*.Partner*XX*.local** (where *YY* is your partner's assigned student number and *XX* is your student number), and then click **Resolve**. Click **OK** to close the New Resource Record window, and then click **Apply**.

8. Click the **Start of Authority (SOA)** tab. Set the Refresh Interval option to **1** minute between refreshes, and then click **Apply**.

9. Click the **Zone Transfers** tab, and then click **Notify** to open the Notify window. Click the **The following server** option button and in the IP address field, type **192.168.1*XX*.1*YY*** (where *XX* is your student number and *YY* is your partner's assigned student number) and click **Add**. Click **OK** to close the Notify window, and then click **OK** to close the Partner*XX*.local Properties window (where *XX* is your student number).

On the secondary DNS server only:

1. Right-click your DNS server **StudentXX** (where *XX* is your student number), and click **New zone**.

2. In the New Zone Wizard, click **Next**. Click the **Secondary zone** option button, and click **Next**. Click **Next** to accept the Forward lookup zone. In the Zone name text box, type **PartnerXX.local** (where *XX* is your partner's assigned student number), and then click **Next**. In the Master DNS servers IP Address field, enter **192.168.1XX.1XX** (where *XX* is your partner's assigned student number), click **Add**. and then click **Next**. Click **Finish** to create the zone.

On both servers:

1. Refer to the Performance Monitor, dns.log, and DNS Events log to determine the information available from each server.

On the primary DNS server only:

1. In the dsmgmt window, under Forward Lookup Zones, right-click the **PartnerXX.local** zone and click **Properties**. See Figure 8-12.

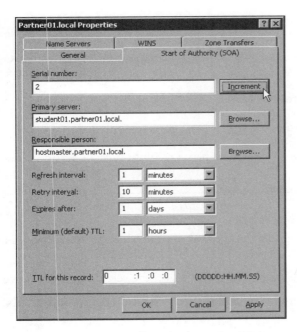

Figure 8-12   Manually increment the SOA record

2. Click the **Start of Authority (SOA)** tab. Click the **Increment** command button once and click **OK** to close the PartnerXX.local Properties window (where *XX* is your student number).

3. Check the Performance Monitor, events log, and dns.log for changed information.

4. In the Command Prompt window, you need to use the DNSCmd command to add a new host. Type **dnscmd Student*XX* /recordadd partner*XX*.local test1 A 10.1.1.1** (where *XX* is your student number) and press **Enter**.

On the secondary DNS server only:

1. Check the Performance Monitor, Event Viewer, and dns.log over the next two minutes to see the results of the automated refresh of data from the primary DNS server.

On both servers:

1. In the dnsmgmt window, under Forward Lookup Zones, right-click your DNS server **Student*XX*** (where *XX* is your student number), and click **Properties**.

2. Click the **Debug Logging** tab. Deselect the **Log packets for debugging** option, and then click **OK** to close the Partner*XX*.local Properties window (where *XX* is your student number). Close the dnsmgmt window. Close Performance Monitor. Close your Command Prompt window.

Certification Objectives

Objectives for Microsoft Exam #70-293: Planning a Microsoft Windows Server 2003 Network:

- Plan zone replication requirements.

- Diagnose and resolve issues related to DNS services.

- Diagnose and resolve issues related to name resolution cache information.

REVIEW QUESTIONS

1. Which of the following sets the amount of time between zone updates initiated by the secondary DNS server?

   a. setting the Refresh Interval in the SOA on the secondary DNS server

   b. setting the Minimum (default) TTL in the SOA on the secondary DNS server

   c. setting the Refresh Interval in the SOA on the primary DNS server

   d. setting the Minimum (default) TTL in the SOA on the primary DNS server

2. Which of the following sets the amount of time that an entry will be cached by DNS clients querying the secondary DNS server?

   a. setting the Refresh Interval in the SOA on the secondary DNS server

   b. setting the Minimum (default) TTL in the SOA on the secondary DNS server

   c. setting the Refresh Interval in the SOA on the primary DNS server

   d. setting the Minimum (default) TTL in the SOA on the primary DNS server

3. Which of the following counters would chart the number of successful full zone transfers from your primary server?

   a. AXFR Success Received

   b. AXFR Success Sent

   c. IXFR Success Received

   d. IXFR Success Sent

4. How can you force a zone update to the secondary server?

   a. Set the refresh interval to 0 seconds.

   b. Increment the SOA serial number.

   c. In the dnsmgmt snap-in, select the zone on the secondary server, and select Reload.

   d. In the dnsmgmt snap-in, select the zone on the secondary server, and select Reload from Master.

5. Which of the following generates events in the DNS event log? (Choose all that apply.)

   a. changing the refresh interval in the SOA record

   b. incrementing the SOA serial number

   c. transferring the zone to a secondary DNS server

   d. adding a new host to the zone

8

LAB 8.5 CONFIRM DNS SERVER RECORDS WITH NSLOOKUP

Objectives

The goal of this lab activity is to demonstrate the NSLookup tool.

Materials Required:

This lab will require the following:

- A Windows Server 2003 system installed and configured according to the instructions at the beginning of this lab manual

Estimated completion time: **15 minutes**

Activity Background

NSLookup is an invaluable tool for a DNS administrator. DNSLint and DNSCmd are available from the Windows Support Tools on the Windows Server 2003 CD. Performance Monitor and other useful logs are available on the server or any computer on your network with permissions to use them. Only NSLookup is available from any Windows NT, 2000, XP, or Server 2003 system. It does not require any special permissions to use and can be used on any DNS on the Internet, not just those that you administer. NSLookup is also the reason that you must allow zone transfers only to specified systems.

Activity

1. If necessary, log on to your server as **Administrator** with a password of **Password!**.

2. Click **Start** and then click **Command Prompt** to open the Command Prompt window. Type the following commands, pressing **Enter** after each one:

   ```
   nslookup
   server 192.168.1.10
   microsoft.com
   set type=mx
   hotmail.com
   set type=NS
   microsoft.com
   set type=ANY
   microsoft.com
   ls -d microsoft.com (Note: This command should fail.)
   exit
   ```

3. Now you will work with your DNS servers. If you have a primary DNS domain called Partner*XX*.local (where *XX* is your student number), skip to Step 5.

4. Type **dnscmd studentXX /zoneadd PartnerXX.local /primary /file PartnerXX.local.dns** (where *XX* is your student number), and press **Enter**.

5. Type the following commands, pressing **Enter** after each. Note that *XX* is your student number:

```
dnscmd StudentXX /recordadd partnerXX.local www A 10.1.1.1
dnscmd StudentXX /recordadd partnerXX.local www A 192.168.
1.200
dnscmd StudentXX /recordadd partnerXX.local mail MX 10 10.
1.1.2
dnscmd StudentXX /recordadd partnerXX.local finance.
partnerXX.local. CNAME studentXX.partnerXX.local
```

6. Type **nslookup** and press **Enter**.

7. Type the following commands, pressing **Enter** after each one:
```
? (This command opens Help.)
set all (This command displays optional settings.)
www
set type=MX
partnerXX.local
set type=ANY
partnerXX.local
ls -d partnerXX.local (This command will be denied.)
```

8. Click **Start**, point to **Administrative Tools**, and then click **DNS**.

9. Click your server. In the right pane, double-click **Forward Lookup Zones**. Right-click the **PartnerXX.local** zone and click **Properties**.

10. Click the **Zone Transfers** tab. Click the option to allow zone transfers to any server, and then click **OK** to close the PartnerXX.local Properties window (where *XX* is your student number).

11. Return to NSLookup.

8

12. Type **ls –d partnerXX.local** (as shown in Figure 8-13), and then press **Enter**. Here you can clearly see that all of your records are visible, including all hosts. With this starting point, a hacker, internal or external, could begin to map your infrastructure.

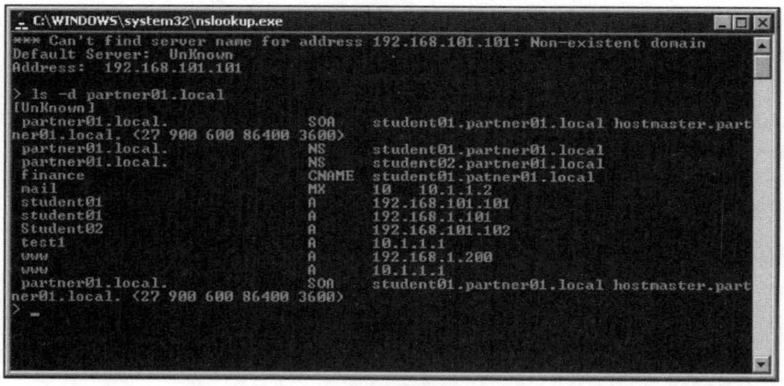

Figure 8-13 NSLookup can download your entire zone file if allowed

13. Close the Command Prompt window, and then close the dnsmgmt window.

14. You now need to join the domain in preparation for the next chapter in this lab manual. Click **Start**, right-click **My Computer**, and click **Properties**.

15. Click the **Computer Name** tab. Click **Change**. Click the **Domain** option button. Click in the Domain box and type **Arctic.local**. Click **OK**. In the Computer Name Changes window, type the User name **Administrator**. Click the Password box. Type **Password!** and click **OK**. Click **OK** to acknowledge the confirmation, and then click **OK** to acknowledge the warning. Click **Yes** to restart your computer.

Certification Objectives

Objectives for Microsoft Exam #70-293: Planning a Microsoft Windows Server 2003 Network:

- Diagnose and resolve issues related to DNS services.

REVIEW QUESTIONS

1. NSLookup is available in which of the following operating systems? (Choose all that apply.)

    a. Windows 2003 Server

    b. Windows 95

    c. Windows 98 SE

    d. Windows NT Workstation

    e. Windows 2000

    f. Windows XP pro

    g. Linux

    h. FreeBSD

    i. Windows ME

2. Which of the following record types, once set, will allow you to see the configured mail servers for a domain? (Choose all that apply.)

    a. NS

    b. MX

    c. SRV

    d. ANY

    e. A

3. Which command will show you the active NSLookup options?

    a. view options

    b. help

    c. set all

    d. set options

4. Which command will show you all aliases in the PartnerXX.local domain?

    a. set type=cname; PartnerXX.local

    b. set type=ANY; PartnerXX.local

    c. ls –a PartnerXX.local

    d. ls –d PartnerXX.local

    e. all of the above

5. What command would you use to force an authoritative answer to your query from your domain server?

a. set querytype=auth

b. set recurse=no

c. set norecurse

d. set root=127.0.0.1

9

PLANNING AND MANAGING CERTIFICATE SERVICES

Labs included in this chapter:

♦ Lab 9.1 Installing Enterprise and Stand-alone Certification Authorities

♦ Lab 9.2 Issuing Certificates Manually

♦ Lab 9.3 Configuring and Testing Autoenrollment

♦ Lab 9.4 Configuring Certificate Mapping

♦ Lab 9.5 Using Certutil to Manage Certificate Services

Microsoft MCSE Exam #70-293 Objectives	
Objective	Lab
Plan a public key infrastructure (PKI) that uses Certificate Services.	9.1, 9.2, 9.3, 9.4, 9.5
Identify the appropriate type of certificate authority to support certificate issuance requirements.	9.1, 9.2, 9.3, 9.5
Plan the enrollment and distribution of certificates.	9.2, 9.3, 9.4, 9.5
Plan for the use of smart cards for authentication.	9.4

Lab 9.1 Installing Enterprise and Stand-alone Certification Authorities

Objectives

The goal of this lab activity is to install and manage Certificate Services. After Certificate Services is installed, you issue and revoke a certificate. You also publish a certificate revocation list (CRL).

Materials Required:

This lab will require the following:

- Windows Server 2003 installed and configured according to the instructions at the beginning of this lab manual

- A partner to complete the exercise with; if a partner is not available, you can play the role of both partners

- IIS (Internet Information Services) installed with processing of ASP (Active Server Pages) scripts enabled

Estimated completion time: **10 minutes**

Activity Background

When Certificate Services is installed on Windows Server 2003, it can be configured as an Enterprise certification authority (CA) or a stand-alone CA. An Enterprise CA integrates with Active Directory. This offers the ability to use Windows security to control access to certificate templates. A stand-alone CA does not integrate with Active Directory and cannot create certificates using certificate templates. All certificates must be manually approved by an administrator. Stand-alone CAs are used when Active Directory is unavailable or not used.

Certification authorities are organized in a hierarchy. The first CA installed is the root certification authority. Other subordinate CAs are then authorized by the root CA. If the certificate for a CA is revoked, then all certificates it has issued are also revoked.

Activity

1. Log on as **Administrator** to the Arctic.local domain with a password of **Password!**.

2. To perform the following lab and ensure proper configuration, remove Certificate Services if it is already installed by performing the following:

   a. Click **Start**, point to **Control Panel**, and click **Add or Remove Programs**.

   b. Click **Add/Remove Windows Components**.

   c. If the Certificate Services check box is checked, then uncheck it. If the Certificate Services check box is unchecked, leave it as it is, click **Cancel**, and continue to Step 3.

   d. Click **Next** to remove Certificate Services.

   e. Click **Finish**.

3. Partner 1, install Certificate Services as an Enterprise root CA by doing the following:

   a. Click **Add/Remove Windows Components**.

   b. Check the **Certificate Services** check box.

   c. Click **Yes** to acknowledge the warning, and click **Next**.

   d. If necessary, click the **Enterprise root CA** option button, as shown in Figure 9-1, and then click **Next**.

9

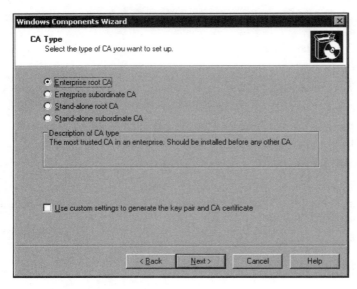

Figure 9-1   Choosing a CA type

e. In the Common name for this CA text box, type *yourname***RootCA** (where *yourname* is your first name), and click **Next**.

f. Click **Next** to accept the default location for the certificate database and certificate database log. Click **Yes** to confirm that IIS will be stopped.

g. If prompted to insert the Windows Server 2003 CD-ROM, insert it and then click **OK**. In the Copy files from text box, type **C:\I386** and click **OK**.

h. Click **Finish** and close the Add or Remove Programs window.

4. Partner 2, install Certificate Services as a stand-alone subordinate CA by doing the following:

   a. Click **Add/Remove Windows Components**.

   b. Check the **Certificate Services** check box.

   c. Click **Yes** to acknowledge the warning, and click **Next**.

   d. Click the **Stand-alone subordinate CA** option button to select it, and click **Next**.

   e. In the Common name for this CA text box, type *yourname***SubCA** (where *yourname* is your first name), and click **Next**.

   f. Click **Next** to accept the default location for the certificate database and certificate database log.

   g. If necessary, select the **Send the request directly to a CA already on the network** option button. In the Computer name text box, type **student*XX*.arctic.local** (where *XX* is the student number of partner 1), and press **Tab**. The Parent CA text box automatically fills in with the name of the root CA running on the server, as shown in Figure 9-2.

9

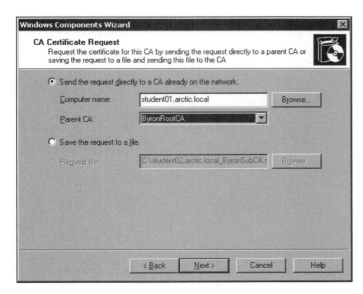

Figure 9-2   Requesting a CA certificate

   h. Click **Next** and click **Yes** to acknowledge the message about stopping IIS.

   i. If prompted to insert the Windows Server 2003 CD-ROM, insert it, and then click **OK**. In the Copy files from text box, type **C:\I386**, and click **OK**.

   j. Click **Finish** and close the Add or Remove Programs window.

5. Partner 1, verify the configuration of the Enterprise CA by doing the following:

   a. Click **Start**, point to **Administrative Tools**, and click **Certification Authority**.

   b. Double-click your CA to expand it. Notice that the option Certificate Templates is available because this is an Enterprise CA.

   c. Click **Issued Certificates** to view the certificate issued to the subordinate CA.

6. Partner 2, verify the configuration of the subordinate CA by doing the following:

   a. Click **Start**, point to **Administrative Tools**, and click **Certification Authority**.

   b. Double-click your CA to expand it. Notice that the option Certificate Templates is not available because this is a stand-alone CA.

   c. Click **Issued Certificates**. Notice that no certificates have been issued by the subordinate CA.

   d. Close the Certification Authority window.

7. Partner 1, revoke the certificate for the subordinate CA with the following steps. (This process would be performed if the certificate for the subordinate CA were somehow compromised or were retired from service.)

   a. Right-click the subordinate CA certificate, point to **All Tasks**, and click **Revoke Certificate**.

   b. In the Reason code list box, click **Key Compromise**, and click **Yes** to revoke the certificate. Any certificates issued by the subordinate CA are also revoked by this procedure.

   c. Click **Revoked Certificates**. Notice that the subordinate CA certificate is now listed here.

   d. Right-click **Revoked Certificates**, point to **All Tasks**, and click **Publish**.

   e. Verify that the default option to publish a new CRL is selected, as shown in Figure 9–3. This option forces the publication of a complete CRL. The CRL is used by Windows to learn about certificates that have been revoked before their expiration date. Click **OK**.

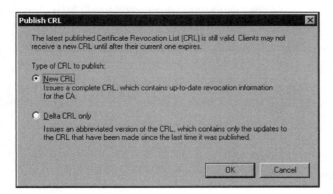

Figure 9-3   CRL publication

   f. Close the Certification Authority window.

8. Partner 2, remove Certificate Services and then reinstall Certificate Services as an Enterprise root CA by performing the following steps. You are removing Certificate Services because the certificate authorizing it has been revoked.

   a. Click **Start**, point to **Control Panel**, and click **Add or Remove Programs**.

   b. Click **Add/Remove Windows Components**.

   c. Uncheck the **Certificate Services** check box.

   d. Click **Next** to remove Certificate Services.

   e. Click **Finish**.

   f. Click **Add/Remove Windows Components**.

   g. Check the **Certificate Services** check box, and click **Yes** to acknowledge the warning.

   h. Click **Next** to begin installing Certificate Services.

   i. Click the **Enterprise root CA** option button to select it, and click **Next**.

   j. In the Common name text box, type *yourname***RootCA** (where *yourname* is your first name), and click **Next**.

   k. Click **Next** to accept the default location for the certificate database and certificate database log. Click **OK** to confirm stopping IIS.

   l. If prompted to insert the Windows Server 2003 CD-ROM, insert it and then click **OK**. In the Copy files from text box, type **C:\I386** and click **OK**.

   m. Click **Finish** and close the Add or Remove Programs window.

Certification Objectives

Objectives for Microsoft Exam #70-293: Planning a Microsoft Windows Server 2003 Network:

- Plan a public key infrastructure (PKI) that uses Certificate Services.

- Identify the appropriate type of certificate authority to support certificate issuance requirements.

REVIEW QUESTIONS

1. Which type of CA integrates with Active Directory?

   a. Enterprise CA

   b. Subordinate CA

   c. Root CA

   d. Stand-alone CA

2. Which type of CA is authorized by another CA?

   a. Enterprise CA

   b. Subordinate CA

   c. Root CA

   d. Stand-alone CA

3. Which type of CA requires an administrator to approve certificate requests?

   a. Enterprise CA

   b. Subordinate CA

   c. Root CA

   d. Stand-alone CA

4. What are two reasons that a certificate could be revoked? (Choose all that apply.)

   a. The certificate has been compromised.

   b. The certificate has expired.

   c. The server using the certificate is being retired.

   d. The certificate has been renewed.

5. What is published to inform users and applications that a certificate has been revoked?

   a. dead certificate list

   b. certificate expiration list

   c. tombstone list

   d. certificate revocation list

LAB 9.2 ISSUING CERTIFICATES MANUALLY

Objectives

The goal of this lab activity is to request certificates from both the Certificates snap-in and the Certificate Services Web pages. You also manually approve these requests in the Certification Authority snap-in.

Materials Required:

This lab will require the following:

- Windows Server 2003 installed and configured according to the instructions at the beginning of this lab manual

- Certificate Services installed on your server as an Enterprise root CA

- IIS installed with processing of ASP scripts enabled

Estimated completion time: **10 minutes**

Activity Background

Manual distribution of certificates can be done using both the Certificates snap-in and Certificate Services Web pages. The Certificates snap-in can only be used with an Enterprise CA. To issue certificates from a Stand-alone CA, the Certificate Services Web pages must be used.

If IIS is installed before Certificate Services, then a virtual directory will be automatically created that links the URL http://server/certsrv to the folder C:\WINDOWS\system32\CertSrv. The Certificate Services Web pages require IIS to be installed and ASP script processing to be allowed.

ACTIVITY

Activity

1. Log on as **Administrator** to the Arctic.local domain with a password of **Password!**.
2. Click **Start**, click **Run**, type **MMC**, and press **Enter**.
3. Click the **File** menu, and click **Add/Remove Snap-in**.
4. Click **Add**, and double-click **Certificates**. If necessary, click the **My user account** option, click **Finish**, click **Close**, and click **OK**.
5. In the left pane, double-click **Certificates – Current User** to expand it, double-click **Personal** to expand it, and click **Certificates** (if present). Notice that no personal certificates have been issued.
6. Right-click **Personal**, point to **All Tasks**, and click **Request New Certificate**.
7. Click **Next** to begin obtaining a certificate.

8. In the Certificate types list box, click **User**, as shown in Figure 9-4, and click **Next**. The list of available certificate types is based on the available certificate templates.

Figure 9-4   Selecting a certificate type

9. In the Friendly name text box, type **UserXX** (where *XX* is your student number), and click **Next**.

10. Click **Finish** to create the certificate, and click **OK** to acknowledge that the certificate was successfully created.

11. In the left pane of the Certificates snap-in, click **Certificates** in the Personal folder to view the certificate you have created.

12. Click the **File** menu, click **Save As**, type **Certificates**, and press **Enter**.

13. Close the Certificates snap-in. If prompted to save console settings, click **Yes**.

14. Click **Start**, point to **All Programs**, and click **Internet Explorer**.

15. You need to lower the default Internet Explorer security settings to create a certificate using the Certificate Services Web pages. Click the **Tools** menu, and click **Internet Options**. Click the **Security** tab, click **Local intranet**, and click the **Sites** button. If necessary, in the Add this Web site to the zone text box, type **http://studentXX.arctic.local** (where *XX* is your student number), and click **Add**. Click **Close** and click **OK**.

16. In the Address Bar, type **http://studentXX.arctic.local/certsrv** and press **Enter**.

17. If prompted, type **Administrator** in the User text box, type **Password!** in the Password text box, and then click **OK**.

18. Click **Request a certificate** to begin obtaining a certificate, click **advanced certificate request**, and click **Create and submit a request to this CA**.

19. In the Certificate Template drop-down list, select **User**, shown in Figure 9-5.

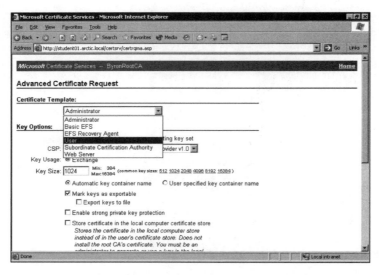

Figure 9-5   Selecting a certificate type in the Certificate Services Web pages

20. Scroll to the bottom of the Web page, and in the Friendly Name text box, type **WebUserXX** (where *XX* is your student number), and then click **Submit**.

21. Click **Yes** to confirm requesting a certificate.

22. Click **Install this certificate**, click **Yes** to indicate that you trust the Web site, and then close Internet Explorer. If a dialog box for Auto Complete appears, click **No**.

23. Click **Start**, point to **Administrative Tools**, and click **Internet Information Services (IIS) Manager**.

24. In the left pane, double-click your server to expand it.

25. In the left pane, click **Web Service Extensions**. Notice that Active Server Pages are allowed. This is required for the Certificate Services Web pages to function properly.

26. In the left pane, double-click **Web Sites** to expand it, and click **Default Web Site**. Notice that there are three virtual directories created to support Certificate Services Web pages, as shown in Figure 9-6. The CertSrv virtual directory points to C:\WINDOWS\system32\CertSrv.

Figure 9-6   Certificate Services Web pages configuration

27. Close the Internet Information Services (IIS) Manager window.

Certification Objectives

Objectives for Microsoft Exam #70-293: Planning a Microsoft Windows Server 2003 Network:

- Plan a public key infrastructure (PKI) that uses Certificate Services.

- Identify the appropriate type of certificate authority to support certificate issuance requirements.

- Plan the enrollment and distribution of certificates.

REVIEW QUESTIONS

1. The Certificates snap-in can only be used to issue certificates from what type of CA?

   a. Root CA

   b. Enterprise CA

   c. Subordinate CA

   d. Stand-alone CA

2. What can be used to request a certificate from a stand-alone CA?

    a. Certificates snap-in

    b. Active Directory Users and Computers

    c. Certificate Services Web pages

    d. Apache Web Server

3. To what directory does the CertSrv virtual directory point?

    a. C:\WINNT\system32\CertSrv

    b. C:\WINDOWS\CertSrv

    c. C:\WINDOWS\system32\CertSrv

    d. C:\WINNT\Certificate

4. What must be in place before installing Certificate Services for the Certificate Services Web pages to install properly? (Choose all that apply.)

    a. IIS must be installed.

    b. The guest account must be enabled.

    c. An FTP site must be configured.

    d. Active Server Pages must be enabled.

5. Which snap-in is used to manage IIS?

    a. Web Manager

    b. Computer Management

    c. Storage Management

    d. Internet Information Services (IIS) Manager

LAB 9.3 CONFIGURING AND TESTING AUTOENROLLMENT

Objectives

The goal of this lab activity is to configure and test autoenrollment for certificates. When the use of certificates for e-mail encryption or other purposes is widespread in a company, manual process for issuing certificates is very burdensome. Many users are not able to perform the relatively complex tasks involved in creating their own certificates.

Materials Required:

This lab will require the following:

- Windows Server 2003 installed and configured according to the instructions at the beginning of this lab manual

- Certificate Services installed on your server as an Enterprise root CA

Estimated completion time: **15 minutes**

Activity Background

Autoenrollment is an automated way for administrators to give users certificates that can be use for authentication, e-mail encryption, or file system encryption. Autoenrollment is a new feature in Windows Server 2003.

Activity

1. Log on as **Administrator** to the Arctic.local domain with a password of **Password!**.

2. Click **Start**, point to **Run**, type **mmc**, and press **Enter**.

3. In the MMC console, click the **File** menu, click **Add/Remove Snap-in**, and click **Add**.

4. Double-click **Active Directory Users and Computers**, double-click **Certificate Templates**, click **Close**, and click **OK**.

5. Double-click **Active Directory Users and Computers** to expand it, and double-click **Arctic.local**.

6. Right-click **Arctic.local**, point to **New**, and click **Organizational Unit**. In the Name text box, type **CertOUXX** (where *XX* is your student number), and click **OK**.

7. Right-click **CertOUXX** (where *XX* is your student number), point to **New**, and click **User**.

8. In the First name text box, type **AutoCert**. In the Last name text box, type **UserXX** (where *XX* is your student number). In the User logon name text box, type **AutoXX** (where *XX* is your student number), and click **Next**.

9. In the Password text box, type **Password!**. In the Confirm password text box, type **Password!**, uncheck the **User must change password at next logon** check box, click **Next**, and click **Finish**.

10. In the left pane, click **Certificate Templates**.

11. In the right pane, right-click **Basic EFS** and click **Duplicate Template**.

12. In the Template display name text box, type **AutoEFS**. The new name AutoEFS describes what the template does and makes it easier for you to manage.

13. Click the **Request Handling** tab, and if necessary, click the **Enroll subject without requiring any user input** option button, as shown in Figure 9-7. This option allows users to get certificates without performing any tasks. If this is not selected, then the user must at minimum confirm that a certificate is being requested.

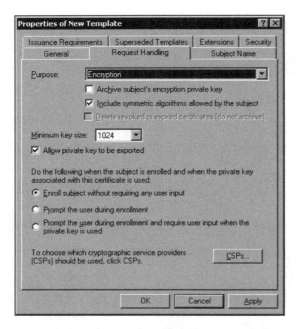

Figure 9-7   Request handling for autoenrollment

14. Click the **Security** tab. You must allow read, enroll, and autoenroll permissions for the user you want to autoenroll. Read permission is allowed by default.

15. Click **Add**, type **AutoXX** (where *XX* is your student number), click the **Check Names** button, and click **OK**.

16. Under the Allow column, check the **Enroll** and **Autoenroll** check boxes to select them, and then click **OK**.

17. Click **Start**, point to **Administrative Tools**, and click **Certification Authority**.

18. Double-click your server to expand it.

19. Right-click **Certificate Templates**, point to **New**, click **Certificate Template to Issue**, click **AutoEFS**, and click **OK**. This process is required to instruct the CA to start using the AutoEFS certificate template.

20. If necessary, click **Certificate Templates** to view the list of available certificate templates.

21. Close the Certification Authority window.

22. In the Active Directory Users and Computers snap-in, in the left pane, right-click **CertOUXX** (where *XX* is your student number), and click **Properties**.

23. Click the **Group Policy** tab, click **New**, and type **AutoXX** (where *XX* is your student number), and press **Enter**.

24. Click **Edit** to open the group policy. Under User Configuration, double-click **Windows Settings**, double-click **Security Settings**, and click **Public Key Policies**.

25. In the right pane, double-click **Autoenrollment Settings**.

26. If necessary, click **Enroll certificates automatically** to select it. This setting is backward compatible with Windows 2000.

27. Check the **Renew expired certificates, update pending certificates, and remove revoked certificates** check box. This option allows all elements of the certificate lifecycle to be performed by autoenrollment.

28. Check the **Update certificates that use certificate templates** check box. When this option is selected, certificates created with Windows 2000 version 1 templates are updated to version 2 templates found in Windows Server 2003.

29. Click **OK**, close the Group Policy Object Editor window, click **Close**, and close MMC. If prompted to save the settings, click **No**.

30. Log off as administrator, and then log on as **AutoXX** (where *XX* is your student number) with the password **Password!**.

31. Click **Start**, click **Run**, type **mmc**, and press **Enter**.

32. In the MMC console, click the **File** menu, click **Add/Remove Snap-in**, click **Add**, double-click **Certificates**, click **Close**, and click **OK**.

33. Double-click **Certificates – Current User**, double-click **Personal**, and click **Certificates**. Notice that there is now a certificate issued to your user for EFS. If the certificate is not there, wait a few minutes and then press the **F5** key to refresh the screen.

34. Close MMC. If prompted to save the settings, click **No**.

Certification Objectives

Objectives for Microsoft Exam #70-293: Planning a Microsoft Windows Server 2003 Network:

- Plan a public key infrastructure (PKI) that uses Certificate Services.

- Identify the appropriate type of certificate authority to support certificate issuance requirements.

- Plan the enrollment and distribution of certificates.

REVIEW QUESTIONS

1. How do you create a new certificate template based on an exiting one?

    a. You copy it.

    b. You clone it.

    c. You duplicate it.

    d. You transform it.

2. What type of CA must be used for certificate autoenrollment?

    a. Root CA

    b. Enterprise CA

    c. Subordinate CA

    d. Stand-alone CA

3. If want the certificate issuing process to be completely automatic, what type of request handling should you choose in the certificate template?

    a. Prompt the user during enrollment

    b. Enroll subject without requiring any user input

    c. Enroll certificate automatically

    d. Renew expired certificates, update pending certificates, and remove revoked certificates

4. What option must be selected in a group policy to enable autoenrollment for users?

    a. Prompt the user during enrollment

    b. Enroll subject without requiring any user input

    c. Enroll certificate automatically

    d. Renew expired certificates, update pending certificates, and remove revoked certificates

5. Which permissions must be assigned to a certificate template to allow autoenrollment? (Choose all that apply.)

    a. Read

    b. Write

    c. Enroll

    d. Autoenroll

LAB 9.4 CONFIGURING CERTIFICATE MAPPING

Objectives

The goal of this lab activity is to configure certificate mapping for authentication. Certificates can be used for authentication in place of a username and password. In such a system the possession of a certificate serves as proof of identity. This is referred to as certificate authentication. Certificate authentication can be used by any application written to use it.

Materials Required:

This lab will require the following:

- Windows Server 2003 installed and configured according to the instructions at the beginning of this lab manual

- Certificate Services installed on your server as an Enterprise root CA

- IIS installed

- Successful completion of Lab 9.1, Lab 9.2, and Lab 9.3

Estimated completion time: **15 minutes**

Activity Background

When a user presents a certificate for certificate authentication, the server looks for a user object that is mapped to the certificate. Certificates can be mapped to users as one-to-one mappings or many-to-one mappings. In a one-to-one mapping, a single certificate is mapped to a single user account. In a many-to-one mapping, many certificates are mapped to a single user account. The Active Directory Users and Computers snap-in is used to perform certificate mapping.

User principal name mapping is a special type of one-to-one mapping in which a user principal name in the certificate is used to identify the user account to which the certificate should be mapped. This type of mapping is automatic and does not have to be configured.

Certificate mapping is also performed when smart cards are used. Users enter a PIN (personal identification number) for a smart card to decrypt a certificate. The certificate is then used to identify the user. The certificate mapping used by smart cards is automatic and not configured using the same process used in this lab.

IIS also has the ability to perform certificate mapping. However, it has its own internal database that is used for certificate mapping.

ACTIVITY

Activity

1. Log on as **AutoXX** (where *XX* is your student number) to the Arctic.local domain with a password of **Password!**.

2. Click **Start**, click **Run**, type **MMC**, and press **Enter**.

3. In MMC, click the **File** menu, click **Add/Remove Snap-in**, click **Add**, double-click **Certificates**, click **Close**, and click **OK**.

4. Double-click **Certificates – Current User**, double-click **Personal**, and click **Certificates**.

5. Right-click **Certificates**, point to **All Tasks**, and click **Request New Certificate**.

6. Click **Next**, click **User**, and click **Next**. In the Friendly name text box, type **UserAuth**, click **Next**, and click **Finish**.

7. Click **OK** to acknowledge the message about issuance being successful.

8. Right-click the new certificate, point to **All Tasks**, and click **Export**.

9. Click **Next**. If necessary, click **Next** to accept the default No, do not export the private key option.

10. The Export File Format page in the wizard provides several format options for exporting the certificate, as shown in Figure 9-8. Click **Next** to accept the default format of DER encoded binary X.509 (.CER).

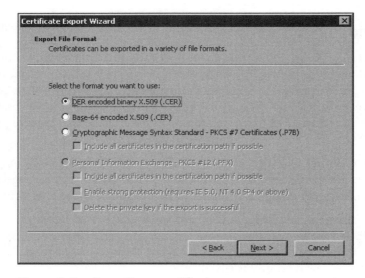

Figure 9-8   Exporting a certificate

11. In the File name box, type **mycert.cer** and click **Next**. This will save the file in C:\Documents and Settings\Auto*XX*\ (where *XX* is your student number).

12. Click **Finish** and click **OK**.

13. Close MMC. Click **No** if asked to save the settings. Log off.

14. Log on as **Administrator** to the Arctic.local domain with a password of **Password!**.

15. Click **Start**, click **Run**, type **mmc**, and press **Enter**.

16. In MMC, click the **File** menu, click **Add/Remove Snap-in**, click **Add**, double-click **Active Directory Users and Computers**, click **Close**, and click **OK**.

17. Click **Active Directory Users and Computers**, click the **View** menu, and click **Advanced Features**.

18. In the right pane, double-click **Arctic.local** and double-click **CertOUXX** (where *XX* is your student number).

19. Right-click **AutoCert UserXX** (where *XX* is your student number), and click **Name Mappings**.

20. Click **Add**. Type **C:\Documents and Settings\AutoXX\mycert.cer** (where *XX* is your student number), and press **Enter**.

21. In the Add Certificate dialog box, you can configure the mapping settings, as shown in Figure 9-9. When the Use Issuer for alternate security identity check box is the only option selected, it is a many-to-one mapping in which all of the certificates with the same subject are mapped to this user account. When the Use Subject for alternate security identity check box is the only option selected, it is a many-to-one mapping in which all of the certificates issued by a particular CA are mapped to this user account. When both of these check boxes are selected, the mapping is one-to-one. Click **OK** to accept the default one-to-one mapping, and click **OK**.

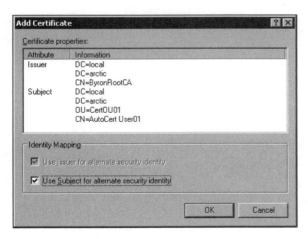

Figure 9-9   Certificate mapping options

22. Close MMC. If prompted to save settings, click **No**.

Certification Objectives

Objectives for Microsoft Exam #70-293: Planning a Microsoft Windows Server 2003 Network:

- Plan a public key infrastructure (PKI) that uses Certificate Services.

- Plan the enrollment and distribution of certificates.

- Plan for the use of smart cards for authentication.

REVIEW QUESTIONS

1. Which snap-in is used to configure certificate mapping between a user account and a certificate?

   a. Certification Authority

   b. Certification Templates

   c. Certificates

   d. Active Directory Users and Computers

2. Which type of certificate mapping allows only a single certificate to a user account?

   a. single-to-single

   b. one-to-one

   c. autonomous

   d. many-to-one

3. Which two options must be selected during the mapping process to create a one-to-one mapping?

   a. Use Issuer for alternate security identity

   b. Use CA for alternate security identity

   c. Use Subject for alternate security identity

   d. Use User Principal Name for alternate security identity

4. How are the certificates in smart cards mapped to user accounts?

   a. using Active Directory Users and Computers

   b. automatically when the smart card is created

   c. using the Certification Authority snap-in

   d. using the Certificates snap-in

5. Which option must be selected in Active Directory Users and Computers to perform certificate mapping?

 a. Mapped in the properties of a user

 b. Advanced Features in the View menu

 c. Certificates in the File menu

 d. Certificates in the Action menu

LAB 9.5 USING CERTUTIL TO MANAGE CERTIFICATE SERVICES

Objectives

The goal of this lab activity is to manage Certificate Services using Certutil. Certutil is a command-line utility that can be used to configure and manage certification authorities running on Windows Server 2003. It cannot be used to issue or request certificates.

Materials Required:

This lab will require the following:

- Windows Server 2003 installed and configured according to the instructions at the beginning of this lab manual

- Certificate Services installed on your server as an Enterprise root CA

- Successful completion of Lab 9.1

Estimated completion time: **10 minutes**

Activity Background

This utility is useful for scripting to perform repetitive maintenance tasks or when a GUI is not available. A GUI may not be available during remote access, or if there is a catastrophic error on the server that disables the GUI.

Activity

1. Log on as **Administrator** to the Arctic.local domain with a password of **Password!**.

2. Click **Start**, click **Run**, type **cmd.exe**, and press **Enter**.

3. Type **certutil –?** and press **Enter**. This command gives you a list of options for the utility. You may find it useful to enlarge the Command Prompt window and make it taller.

4. Scroll in the Command Prompt window to see the available options.

5. Type **certutil -ping -config studentXX** (where *XX* is your student number), and press **Enter**. This command verifies that the certificate request interface is running properly and listening for requests.

6. Type **certutil -pingadmin -config studentXX** (where *XX* is your student number), and press **Enter**. This command verifies that the certificate server administrative interface is running properly and listening for requests.

7. Type **certutil -template** and press **Enter**. This command displays the certificate templates that are installed on the local server.

8. Type **certutil -template -v > C:\tlist.txt** and press **Enter**. The -v option is for verbose output. This much information is difficult to view in the Command Prompt window. The ">" symbol redirects the output from the command to another location. In this case, it is redirected to the file C:\tlist.txt.

9. Type **type c:\tlist.txt | more** to view the contents of the file one page at a time. The type command displays a test file to screen. The more command limits the display of information to one screen at a time. Notice that many details of each certificate are listed. Press the **spacebar** until you reach the end of the file. To stop viewing the file, press **Ctrl+C**.

10. Type **certutil -catemplates** and press **Enter**. This command shows the list of certificate templates that the CA is configured to use.

11. Type **certutil -crl** and press **Enter**. This publishes a new certificate revocation list.

12. Type **certutil -shutdown** and press **Enter**. This stops Certificate Services.

13. Type **certutil -ping -config studentXX** (where *XX* is your student number), and press **Enter**. You will receive an error message this time because the service is no longer running. The error message indicates that the server could not be reached and that access is denied.

14. Close the Command Prompt window.

Certification Objectives

Objectives for Microsoft Exam #70-293: Planning a Microsoft Windows Server 2003 Network:

- Plan a public key infrastructure (PKI) that uses Certificate Services.

- Identify the appropriate type of certificate authority to support certificate issuance requirements.

- Plan the enrollment and distribution of certificates.

REVIEW QUESTIONS

1. Which of the following can you not perform with the Certutil utility?

   a. stopping Certificate Services

   b. publishing a CRL

   c. viewing a list of certificate templates installed on the server

   d. requesting a certificate

2. Which command verifies that the server is listening for certificate requests?

   a. certutil –ping –config server

   b. certutil –crl

   c. certutil –shutdown

   d. certutil –pingadmin

3. Which command displays a list of certificate templates installed on the local server?

   a. certutil –crl

   b. certutil –pingadmin

   c. certutil –templates

   d. certutil –catemplates

4. Which command displays a list of options available for Certutil?

   a. certutil –help

   b. certutil –?

   c. help certutil

   d. certutil –crl

5. Which character can be used to redirect output from the screen to a file?

   a. @

   b. ^

   c. <

   d. >

9

PLANNING AND MANAGING IPSEC

Labs included in this chapter:

♦ 10.1 Enabling IPSec Through Group Policy

♦ 10.2 Implementing IPSec in Transport Mode

♦ 10.3 Viewing Differences in ESP and AH Mode

♦ 10.4 Configuring IPSec Policies with Netsh

♦ 10.5 Creating a Custom IPSec Policy for Application Traffic

Microsoft MCSE Exam #70-293 Objectives	
Objective	Lab
Create and implement an IPSec policy.	10.1, 10.2, 10.3, 10.4, 10.5
Configure IPSec policy settings.	10.2, 10.3, 10.4, 10.5
Configure protocol security by using IPSec policies.	10.1, 10.2, 10.3, 10.5
Specify the required ports and protocols for specified network services.	10.5
Plan an IPSec policy for secure network communications.	10.1, 10.2, 10.3, 10.4, 10.5
Secure data transmission between client computers to meet security requirements.	10.1, 10.2, 10.3, 10.5
Secure data transmission by using IPSec.	10.1, 10.2, 10.3, 10.5
Plan for network protocol security.	10.1, 10.2, 10.3, 10.4, 10.5
Plan security for data transmission.	10.1, 10.2, 10.3, 10.4, 10.5

Lab 10.1 Enabling IPSec Through Group Policy

Objectives

The goal of this lab activity is to implement IPSec (IP Security) policies through a group policy. IPSec policies can be configured and assigned through the local security policy on servers and workstations. However, in a large environment, manually going to each computer and assigning IPSec policies would be needlessly repetitive and inefficient. You can use Group Policy to distribute and assign IPSec policies instead.

Materials Required:

This lab will require the following:

- Windows Server 2003 installed and configured according to the instructions at the beginning of this lab manual

Estimated completion time: **15 minutes**

Activity Background

When Group Policy is used to distribute and assign IPSec policies, the task needs to be performed only once. Then all of the workstations and servers will read the IPSec policy from Group Policy. This is much faster than configuring each computer individually. It is also less prone to configuration errors because the task is performed only once.

Different groups of computers can be assigned different IPSec policies by placing the computers in organizational units (OUs). This allows you to put a different group policy in place for each OU.

When enabling IPSec policies through Group Policy, you need to be aware of how Group Policies are assigned. Domain controllers update Group Policies every five minutes. However, member servers and workstations only update Group Policies every 90 minutes. When implementing restrictive Group Policies, you also need to ensure that you do not restrict communication with a domain controller so much that member servers and workstations cannot communicate with it. For example, if you configure a Group Policy that assigns an IPSec policy that limits communication to only IPSec-secured communication for domain controllers, member servers, and workstations, then the domain controllers will read the Group Policy first, assign the IPSec policy, and prevent member servers and workstations from reading the Group Policy.

ACTIVITY

Activity

1. Log on as **Administrator** to the Arctic.local domain with a password of **Password!**.

2. Click **Start**, click **Run**, type **mmc**, and press **Enter**.

3. Click the **File** menu, click **Add/Remove Snap-in**, and click **Add**.

4. Double-Click **Active Directory Users and Computers**, click **Close**, and then click **OK**.

5. Double-click **Active Directory Users and Computers** to expand it, and double-click **Arctic.local**.

6. If necessary, create an OU named OU*XX*, where *XX* is your student number. Right-click **Arctic.local**, point to **New**, and click **Organizational Unit**. In the Name text box, type **OU*XX*** (where *XX* is your student number), and click **OK**.

7. Click the **Computers** OU to view the contents.

8. Right-click **STUDENT*XX*** (where *XX* is your student number), and click **Move**.

9. Click **OU*XX*** (where *XX* is your student number), and click **OK**.

10. Click **OU*XX*** (where *XX* is your student number), to view your computer in the OU.

11. Right-click **OU*XX*** (where *XX* is your student number), click **Properties**, and click the **Group Policy** tab.

12. Click **New**, type **IPSec*XX*** (where *XX* is your student number), and press **Enter**.

13. Double-click **IPSec*XX*** (where *XX* is your student number), to open it for editing.

14. In the left pane under Computer Configuration, double-click **Windows Settings** to expand it, double-click **Security Settings** to expand it, and click **IP Security Policies on Active Directory (arctic.local)**.

15. Right-click **Server (Request Security)** and click **Assign**.

16. Close the Group Policy Object Editor window, click **Close**, and close the MMC. If asked to save settings, click **No**.

17. Click **Start**, click **Run**, type **cmd.exe**, and press **Enter**.

18. Type **gpupdate /force** and press **Enter**. The Gpupdate utility causes Group Policy to update immediately. If you did not perform this step, it would take up to 90 minutes for Group Policy to update.

10

19. Type **gpresult** and press **Enter**. This command compiles a list of Group Policies that apply to the local user and the local computer. When the command is finished generating results, scroll up in the window to view the computer section. It shows that the Group Policy IPSec*XX* (where *XX* is your student number), has been applied, as shown in Figure 10-1. Close the Command Prompt window.

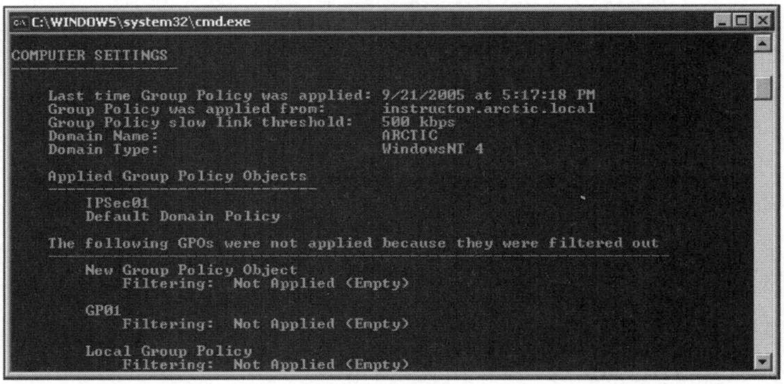

Figure 10-1   Output from gpresult

20. Click **Start**, point to **Run**, type **mmc**, and press **Enter**.

21. Click the **File** menu, click **Add/Remove Snap-in**, and click **Add**.

22. Double-Click **Active Directory Users and Computers**, click **Close**, and click **OK**.

23. Double-click **Active Directory Users and Computers** to expand it, and double-click **Arctic.local**.

24. Right-click **OU*XX*** (where *XX* is your student number), click **Properties**, and click the **Group Policy** tab.

25. Right-click **IPSec*XX*** (where *XX* is your student number), click **Delete**, click the **Remove the link and delete the Group Policy Object permanently** option, click **OK**, and click **Yes**. This removes the group policy so that it does not interfere with later labs.

26. Click **Close**, and close the MMC. If prompted to save settings, click **No**.

27. Click **Start**, click **Run**, type **gpupdate**, and press **Enter**.

Certification Objectives

Objectives for Microsoft Exam #70-293: Planning a Microsoft Windows Server 2003 Network:

- Create and implement an IPSec policy.

- Configure protocol security by using IPSec policies.

- Plan an IPSec policy for secure network communications.

- Secure data transmission between client computers to meet security requirements.

- Secure data transmission by using IPSec.

- Plan for network protocol security.

- Plan security for data transmission.

REVIEW QUESTIONS

1. Which command-line utility can be used to force the immediate application of Group Policy?

   a. Gpresult

   b. Gpupdate

   c. Gpi

   d. Secedit

2. Which command-line utility can be used to view the effective Group Policies on a workstation?

   a. Gpresult

   b. Gpupdate

   c. Gpi

   d. Gpdown

3. To what type of Active Directory object is a Group Policy linked?

   a. user

   b. group

   c. computer

   d. OU

4. How do you configure a computer to use an IPSec policy?

   a. You enforce it.

   b. You enable it.

   c. You assign it.

   d. You apply it.

5. How often do member servers download Group Policies?

    a. every 5 minutes

    b. every 15 minutes

    c. every 60 minutes

    d. every 90 minutes

LAB 10.2 IMPLEMENTING IPSEC IN TRANSPORT MODE

Objectives

The goal of this lab activity is to implement IPSec in transport mode. IPSec can be configured to run in transport mode or tunnel mode.

Materials Required:

This lab will require the following:

- Windows Server 2003 installed and configured according to the instructions at the beginning of this lab manual

- A partner to complete the exercise with; if a partner is not available you can play the role of both partners by using two computers. All parts of this lab are completed by both partners

Estimated completion time: **15 minutes**

Activity Background

Transport mode is used when IPSec is to be used only for communication between two end-points (computers). This is most appropriate when you are securing communication within a LAN.

Tunnel mode is designed for use with routers. Two routers negotiate an IPSec tunnel and then information routed between them is protected by IPSec. This is most common for securing communication between two areas within a LAN or between two locations across the Internet.

Several options are available for authentication when IPSec is implemented:

- Kerberos is the easiest authentication method to use when all computers are part of the same Active Directory forest.

- A preshared key is the simplest authentication method to use when the computers are not part of the same forest.

- Certificates can also be used for authentication when the computers are not part of the same forest. If certificates are used for authentication, they must be issued from certification authorities (CAs) in the same certificate trust chain.

Activity

1. Log on as **Administrator** to the Arctic.local domain with a password of **Password!**.

2. Click **Start**, point to **Administrative Tools**, and click **Local Security Policy**.

3. In the Local Security Settings window, right-click **IP Security Policies on Local Computer**, and click **Create IP Security Policy**.

4. Click **Next** to begin the IP Security Policy Wizard.

5. In the Name text box, type **Transport Mode** and then click **Next**.

6. Click **Next** to accept the default of the default response rule being activated. The default response rule allows the negotiation of an IPSec security association for all IP traffic for which no rules are defined.

7. Click the **Use this string to protect the key exchange (preshared key)** option button, and in the text box below it, type **MySecretKey**, as shown in Figure 10-2. The key chosen here is simple to make it easier to complete the lab. In a real life situation, you should pick a key that is a combination of uppercase letters, lowercase letters, numbers, and punctuation. In addition, a longer key is more secure. Click **Next** to continue.

10

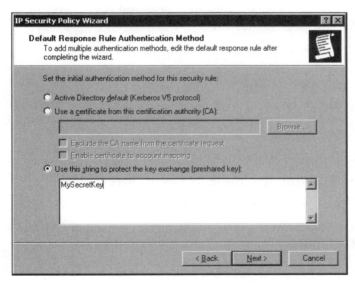

Figure 10-2   Entering a preshared key

8. If necessary, check the **Edit properties** check box, and click **Finish**.

9. On the Rules tab, click **Add** and click **Next** to start the Create IP Security Rule Wizard.

10. Select the **This rule does not specify a tunnel** option button, and click **Next**.

11. Click the **Local area network (LAN)** option button. Selecting this option means that the rule will apply only to network traffic from LAN connections. If this server were a Remote Access server, the network traffic from dial-up and VPN connections would not be affected by this rule. Click **Next** to continue.

12. Select the **All IP Traffic** option button. When this option is selected, the rule will apply to all IP traffic except broadcasts, multicasts, Kerberos packets, RSVP packets, and ISAKMP (IKE) packets. The other option—All ICMP Traffic—lets you create rules for ICMP traffic, such as ping packets and tracert packets. Click **Next** to continue.

13. Select the **Request Security (Optional)** option button. When this option is selected, the rule will attempt to negotiate an IPSec security association, but if it is not possible, the rule will permit the traffic anyway. Click **Next** to continue.

14. Select the **Use this string to protect the key exchange (preshared key)** option button, and in the text box below it, type **MySecretKey**. Click **Next** to continue.

15. Uncheck the **Edit properties** check box, and click **Finish**.

16. Click **OK** to close the Transport Mode Properties dialog box.

17. In the left pane of the Local Security Settings window, if necessary click **IP Security Policies on Local Computer**, then right-click **Transport Mode**, and click **Assign**.

18. Click **Start**, click **Run**, type **cmd**, and press **Enter**.

19. When your partner has also completed the exercise to this point, type **ping 192.168.1.1XX** (where *XX* is your partner's student number), and press **Enter**. You may receive a message that says "Negotiating IP Security." This indicates that IPSec is attempting to create a security association. Out of the four ping packets, at least the final two should get a reply.

20. Close the Command Prompt window.

21. Click **Start**, click **Run**, type **mmc**, and press **Enter**.

22. Click the **File** menu, click **Add/Remove Snap-in**, and click **Add**.

23. Scroll down in the list of snap-ins, double-click **IP Security Monitor**, click **Close**, and click **OK**.

24. Double-click **IP Security Monitor** to expand it, double-click your server to expand it, and click **Active Policy**. This shows the IPSec policy that is currently assigned to your server. Notice that the policy name is Transport Mode. In addition, notice that Policy Store, which indicates the location of the policy, is set to Local Store, which means it is stored locally on your server. If Policy Store is set to Domain Store, then it indicates that the IPSec policy is part of a group policy.

25. Double-click **Quick Mode** to expand it, and click **Security Associations**. In the list of security associations, there will be an entry with your partner's IP address listed as a peer, as shown in Figure 10-3. Other security associations may also be listed here.

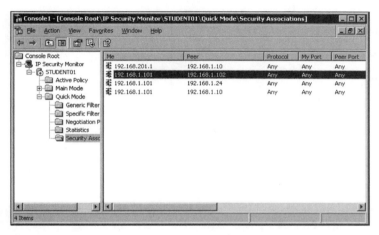

Figure 10-3   Viewing security associations

26. Close MMC. If prompted to save the console settings, click **No**.

27. In the Local Security Settings window, right-click **Transport Mode** and click **Un-assign**.

28. Close the Local Security Settings window.

Certification Objectives

Objectives for Microsoft Exam #70-293: Planning a Microsoft Windows Server 2003 Network:

- Create and implement an IPSec policy.

- Configure IPSec policy settings.

- Configure protocol security by using IPSec policies.

- Plan an IPSec policy for secure network communications.

■ Secure data transmission between client computers to meet security requirements.

■ Secure data transmission by using IPSec.

■ Plan for network protocol security.

■ Plan security for data transmission.

REVIEW QUESTIONS

1. Which IPSec mode would you choose when encrypting traffic across the Internet between two locations?

    a. transport mode

    b. internet mode

    c. local mode

    d. tunnel mode

2. Which IPSec mode would you choose when encrypting traffic between two hosts on a local area network?

    a. transport mode

    b. internet mode

    c. local mode

    d. tunnel mode

3. Which options are available for authenticating IPSec connections? (Choose all that apply.)

    a. preshared key

    b. ESP mode

    c. AH mode

    d. certificates

4. Which IPSec authentication option is the easiest to implement if all computers are part of the same Active Directory forest?

    a. preshared key

    b. certificates

    c. Kerberos

    d. ESP mode

5. Which utility can be used to view IPSec security associations?

   a. Local Security Policy

   b. Active Directory Users and Computers

   c. IP Security Monitor

   d. IP Security Policy Management

LAB 10.3 VIEWING DIFFERENCES IN ESP AND AH MODE

Objectives

The goal of this lab activity is to view the differences between IPSec in ESP mode and IPSec in AH mode. In addition to functioning in tunnel mode and transport mode, IPSec also has the ability to function in Encapsulated Secure Payload (ESP) mode and Authentication Headers (AH) mode. ESP mode and AH mode are independent of tunnel mode and transport mode. That is, when configuring IPSec, you must choose either tunnel mode or transport mode, and also choose either ESP mode or AH mode.

Materials Required:

This lab will require the following:

- Windows Server 2003 installed and configured according to the instructions at the beginning of this lab manual

- Network Monitor installed on your server

- A partner to complete the exercise with; if a partner is not available you can play the role of both partners by using two computers. All parts of this lab are completed by both partners

- Successful completion of Lab 10.2

Estimated completion time: **15 minutes**

Activity Background

When AH mode is used, only the header is encrypted and the packets will be authenticated with digital signatures. This will protect against spoofing, and provides non-repudiation. However, AH mode does not encrypt the data in the packets.

ESP mode is required to encrypt data in the packets. When ESP mode is used, data encryption is optional. However, most implementations of IPSec do perform data encryption.

Activity

1. Log on as **Administrator** to the Arctic.local domain with a password of **Password!**.

2. Click **Start**, point to **Administrative Tools**, and click **Local Security Policy**.

3. Click **IP Security Policies on Local Computer**, right-click **Transport Mode**, and click **Properties**.

4. Double-click **All IP Traffic** to open the rule for editing.

5. Click the **Filter Action** tab, click **Add**, and click **Next** to begin the IP Security Filter Action Wizard.

6. In the Name text box, type **MyAction**, and click **Next**.

7. Click **Next** to accept the default setting of Negotiate security. This setting indicates that an IPSec security association should be negotiated. Other filter actions available are Permit and Block. Permit allows traffic without IPSec, whereas Block stops traffic.

8. Select the **Fall back to unsecured communication** option button, and click **Next**. This option is required if you want your server to communicate with other computers that do not support IPSec.

9. Select the **Custom** option button, and click **Settings**. This will open the Custom Security Method Settings dialog box, as shown in Figure 10-4.

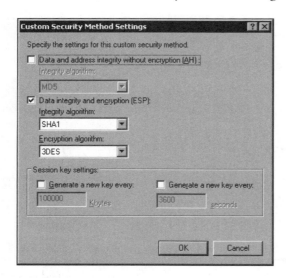

Figure 10-4   Custom Security Method Settings dialog box

10. If necessary, uncheck the **Data and address integrity without encryption (AH)** check box. This check box turns on AH mode.

11. If necessary, check the **Data integrity and encryption (ESP)** check box. This check box turns on ESP mode.

12. Click the **Integrity algorithm** drop-down arrow. This shows you the available options for the hashing algorithm used for the digital signatures. If <None> is chosen, integrity checking will not be performed. MD5 produces a 128-bit hash and is slightly faster than SHA1, which produces a 160-bit hash. However, SHA1 is more secure. Click **SHA1**.

13. Click the **Encryption algorithm** drop-down arrow. This shows you the available options for the algorithm used to encrypt the data. If <None> is selected, the data will not be encrypted. DES uses a 56-bit key to encrypt data and is less secure than 3DES, which uses three 56-bit keys to encrypt data. Because 3DES encrypts the data three times, it is slower than DES. Click **3DES**.

14. Check the **Generate a new key every** check box on the left side of the dialog box. When this check box is selected, a new session key is generated after a certain amount of data has been sent. Changing the session key regularly keeps data more secure because if the key is cracked by using brute force, the amount of data that can be decrypted is limited. The default setting when enabled changes the key for every 100 MB of data transmitted. You also have the ability to change the session key based on a period of time.

15. Click **OK**, click **Next**, and then click **Finish**.

16. In the Edit Rule Properties dialog box, click the **MyAction** option button, click **Apply**, click **OK**, and click **OK**.

17. Right-click **Transport Mode** and click **Assign**.

18. Close the Local Security Settings window. Do not proceed further until your partner has completed the exercise this far.

19. Click **Start**, point to **Administrative Tools**, and click **Network Monitor**.

20. If necessary, click **OK** to clear the message about selecting a network.

21. If necessary, in the Select a network dialog box, expand **Local Computer**, click **Classroom**, and click **OK**.

22. Press **F10** to start capturing packets.

23. Click **Start**, click **Run**, type **cmd**, and press **Enter**.

24. Type **ping 192.168.1.1XX** (where *XX* is your partner's student number), and press **Enter**.

25. Close the Command Prompt window.

26. In Network Monitor, press **F11** to stop the capture, and then press **F12** to view the capture.

27. Click the **Display** menu and click **Filter**.

10

28. Double-click **Protocol == Any** and click **Disable All**. The results are shown in Figure 10-5.

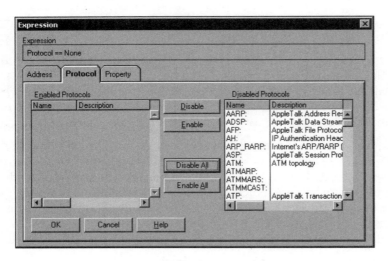

Figure 10-5   Expression dialog box

29. Scroll down in the Disabled Protocols box, double-click **ICMP**, click **OK,** and then click **OK**. A message appears, indicating that there are no frames to display. This is because the ICMP packets from the ping command were inside IPSec packets. Click **OK** to close the message.

30. Click the **Display** menu and click **Filter**.

31. Double-click **Protocol == ICMP** and click **Disable All**.

32. Scroll down in the Disabled Protocols box, double-click **ESP**, click **OK**, and then click **OK**. Between six and sixteen packets are listed after the filter is applied. Double-click the first packet.

33. In the middle pane, expand **ESP** and click **ESP: Rest of Frame (encrypted) Number of data bytes remaining = 68 (0x0044)**. This highlights the encrypted data in the lower pane. The right side of the lower pane shows the data in text format. Notice that it is encrypted and you are unable to read the contents. This is shown in Figure 10-6.

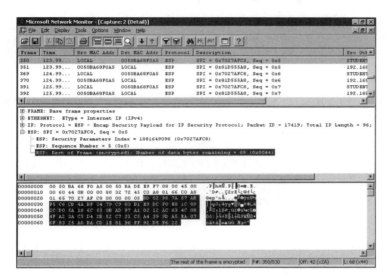

Figure 10-6   ESP mode packet

34. Click the **File** menu and click **Close**.

35. Minimize Network Monitor.

36. Wait until your partner has completed up to this point in the lab before continuing. Click **Start**, point to **Administrative Tools**, and click **Local Security Policy**.

37. If necessary, click **IP Security Policies on Local Computer** to select it, right-click **Transport Mode**, and click **Un-assign**.

38. Right-click **Transport Mode** and click **Properties**.

39. Double-click **All IP Traffic** to edit the rule, click the **Filter Action** tab, and click **Add**.

40. Click **Next**, type **AH Mode** in the Name text box, and click **Next**.

41. Click **Next** to accept the default setting to negotiate security, select the **Fall back to unsecured communication** option button, and click **Next**.

42. Select the **Custom** option button, and click **Settings**.

43. If necessary, check the **Data and address integrity without encryption (AH)** check box. This check box turns on AH mode.

44. If necessary, uncheck the **Data integrity and encryption (ESP)** check box. This check box turns on ESP mode.

45. Click **OK**, click **Next**, and click **Finish**.

46. Select the **AH Mode** option button, click **Apply**, click **OK**, and click **OK**.

47. Right-click **Transport Mode** and click **Assign**.

48. Close Local Security Settings. Wait until your partner has completed the exercise to this point before continuing.

49. In Network Monitor, press **F10** to start capturing packets, and click **No** to saving the capture.

50. Click **Start**, click **Run**, type **cmd**, and press **Enter**.

51. Type **ping 192.168.1.1XX** (where *XX* is your partner's student number), and press **Enter**.

52. Close the Command Prompt window.

53. In Network Monitor, press the **F11** key to stop the capture, and then press the **F12** key to view the capture.

54. Click the **Display** menu and click **Filter**.

55. Double-click **Protocol == Any** and click **Disable All**.

56. Scroll down in the Disabled Protocols box, double-click **AH**, click **OK**, and click **OK**.

57. Double-click the first packet in the list. Read the information in the middle pane. Notice that there is an ICMP section because the data in the packet is not encrypted when using AH mode.

58. In the middle pane, double-click the **ICMP: Echo:** line to expand it, and click **ICMP: Data: Number of data bytes remaining = 32 (0x0020)**. This highlights the data in the lower pane. Notice that the data is readable. A ping packet includes a string of characters from the alphabet as data. This is shown in Figure 10-7.

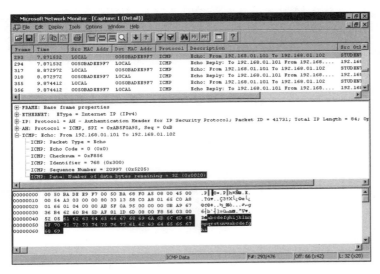

Figure 10-7   AH mode packet

59. Close Network Monitor. If prompted to save the capture, click **No**.

60. Wait until your partner has completed up to this point in the lab before continuing. Click **Start**, point to **Administrative Tools**, and click **Local Security Policy**.

61. If necessary, click **IP Security Policies on Local Computer** to select it, right-click **Transport Mode**, and click **Un-assign**.

62. Close Local Security Policy.

Certification Objectives

Objectives for Microsoft Exam #70-293: Planning a Microsoft Windows Server 2003 Network:

- Create and implement an IPSec policy.

- Configure IPSec policy settings.

- Configure protocol security by using IPSec policies.

- Plan an IPSec policy for secure network communications.

- Secure data transmission between client computers to meet security requirements.

10

- Secure data transmission by using IPSec.

- Plan for network protocol security.

- Plan security for data transmission.

REVIEW QUESTIONS

1. Which IPSec mode is required to perform encryption of data?

    a. ESP mode

    b. AH mode

    c. tunnel mode

    d. transport mode

2. Which options are available when selecting an integrity algorithm? (Choose all that apply.)

    a. SHA1

    b. DES

    c. SHA3

    d. MD5

    e. <None>

3. Which options are available when selecting an encryption algorithm? (Choose all that apply.)

    a. DES

    b. MPPE

    c. 3DES

    d. <None>

    e. SHA1

4. Why would you configure an IPSec filter action to change the session key?

    a. to replace a lost key

    b. to replace a stolen key

    c. to limit the amount of data that can be decrypted with a cracked key

    d. to change the key every 10 minutes, which is a requirement

5. Based on what two criteria can you force changing of the session key? (Choose all that apply.)

   a. the amount of data that has been transferred

   b. the application protocol being encrypted

   c. the amount of time that has passed

   d. the time of day

LAB 10.4 CONFIGURING IPSEC POLICIES WITH NETSH

Objectives

The goal of this lab activity is to configure IPSec policies with the Netsh utility.

Materials Required:

- Windows Server 2003 installed and configured according to the instructions at the beginning of this lab manual

- Successful completion of Lab 10.3

10

Estimated completion time: **15 minutes**

Activity Background

Most of the time, you will configure IPSec policies on individual computers using the Local Security Policy. If you need to configure many computers at once, you can configure and apply IPSec policies using Group Policy. However, there may be situations in which you would like to script the implementation of IPSec policies. To script IPSec policies you can use the Netsh utility.

Netsh has some features that are not available in the IP Security Policy Management snap-in. These features include: IPSec diagnostics, default traffic exemptions, strong certificate revocation list (CRL) checking, IKE (Oakley) logging, logging intervals, computer startup security, and computer startup traffic exemptions.

Activity

1. Log on as **Administrator** to the Arctic.local domain with a password of **Password!**.

2. Click **Start**, click **Run**, type **cmd**, and press **Enter**.

3. Type **netsh** and press **Enter**.

4. Type **?** and press **Enter**. This shows you a list of available commands. Notice that one of the available commands is ipsec. To make it easier to see command results, you may want to expand the size of the Command Prompt window to make it taller.

5. Type **ipsec** and press **Enter**, and then type **?** and press **Enter**. This changes to the ipsec context in Netsh and then shows a list of available commands in the ipsec context. These are the commands you are concerned about right now.

6. Type **dump** and press **Enter**. This command does not return any results to the screen. Even though it is listed as available, it does not have any effect for the ipsec context of Netsh.

7. There are two subcontexts available in ipsec. The first is dynamic, which makes adjustments to the current IPSec configuration immediately. This is normally not used because it is very easy to make configuration mistakes. The second is static, which makes adjustments to IPSec policies the same way as the IP Security Policy Management snap-in does. Type **static** and press **Enter**.

8. Type **help** and press **Enter** to view the list of available commands in the static context. Notice that the help command is equivalent to the ? command.

9. Type **show policy all** and press **Enter**. This command shows the four IPSec policies that are configured on your server. This includes when they were last modified and whether they are assigned. Notice that by default they refresh their settings every 180 minutes. This is listed as Polling Interval.

10. Type **show gpoassignedpolicy** and press **Enter**. This results in an error indicating that there is no currently assigned policy through Group Policy. You have not configured an IPSec policy through Group Policy. If you had, this command would have displayed information about the IPSec policy in use.

11. Type **set policy** and press **Enter**. This shows the list of commands that can be used to configure policies.

12. Type **set policy name="Transport Mode" assign=y** and press **Enter**. This assigns the Transport Mode IPsec policy.

13. Type **show policy name="Transport Mode"** and press **Enter**. This shows information for only the Transport Mode IPSec policy. Notice that Assigned is now set to YES.

14. Type **set policy name="Transport Mode" assign=n** and press **Enter**. This un-assigns the Transport Mode IPsec policy.

15. Type **set policy name="Transport Mode" newname="RenamedPolicy"** and press **Enter**. This completes the renaming. Type **show policy all** and press **Enter** to confirm the rename.

16. Type **add policy name="NewPolicy" activatedefaultrule=y pollinginterval=30 assign=n** and press **Enter**. This creates a new IPSec policy with the default response rule activated and a polling interval of 30 minutes, which is not assigned.

17. Type **show policy all** and press **Enter** to confirm the creation of NewPolicy.

18. Type **delete policy name="NewPolicy"** and press **Enter**. This deletes the IPSec policy named NewPolicy.

19. Type **show policy all** and press **Enter** to confirm the deletion of NewPolicy.

20. Type **delete policy all** and press **Enter**. This deletes all of the local IPSec policies. To confirm that all of the IPSec policies are deleted, type **show policy all** and press **Enter**. You should see the message "ERR IPSec[05072] : No Policies in Policy Store" on the screen.

21. To restore the default IPSec policies, type **restorepolicyexamples release=win2003** and press **Enter**.

22. To verify that the default IPSec policies have been restored, type **show policy all** and press **Enter**.

23. Type **Exit** and press **Enter** to exit the Netsh utility.

24. Close the Command Prompt window.

Certification Objectives

Objectives for Microsoft Exam #70-293: Planning a Microsoft Windows Server 2003 Network:

- Create and implement an IPSec policy.

- Configure IPSec policy settings.

- Plan an IPSec policy for secure network communications.

- Plan for network protocol security.

- Plan security for data transmission.

10

REVIEW QUESTIONS

1. In Netsh, which context located below ipsec configures IPSec settings immediately?

   a. static

   b. current

   c. dynamic

   d. assigned

2. Which command in the ipsec static context of Netsh restores the default IPSec policies?

   a. restorepolicyexamples

   b. restoredefaultpolicies

   c. recreatedefaultpolicies

   d. recreatepolicyexamples

3. Which command in the ipsec static context of Netsh deletes all IPSec policies?

   a. delete policy name=*

   b. delete policy name=all

   c. delete policy all

   d. remove all

4. What is the default polling interval used to refresh IPSec policy settings?

   a. 5 minutes

   b. 30 minutes

   c. 90 minutes

   d. 180 minutes

5. Which command in the ipsec static context of Netsh displays only IPSec policies assigned through Group Policy?

   a. show policy all

   b. show policy type=gpo

   c. show gpoassignedpolicy

   d. show policy name=gpo

Lab 10.5 Creating a Custom IPSec Policy for Application Traffic

Objectives

The goal of this lab activity is to create a new IPSec policy that will encrypt communication between your server on TCP port 1433 and any other host. This is the process you can use to protect traffic to a SQL server running on your server.

Materials Required:

This lab will require the following:

- Windows Server 2003 installed and configured according to the instructions at the beginning of this lab manual

Estimated completion time: **10 minutes**

Activity Background

The default IPSec filter lists that are installed with Windows Server 2003 are All ICMP Traffic and All IP Traffic. The All ICMP Traffic filter list applies to all ICMP packets. It is normally used to stop IPSec from being used for ICMP packets because these packets seldom have information worth protecting. The All IP Traffic filter list applies to all traffic except broadcasts, multicasts, Kerberos packets, RSVP packets, and ISAKMP (IKE) packets. This filter list is used as a catch-all to apply IPSec to all network communication.

The default filter lists are useful as a starting point when working with IPSec, but you might also need to protect only required traffic on your networks. Protecting only required traffic will reduce the load on computer processors and speed up network traffic. For example, if you want to use IPSec to protect a SQL-based application, only traffic on TCP port 1433 need to be encrypted. All other traffic can be permitted without being encrypted.

10

ACTIVITY

Activity

1. Log on as **Administrator** to the Arctic.local domain with a password of **Password!**.

2. Click **Start**, point to **Administrative Tools**, and click **Local Security Policy**.

3. If necessary, click **IP Security Policies on Local Computer**.

4. Right-click **IP Security Policies on Local Computer**, and click **Manage IP filter lists and filter actions**.

5. Click **Add** to begin creating a new IP filter list.

6. In the Name text box, type **SQL Traffic** and then type **Protects SQL Server Traffic** in the Description text box.

7. Click **Add** to add a new IP filter.

8. Click **Next** to start the IP Filter Wizard.

9. In the Description text box, type **TCP Port 1433**.

10. If necessary, check the **Mirrored. Match packets with the exact opposite source and destination addresses** check box. This option ensures that traffic is properly encrypted when both sending and receiving. When IPSec is used in tunnel mode, mirroring cannot be used. Click **Next** to continue.

11. Click the **Source address** drop-down arrow to view the options that are available, as shown in Figure 10-8. The most common source address choices are My IP Address and Any IP Address. The options A specific DNS Name, A specific IP Address, and A specific IP Subnet are most commonly used when using IPSec in tunnel mode. The dynamic options change based on the configuration of the host to which the policy is applied. For example, if you do not want to encrypt data going to the default gateway, you can create an IP filter that uses the Default Gateway <dynamic> option. Each computer on which this IP filter is configured would insert the IP address of its own default gateway.

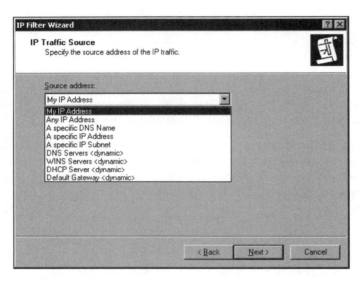

Figure 10-8   Source address options

12. Select **My IP Address**, and click **Next**.

13. Click the **Destination address** drop-down arrow, select **Any IP Address**, and click **Next**.

14. Click the **Select a protocol type** drop-down arrow, select **TCP**, and click **Next**.

15. Select the **From this port** option button, and type **1433** in the text box below it. This is the port of the SQL server and is matched with the source IP address from Step 12.

16. If necessary, select the **To any port** option button, and click **Next**. Most client applications use a random port number 1024 or above to initiate communication. Because this port cannot be predicted, you have chosen to apply this IP filter to all TCP ports on the client computers.

17. Click **Finish** and click **OK**.

18. Click **Close** to close the Manage IP filter lists and filter actions dialog box.

19. Right–click **IP Security Policies on Local Computer**, and click **Create IP Security Policy**.

20. Click **Next** to begin the IP Security Policy Wizard.

21. In the Name text box, type **SQL Policy** and click **Next**.

22. Click **Next** to accept the default of activate the default response rule.

23. Click **Next** to accept the default of using Active Directory default (Kerberos V5 protocol).

24. If necessary, check the **Edit properties** check box, and click **Finish**.

25. On the Rules tab, click **Add** to create a new rule.

26. Click **Next** to start the Create IP Security Rule Wizard.

27. If necessary, select the **This rule does not specify a tunnel** option, and click **Next**.

28. If necessary, select the **All network connections** option, and click **Next**.

29. Select the **SQL Traffic** option. This is the IP filter list you created earlier in the exercise. Click **Next**.

30. Select the **Require Security** option button, and click **Next**. The Require Security option will not communicate without an IPSec security association. The Request Security (Optional) option will attempt to negotiate an IPSec security association, but will fall back to unsecured communication for backward compatibility with non-IPSec clients. The Permit option sends packets without an IPSec security association.

31. If necessary, select the **Active Directory default (Kerberos V5 protocol)** option button, and click **Next**.

32. If necessary, uncheck the **Edit properties** check box, and click **Finish**. This policy now defines that traffic to TCP port 1433 on your server will be encrypted. Now you will add a rule that permits all other IP traffic.

33. Click **Add** and click **Next**.

34. If necessary, select the **This rule does not specify a tunnel** option button, and click **Next**.

35. If necessary, select the **All network connections** option button, and click **Next**.

36. Select the **All IP Traffic** option button, and click **Next**.

37. Select the **Permit** option button, and click **Next**.

38. If necessary, uncheck the **Edit properties** check box, and click **Finish**. When multiple rules are configured, the most specific will be applied first. In this case the SQL Traffic rule will be applied first, the All IP Traffic rule will be applied second, and the Default Response rule will be applied last. This allows you to be very specific in controlling which traffic is affected by different rules.

10

39. Click **OK**.

40. Close Local Security Settings.

Certification Objectives

Objectives for Microsoft Exam #70-293: Planning a Microsoft Windows Server 2003 Network:

- Create and implement an IPSec policy.

- Configure IPSec policy settings.

- Configure protocol security by using IPSec policies.

- Specify the required ports and protocols for specified services.

- Plan an IPSec policy for secure network communications.

- Secure data transmission between client computers to meet security requirements.

- Secure data transmission by using IPSec.

- Plan for network protocol security.

- Plan security for data transmission.

REVIEW QUESTIONS

1. Which filter action would you use if you required backward compatibility with Windows 9x clients?

   a. A custom filter action must be created.

   b. Permit

   c. Request Security (Optional)

   d. Require Security

2. Which IP filter option cannot be used with tunnel mode?

   a. Permit

   b. Blocked

   c. Negotiate security

   d. Mirrored

3. Which of the following options for source address are variables that will change depending on the computer to which the policy is applied? (Choose all that apply.)

   a. My IP Address

   b. Any IP Address

   c. A specific IP Subnet

   d. DHCP Server <dynamic>

4. In what order are IPSec rules applied?

   a. alphabetical

   b. the order you set

   c. most general to most specific

   d. most specific to most general

5. Which types of packets are not affected by the All IP Traffic filter list? (Choose all that apply.)

   a. unicast

   b. multicast

   c. HTTP

   d. ICMP

10

PLANNING NETWORK ACCESS

Labs included in this chapter:

- ◆ Lab 11.1 Configuring a Dial-up Server and Modem Pool
- ◆ Lab 11.2 Configuring Demand-Dial Routing
- ◆ Lab 11.3 Configuring IAS Accounting
- ◆ Lab 11.4 Configuring RRAS Logging
- ◆ Lab 11.5 Configuring ANI/CLI Authentication

Microsoft MCSE Exam #70-293 Objectives	
Objective	Lab
Plan security for remote access users.	11.1, 11.2, 11.5
Implement secure access between private networks.	11.2
Plan for security monitoring.	11.3, 11.4
Plan remote access policies.	11.5
Plan authentication methods for remote access clients.	11.5

Lab 11.1 Configuring a Dial-up Server and Modem Pool

Objectives

The goal of this lab activity is to learn how to configure the most common dial-up configuration, a modem pool.

Materials Required:

This lab will require the following:

- A Windows Server 2003 system installed and configured according to the instructions at the beginning of this lab manual

Estimated completion time: **10 minutes**

Activity Background

As an administrator of a Windows Server 2003 server, you may need to provide network access to many users that only have access to a standard telephone line, also known as a POTS (Plain Old Telephone System) line. At a minimum, you could install several modems in your server and configure Routing and Remote Access Service (RRAS) to allow dial-up users on to your network. A more common configuration is to install a multiport modem, which can act as several modems on one card. In coordination with your phone company, you could have all of your lines configured to use one phone number to simplify access for your users.

In this lab you will create a modem pool of two standard modem cards. Your server does not actually have a modem installed, so you cannot test the configuration.

Activity

1. If necessary, log on as **Administrator** to the Arctic.local domain with a password of **Password!**.

2. Close any open windows.

3. Click **Start**, point to **Control Panel**, and then click **Phone and Modem Options**.

4. In the Phone and Modem Options window, click the **Modems** tab.

5. Click **Add**, check the **Don't detect my modem, I will select it from a list** check box to select it, and then click **Next**.

6. The left pane should default to [Standard Modem Types]. In the right pane, click **Standard 56000 bps Modem**, click **Next**, click **COM1** in the Selected ports list box, click **Next**, and then click **Finish**.

7. To add a second modem, follow the same procedure, except select COM2. Click **Add**, check the **Don't detect my modem, I will select it from a list** check box, click **Next**, click **Standard 56000 bps Modem**, click **Next**, click **COM2** in the Selected ports list box, click **Next**, and then click **Finish**.

8. Click **OK** to close the Phone and Modem Options window.

9. Click **Start**, point to **Administrative Tools**, and then click **Routing and Remote Access**.

10. Right-click the **StudentXX** server (where *XX* is your student ID), and then click **Disable Routing and Remote Access**. Click **Yes** in the confirmation dialog box. Right-click the **StudentXX** server (where *XX* is your student ID), click **Configure and Enable Routing and Remote Access**, and then click **Next**. Click **Next** to select the default "Remote Access (dial-up or VPN)" option and to continue.

11. Click **Dial-up** and click **Next**.

12. Click the **Classroom** connection, and then click **Next**.

13. Click **From a specified range of addresses**, and then click **Next**.

14. Click **New**. In the New Address Range box, type **10.1.1.1** for the start IP address. In the Number of addresses box, type **2**. The End IP address value will fill in for you, as shown in Figure 11-1. Click **OK** and then click **Next**.

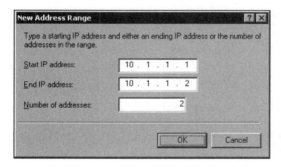

Figure 11-1   Configuring address range

15. Click **Next** to accept the default "No, Use Routing and Remote Access to authenticate connection requests" option. Click **Finish** and then click **OK** to acknowledge the warning.

16. In the Routing and Remote Access window, click **Ports**. Note the two standard modems added earlier.

17. Right-click **Ports** and click **Properties**. Double-click **Standard 56000 bps Modem**. The Maximum ports value is set to 1 and grayed out. Common dial-up server configurations would include a multiport modem, and you would configure how many ports are available for dial-up access here. Click **OK**.

18. Click **OK** to close the Ports Properties window. Close the Routing and Remote Access window.

Certification Objectives

Objectives for Microsoft Exam #70-293: Planning a Microsoft Windows Server 2003 Network:

- Plan security for remote access users.

REVIEW QUESTIONS

1. How many COM ports are available to you when you do not allow the operating system to detect your modem?

   a. 1

   b. 2

   c. 8

   d. 10

2. Which of the following activities can be done in the Phone and Modem Options applet? (Choose all that apply.)

   a. perform modem diagnostics

   b. view call logs

   c. enable modem logs

   d. configure calling cards

3. Where could you add AT strings to modify your modem's initialization parameters?

   a. Dial-up connection

   b. RRAS Ports properties

   c. Device Manager Modem properties

   d. Device Manager COM port properties

4. Which of the following modems could dial into an RRAS dial-up server? (Choose all that apply.)

   a. ADSL modem

   b. asynchronous modem

   c. ISDN modem

   d. cable modem

5. What is the maximum upload speed of a V.92 modem?

    a. 33.6 Kbps

    b. 48000 bps

    c. 56 Kbps

    d. 115200 bps

LAB 11.2 CONFIGURING DEMAND-DIAL ROUTING

Objectives

The goal of this lab activity is to learn how to configure demand-dial routing.

Materials Required:

This lab will require the following:

- A Windows Server 2003 system installed and configured according to the instructions at the beginning of this lab manual

Estimated completion time: **10 minutes**

11

Activity Background

Demand-dial routing is used to provide access between two networks only when required. When you have to connect a remote location to the main network, you have several options. The most readily available is likely to be setting úp the remote location server as a dial-up client and simply dial into the main network. However, maintaining that connection can be expensive if there are long-distance charges. Instead, you can set up demand-dial routing. When demand-dial is configured, a dial-up (or VPN) connection can be initiated, from either end, whenever a network device requests communication with the remote network.

Activity

1. If necessary, log on as **Administrator** to the Arctic.local domain with a password of **Password!**.

2. Click **Start**, point to **Administrative Tools**, and then click **Routing and Remote Access**.

3. Right-click the **StudentXX** server (where *XX* is your student ID) and click **Disable Routing and Remote Access**, then click **Yes** to acknowledge the warning message.

4. Right-click the **StudentXX** server (where *XX* is your student ID) and click **Configure and Enable Routing and Remote Access**.

5. In the Routing and Remote Access Server Setup Wizard, click **Next**.

6. Click **Secure connection between two private networks**, and then click **Next**.

7. To use a demand-dial connection to access the remote network, click **Next** to accept the default option of Yes.

8. Click **Next** to accept the default option of Automatically. DHCP will assign addresses from this connection. Click **Finish**.

9. Click **Next** to begin the Demand-Dial Interface Wizard.

10. In the Interface Name text box, type **RemoteXX** (where *XX* is your student number), and then click **Next**.

11. Click **Next** to accept the default "Connect using a modem, ISDN adapter, or other physical device" option.

12. Click **Standard 56000 bps Modem (COM1)**, and then click **Next**.

13. In the Phone number or address text box, type **555-1212**.

14. Click **Alternates**, type **555-1213** in the New phone number or address text box, click **Add**, click **Move successful number or address to the top of the list on connection**, and then click **OK**.

15. Click **Next** to accept the phone number configuration.

16. In addition to the Route IP packets on this interface, check the **Add a user account so a remote router can dial in** check box. Click **Next**.

17. Click **Add** to add a new static route. In the Destination text box, type **10.10.10.0**. In the Network Mask text box, type **255.255.255.0**. In the Metric box, type **10** (as shown in Figure 11-2). Click **OK** and then click **Next**.

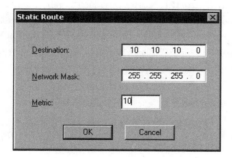

Figure 11-2   New static route

18. To set a password for the remote user, type and then retype to confirm the password **Password!**.

19. To set your server's dial-out credentials, type **CorpXX** (where *XX* is your student number) as the user name. Type the domain as **RemoteDomain** (as shown in Figure 11-3). Type and then retype to confirm the password **Password!**, and then click **Next**.

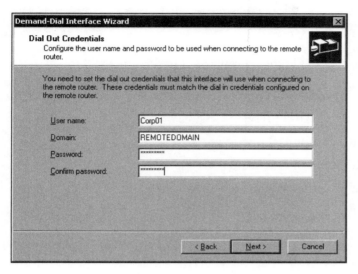

Figure 11-3 Configuring dial-out credentials

20. Click **Finish** and then close the Routing and Remote Access window.

Certification Objectives

Objectives for Microsoft Exam #70-293 Planning and Maintaining a Microsoft Windows Server 2003 Network Infrastructure:

- Plan security for remote access users.

- Implement secure access between private networks.

REVIEW QUESTIONS

1. Which of the following parameters are required in a static route?

   a. network mask

   b. metric

   c. destination network IP address

   d. all of the above

2. What is a metric?

   a. a logical number that represents the cost of a route

   b. a physical number that counts the number of routers between source and destination

   c. an admin preference ID; the higher the number the more preferred the route

   d. the weight of a route; with multiple routes to the same destination, this number determines the percentage of packets that will follow this route.

3. Where must demand-dial routing be configured?

   a. on the source RRAS server

   b. on the destination RRAS server

   c. on both source and destination RRAS servers

   d. with the phone company

4. What advantage does a dial-up connection have over a VPN?

   a. cost

   b. reliability

   c. security

   d. server need not be on the Internet

5. Who initiates a dial-on-demand routing connection?

   a. local RRAS server

   b. remote RRAS server

   c. either a local or a remote RRAS server

   d. connection manually initiated by the administrator

LAB 11.3 CONFIGURING IAS ACCOUNTING

Objectives

The goal of this lab activity is to understand that Remote Access Dial-In User Authentication Service (RADIUS) is a protocol designed to centralize the authentication process for large distributed networks. Accounting is a very important part of providing RADIUS services. Internet Authentication Service (IAS) is Microsoft's implementation of RADIUS.

Materials Required:

This lab will require the following:

- A Windows Server 2003 system installed and configured according to the instructions at the beginning of this lab manual

- IAS, as configured in Activity 11-11 in Chapter 11 of your textbook

Estimated completion time: **5 minutes**

Activity Background

If you are charging for network access, RADIUS accounting is the only tool you have to provide billing information. Even if you are not billing, the accounting logs can provide useful information to indicate and track hacker attacks and breaches.

ACTIVITY

Activity

1. If necessary, log on as **Administrator** to the Arctic.local domain with a password of **Password!**.

2. Click **Start**, point to **Administrative Tools**, and then click **Internet Authentication Service**.

3. Click **Remote Access Logging**.

4. In the right pane, double-click **Local File**.

5. In the Settings tab, check the **Accounting requests** check box.

6. Click the **Log File** tab.

7. In the Format section, select the **Database-compatible** option button. IAS format should be used only if you have NT4 IAS servers in production or your parser and billing systems are already built to support it.

11

8. At the top of the window, note the default log file name: INyymm.log. In the Create a new log file section, click the **Weekly** option button. Note the change in file name (as shown in Figure 11-4). Click **OK**.

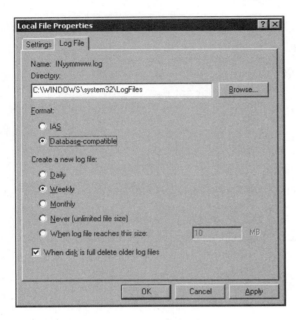

Figure 11-4 Accounting log properties

9. Close the IAS window. Your lab server isn't equipped to accept modem calls, so the lab cannot continue further. Note that a typical IAS accounting log would look like Figure 11-5. It is very difficult to read in this format; however, because it has a predictable comma-delimited format it can easily be imported into a database or spreadsheet for analysis or billing, as shown in Table 11-1.

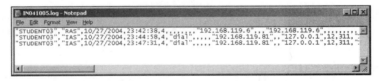

Figure 11-5 A portion of an IAS accounting log

Table 11-1 Fields and their values from the log in Figure 11-5 (omitting empty values)

Accounting-On	Accounting-Start	Accounting-Stop	Attribute	Represents
STUDENT03	STUDENT03	STUDENT03	Computer Name	Server where the packet was received
RAS	IAS	IAS	ServiceName	Service that generated the record—IAS or RAS
10/27/2004	10/27/2004	10/27/2004	Record-Date	Date
23:42:38	23:44:58	23:47:31	Record-Time	Time
4	4	4	Packet-Type	Type of packet, which can be: 1 = Accept-Request 2 = Access-Accept 3 = Access-Reject 4 = Accounting-Request
	dial	dial	User-Name	User identity, as specified by the user
	192.168.119.81	192.168.119.81	Framed-IP-Address	Framed address to be configured for the user
192.168.119.6	127.0.0.1	127.0.0.1	NAS-IP-Address	IP address of the NAS originating the request
	12	12	NAS-Port	Physical port number of the NAS originating the request
	311	311	Client-Vendor	Manufacturer of the NAS
192.168.119.6	192.168.119.6	192.168.119.6	Client-IP-Address	IP address of the RADIUS client
	localhost	localhost	Client-Friendly-Name	Friendly name for the RADIUS client
	10/28/2004 06:44:58	10/28/2004 06:47:29	Event-Timestamp	Date and time that this event occurred on the NAS
	CONNECT 31200/ARQ/V34 /LAPM/V42BIS	CONNECT 31200/ARQ/V34 /LAPM/V42BIS	Connect-Info	Type of connection made; information includes connection speed and data encoding protocols

11

Accounting-On	Accounting-Start	Accounting-Stop	Attribute	Represents
	1	1	Framed-Protocol	Protocol to be used
	2	2	Service-Type	Type of service that the user has requested
0	0	0	Reason-Code	Reason for rejecting a user
	311 1 192.168.119.6 10/27/2004 23:20:21 6	311 1 192.168.119.6 10/27/2004 23:20:21 6	Class	Attribute that is sent to client in an Access-Accept packet
8	1	2	Acct-Status-Type	Specifies whether an accounting packet starts or stops a session
		8216	Acct-Input-Octets	Octets received during the session
		13568	Acct-Output-Octets	Octets sent during the session
4	8	8	Acct-Session-Id	Unique numeric string that identifies the server session
	1	1	Acct-Authentic	Specifies which server authenticated an incoming call
		152	Acct-Session-Time	Length of time (in seconds) the session has been active
		129	Acct-Input-Packets	Packets received during the session
		173	Acct-Output-Packets	Packets sent during the session
		1	Acct-Terminate-Cause	Reason connection was terminated
	MSRASV5.20	MSRASV5.20	MS-RAS-Version	RRAS attribute; for more information, see RFC 2548

Accounting-On	Accounting-Start	Accounting-Stop	Attribute	Represents
	311	311	MS-RAS-Vendor	RRAS attribute; for more information, see RFC 2548
	0x0053545544454E543033	0x0053545544454E543033	MS-CHAP-Domain	RRAS attribute; for more information, see RFC 2548
	4	4	MS-MPPE-Encryption-Types	RRAS attribute; for more information, see RFC 2548

Certification Objectives

Objectives for Microsoft Exam #70–293: Planning a Microsoft Windows Server 2003 Network:

- Plan for security monitoring.

REVIEW QUESTIONS

11

1. Which of the following types of requests are logged in the accounting log?

    a. accounting–off

    b. accounting–start

    c. accounting–stop

    d. all of the above

2. Which of the following are required to form a valid billing record? (Choose all that apply.)

    a. accounting–start

    b. accounting–stop

    c. authentication accept

    d. authentication reject

3. If you are validating users from the domain and you see an unexpected number of authentication rejects in the IAS log, what else would you expect to see?

   a. a corresponding rise in the number of accounting-stop requests

   b. locked-out users on the domain

   c. deleted users on the domain

   d. a corresponding rise in the number of authentication retry requests

4. Which log format is recommended if there are no previous NT4 IAS systems with which to integrate?

   a. ISA

   b. IAS

   c. MySQL

   d. Database-Compatible

5. Authentication and accounting records from a call to a Microsoft RRAS server must be logged on a Microsoft platform. True or false?

LAB 11.4 CONFIGURING RRAS LOGGING

Objectives

The goal of this lab activity is to learn how to configure the logging options of RRAS for troubleshooting purposes.

Materials Required:

This lab will require the following:

- A Windows Server 2003 system installed and configured according to the instructions at the beginning of this lab manual

Estimated completion time: **5 minutes**

Activity Background

Troubleshooting remote access can be the most frustrating part of an administrator's job because so much of the process is out of your control. The problem could easily be with the client configuration, the telephone system (dial-up) configuration, or the Internet (VPN) configuration.

The main textbook that this lab manual accompanies demonstrated how to enable modem logging as a troubleshooting tool in Activity 11-15. However, there are two additional troubleshooting mechanisms built in to RRAS. You can configure RRAS to send more detailed events to the event log, which will provide you with information on each connection to your RRAS server. You can also enable debug logging, which generates an extremely detailed log of connection information.

Activity

1. If necessary, log on as **Administrator** to the Arctic.local domain with a password of **Password!**.

2. Click **Start**, point to **Administrative Tools**, and then click **Routing and Remote Access**.

3. Right-click the **StudentXX** server (where *XX* is your student ID) and click **Properties**.

4. Click the **Logging** tab, and then click the **Log all events** option button. All events will now be logged to the System event log.

5. Check the **Log additional Routing and Remote Access information (used for debugging)** check box, as shown in Figure 11-6. Click **OK**. The debug log will be in C:\WINDOWS\tracing\ppp.log.

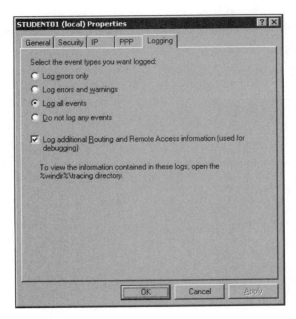

Figure 11-6   RRAS logging options

6. Your lab server isn't equipped to accept modem calls. For your reference, the following four figures (Figures 11-7 through 11-10) show the events generated by a standard modem call from connection to disconnection.

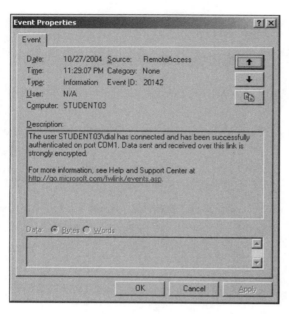

Figure 11-7   User dial connected event

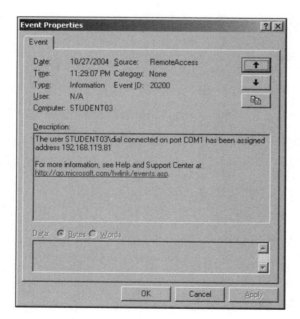

Figure 11-8   Address assignment event

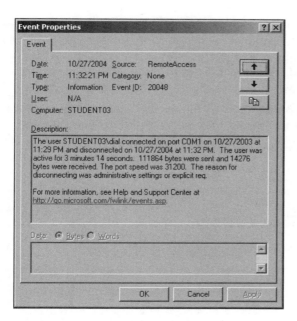

Figure 11-9   User dial disconnected event

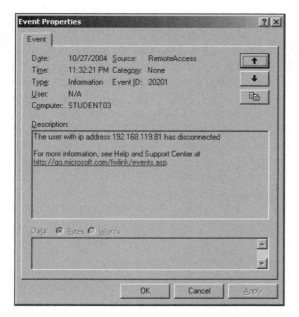

Figure 11-10   Address release event

11

7. The following text is the contents of the C:\WINDOWS\tracing\ppp.log after the same modem dial-up call. It is edited to show only the key points of the connection and disconnection phase. Review the text below. As you can see, the log is very detailed and quite difficult to read. Debug logging is a tool you will want to use only when you are experiencing errors.

Point to Point Protocol (PPP) initialization phase. PPP is an industry standard suite of protocols for the use of point-to-point links.

```
[1900] 10-27 23:29:06:167: Line up event occurred on port 12
[1900] 10-27 23:29:06:167: PortName: COM1
[1900] 10-27 23:29:06:167: Starting PPP on link with IfType=0x0,IPIf=0x0,IPXIf=0x0
[1900] 10-27 23:29:06:167: RasGetBuffer returned 3890498 for SendBuf
[1900] 10-27 23:29:06:167: FsmInit called for protocol = c021, port = 12
[1900] 10-27 23:29:06:167: ConfigInfo = 80a70a
[1900] 10-27 23:29:06:167: APs available = 7
[1900] 10-27 23:29:06:167: FsmReset called for protocol = c021, port = 12
[1900] 10-27 23:29:06:167: Inserting port in bucket # 12
[1900] 10-27 23:29:06:167: Inserting bundle in bucket # 0
[1900] 10-27 23:29:06:167: FsmOpen event received for protocol c021 on port 12
[1900] 10-27 23:29:06:167: FsmThisLayerStarted called for protocol = c021, port = 12
[1900] 10-27 23:29:06:167: FsmUp event received for protocol c021 on port 12
[1900] 10-27 23:29:06:167: <PPP packet sent at 10/28/2003 06:29:06:167
[1900] 10-27 23:29:06:167: <Protocol = LCP, Type = Configure-Req, Length = 0x3c, Id = 0x0, Port = 12
[1900] 23:29:06:167: <C0 21 01 00 00 3A 02 06 00 00 00 00 03 04 C2 27  |.!...:.........'|
[1900] 23:29:06:167: <05 06 7B 56 73 78 07 02 08 02 0D 03 06 11 04 06  |..{Vsx..........|
[1900] 23:29:06:167: <4E 13 17 01 7D 76 B9 AC E3 6E 49 CF AB 8F 56 0F  |N..}v...nI...V.|
[1900] 23:29:06:167: <D8 58 63 6C 00 00 00 00 17 04 00 04 00 00 00 00  |.Xcl............|
```

Link Control Protocol (LCP) initialization phase. LCP establishes the framing of the data to be transmitted on the Wide-Area Network (WAN). Using an LCP standardized framing allows all vendor devices to communicate regardless of the format of the data to be transmitted.

```
[1900] 10-27 23:29:06:167:
[1900] 10-27 23:29:06:167: InsertInTimerQ called portid=8,Id=0,Protocol=c021, EventType=0,fAuth=0
[1900] 10-27 23:29:06:167: InsertInTimerQ called portid=0,Id=0,Protocol=0,EventType=3, fAuth=0
[1900] 10-27 23:29:06:167: >PPP packet received at 10/28/2003 06:29:06:167
[1900] 10-27 23:29:06:167: >Protocol = LCP, Type = Configure-Req, Length = 0x19, Id = 0x0,
Port = 12
[1900] 23:29:06:167: >C0 21 01 00 00 17 02 06 00 00 00 00 05 06 1D 17  |..!.............|
[1900] 23:29:06:167: >5A D0 07 02 08 02 0D 03 06 00 00 00 00 00 00 00  |Z...............|
[1900] 10-27 23:29:06:167:
[1900] 10-27 23:29:06:167: <PPP packet sent at 10/28/2003 06:29:06:167
[1900] 10-27 23:29:06:167: <Protocol = LCP, Type = Configure-Ack, Length = 0x19, Id = 0x0,
Port = 12
[1900] 23:29:06:167: <C0 21 02 00 00 17 02 06 00 00 00 00 05 06 1D 17  |..!.............|
[1900] 23:29:06:167: <5A D0 07 02 08 02 0D 03 06 00 00 00 00 00 00 00  |Z...............|
[1900] 10-27 23:29:06:167:
[1844] 10-27 23:29:06:317: Packet received (37 bytes) for hPort 12
[1900] 10-27 23:29:06:317: >PPP packet received at 10/28/2003 06:29:06:317
[1900] 10-27 23:29:06:317: >Protocol = LCP, Type = Configure-Reject, Length = 0x25,  Id = 0x0,
Port = 12
[1900] 23:29:06:317: >C0 21 04 00 00 23 11 04 06 4E 13 17 01 7D 76 B9  |.!...#...N...}v.|
[1900] 23:29:06:317: >AC E3 6E 49 CF AB 8F 56 0F D8 58 63 6C 00 00 00  |..nI...V..Xcl...|
[1900] 23:29:06:317: >00 17 04 00 04 00 00 00 00 00 00 00 00 00 00 00  |................|
[1900] 10-27 23:29:06:317:
[1900] 10-27 23:29:06:317: RemoveFromTimerQ called portid=8,Id=0,Protocol=c021,
EventType=0,fAuth=0
[1900] 10-27 23:29:06:317: <PPP packet sent at 10/28/2003 06:29:06:317
[1900] 10-27 23:29:06:317: <Protocol = LCP, Type = Configure-Req, Length = 0x1d, Id = 0x1,
Port = 12
[1900] 23:29:06:317: <C0 21 01 01 00 1B 02 06 00 00 00 00 03 04 C2 27  |.!.............'|
[1900] 23:29:06:317: <05 06 7B 56 73 78 07 02 08 02 0D 03 06 00 00 00  |..{Vsx..........|
```

LCP completion.

```
[1900]  10-27 23:29:06:608:
[1900]  10-27 23:29:06:608: RemoveFromTimerQ called portid=8,Id=2,Protocol=c021,EventType=0,fAuth=0
[1900]  10-27 23:29:06:608: FsmThisLayerUp called for protocol = c021, port = 12
[1900]  10-27 23:29:06:608: LCP Local Options-------------
[1900]  10-27 23:29:06:608:    MRU=1500,ACCM=0,Auth=c223,MagicNumber=2069263224,PFC=ON,ACFC=ON
[1900]  10-27 23:29:06:608: Recv Framing = PPP,SSHF=OFF,MRRU=1500,LinkDiscrim=4,BAP=OFF
[1900]  10-27 23:29:06:608: LCP Remote Options-------------
[1900]  10-27 23:29:06:608: MRU=1500,ACCM=0,Auth=0,MagicNumber=488069840,PFC=ON,ACFC=ON
[1900]  10-27 23:29:06:608: Send Framing = PPP,SSHF=OFF,MRRU=1500,LinkDiscrim=0
[1900]  10-27 23:29:06:608: LCP Configured successfully
```

Authentication phase. Note that Challenge Handshake Authentication Protocol (CHAP) has been used to authenticate the user.

```
[1900]  10-27 23:29:06:608: Authenticating phase started
[1900]  10-27 23:29:06:608: Calling APWork in APStart
[1844]  10-27 23:29:06:608: Packet received (20 bytes) for hPort 12
[1900]  10-27 23:29:06:608: <PPP packet sent at 10/28/2004 06:29:06:608
[1900]  10-27 23:29:06:608: <Protocol = CHAP, Type = Protocol specific, Length = 0x20, Id = 0x0,
Port = 12
[1900]  23:29:06:608: <C2 23 01 00 00 1E 10 E2 6A BD 52 C9 1F EC 7D 2B  |.#......j.R...}+|
[1900]  23:29:06:608: <31 B1 92 91 03 C0 29 53 54 55 44 45 4E 54 30 33  |1.....)STUDENT03|
[1900]  10-27 23:29:06:608:
[1900]  10-27 23:29:06:608: Identification packet received
[1900]  10-27 23:29:06:608: Remote identification = MSRASV5.00
[1844]  10-27 23:29:06:608: Packet received (25 bytes) for hPort 12
[1900]  10-27 23:29:06:608: >PPP packet received at 10/28/2004 06:29:06:608
[1900]  10-27 23:29:06:608: >Protocol = LCP, Type = Identification, Length = 0x19, Id = 0x2,
Port = 12
[1900]  23:29:06:608: >C0 21 0C 02 00 17 1D 17 5A D0 4D 53 52 41 53 2D  |.!......Z.MSRAS-|
[1900]  23:29:06:608: >31 2D 4B 52 45 49 44 32 4B 00 00 00 00 00 00 00  |1-KREID2K.......|
[1900]  10-27 23:29:06:608:
[1900]  10-27 23:29:06:608: Identification packet received
[1900]  10-27 23:29:06:608: Remote identification = MSRAS-1-KREID2K
[1844]  10-27 23:29:06:748: Packet received (60 bytes) for hPort 12
[1900]  10-27 23:29:06:748: >PPP packet received at 10/28/2004 06:29:06:748
[1900]  10-27 23:29:06:748: >Protocol = CHAP, Type = Protocol specific, Length = 0x3c, Id = 0x0,
Port = 12
[1900]  23:29:06:748: >C2 23 02 00 00 3A 31 1A DB 6F 90 65 A2 CE BB E2  |.#...:1..o.e....|
[1900]  23:29:06:748: >7D D7 0F EA 83 79 24 00 00 00 00 00 00 00 00 5A  |}....y$........Z|
[1900]  23:29:06:748: >FE 25 A8 68 96 DA C7 0F B1 78 7B 01 FB BD 18 73  |.%.h.....x{....s|
[1900]  23:29:06:748: >F7 2E 91 EB 18 9C C9 00 64 69 61 6C 00 00 00 00  |........dial....|
```

Encryption phase. Microsoft Point to Point Encryption (MPPE) with a strong (128-bit) key is used for this connection.

```
[1900]  10-27 23:29:06:758:
[1900]  10-27 23:29:06:758: Encryption
[1900]  10-27 23:29:06:758: Strong encryption
[1900]  10-27 23:29:06:758: MPPE-Send/Recv-Keys set
[1900]  10-27 23:29:06:758: Auth Attribute Domain = STUDENT03
[1900]  10-27 23:29:06:758: Auth Attribute Idle Timeout Seconds = 0
[1900]  10-27 23:29:06:758: AuthAttribute MaxChannelsAllowed = -1
[1900]  10-27 23:29:06:758: FsmThisLayerUp called for protocol = c223, port = 12
[1900]  10-27 23:29:06:758: NotifyCaller(hPort=12, dwMsgId=17)
[[1900]  10-27 23:29:06:758: <PPP packet sent at 10/28/2004 06:29:06:758
[1900]  10-27 23:29:06:758: <Protocol = CBCP, Type = Protocol specific, Length = 0x8, Id = 0x1,
Port = 12
[1900]  23:29:06:758: <C0 29 01 01 00 06 01 02 00 00 00 00 00 00 00 00  |.)..............|
```

11

Network Control phase. Internet Protocol Control Protocol (IPCP) is the Network Control Protocol used to configure TCP/IP for the connection.

```
[1900] 10-27 23:29:06:938:
[1900] 10-27 23:29:06:938: InsertInTimerQ called portid=8,Id=4,Protocol=80fd,EventType=0,fAuth=0
[1900] 10-27 23:29:06:938: FsmOpen event received for protocol 8021 on port 12
[1900] 10-27 23:29:06:938: FsmThisLayerStarted called for protocol = 8021, port = 12
[1900] 10-27 23:29:06:938: FsmUp event received for protocol 8021 on port 12
[1900] 10-27 23:29:06:938: <PPP packet sent at 10/28/2004 06:29:06:938
[1900] 10-27 23:29:06:938: <Protocol = IPCP, Type = Configure-Req, Length = 0x12, Id = 0x5,
Port = 12
[1900] 23:29:06:938: <80 21 01 05 00 10 02 06 00 2D 0F 01 03 06 C0 A8 |.!.......-......|
[1900] 23:29:06:938: <77 50 00 00 00 00 00 00 00 00 00 00 00 00 00 00 |wP.............|
```

Disconnection phase.

```
[1900] 10-27 23:32:22:159: Line down event occurred on port 12
[1900] 10-27 23:32:22:169: FsmDown event received for protocol c021 on port 12
[1900] 10-27 23:32:22:169: RemoveFromTimerQ called portid=8,Id=2,Protocol=c021,EventType=0,fAuth=0
[1900] 10-27 23:32:22:169: FsmReset called for protocol = c021, port = 12
[1900] 10-27 23:32:22:169: RemoveFromTimerQ called portid=8,Id=0,Protocol=0,EventType=3,fAuth=0
[1900] 10-27 23:32:22:169: RemoveFromTimerQ called portid=8,Id=0,Protocol=0,EventType=7,fAuth=0
[1900] 10-27 23:32:22:169: RemoveFromTimerQ called portid=8,Id=0,Protocol=0,EventType=2,fAuth=0
[1900] 10-27 23:32:22:169: RemoveFromTimerQ called portid=8,Id=0,Protocol=0,EventType=1,fAuth=0
[1900] 10-27 23:32:22:169: RemoveFromTimerQ called portid=8,Id=0,Protocol=0,EventType=4,fAuth=0
[1900] 10-27 23:32:22:169: RemoveFromTimerQ called portid=8,Id=0,Protocol=0,EventType=6,fAuth=0
[1048] 10-27 23:32:22:169: Stopping Accounting for port 12
[1900] 10-27 23:32:22:169: LcpEnd
[1900] 10-27 23:32:24:172: Post line down event occurred on port 12
[1900] 10-27 23:32:24:172: NotifyCaller(hPort=12, dwMsgId=23)
```

8. Close all windows.

Certification Objectives

Objectives for Microsoft Exam #70-293: Planning a Microsoft Windows Server 2003 Network:

- Plan for security monitoring.

REVIEW QUESTIONS

1. RRAS events can be filtered from the event log and saved to a file. True or false?

2. RRAS events will be added to which event log?

   a. Application

   b. Security

   c. System

   d. RRAS

3. If you turn on debug logging, detailed information will be written to which log?

   a. System event

   b. C:\Windows\System32\LogFiles\INyymm.

   c. C:\Windows\Tracing\ppp.

   d. C:\Windows\Modem

4. Where is modem logging activated?

   a. Diagnostics tab of modem properties

   b. RRAS Ports properties

   c. IAS Ports properties

   d. Remote Logging tab of IAS

5. IAS can act as which of the following? (Choose all that apply.)

   a. RADIUS client

   b. RADIUS server

   c. RADIUS proxy

   d. RADIUS redirector

11

LAB 11.5 CONFIGURING ANI/CLI AUTHENTICATION

Objectives

The goal of this lab activity is to learn how to configure authentication by calling number.

Materials Required:

This lab will require the following:

- A Windows Server 2003 system installed and configured according to the instructions at the beginning of this lab manual

Estimated completion time: **30 minutes**

Activity Background

Automatic Number Identification/Calling Line Identification (ANI/CLI) is more commonly known as caller ID. ANI authentication is most commonly used by schools that provide Internet access to students and their families. The concept is to simplify the logon process for the students, which will reduce the amount of technical support required. It involves removing all other forms of authentication and configuring the students' home phone numbers as the user names so that the network is not available from anywhere else.

Activity

1. If necessary, log on as **Administrator** to the Arctic.local domain with a password of **Password!**.

2. To eliminate the domain password policies, you need to remove the server from the domain. Click **Start**, right-click **My Computer**, and then click **Properties**.

3. Click the **Computer Name** tab, and then click **Change**. In the Member of section, click **Workgroup**, type **WORKGROUP**, and then click **OK**. Type **Administrator** as your username and type **Password!** as your password, and then click **OK**. Click **OK** to acknowledge the Welcome window, and then click **OK** to acknowledge the resulting message. Click **OK** to close the System Properties window. Click **Yes** to restart your server.

4. Log in to your server as **Administrator** with a password of **Password!**.

5. Click **Start**, point to **Administrative Tools**, and then click **Computer Management**.

6. Double-click **Local Users and Groups**, right-click **Groups**, and then click **New Group**. In the Group name, type **ANI Users**, click **Create**, click **Close**, and then close the Computer Management window.

7. Click **Start**, point to **Administrative Tools**, and then click **Routing and Remote Access**.

8. Right-click the **StudentXX** server (where *XX* is your student ID) and click **Properties**. Click the **Security** tab, and then click **Authentication Methods**. Click the **Allow remote systems to connect without authentication** check box, as shown in Figure 11-11. Click **OK** to close the Authentication Methods window, and then click **OK** to close the Server Properties window. Click **No** to the warning.

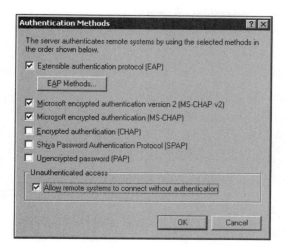

Figure 11-11   Authentication Methods window

9. Expand **ServerXX**, if necessary, right-click **Remote Access Policies**, and then click **New Remote Access Policy**.

10. Click **Next** to start the wizard. Click the **Set up a custom policy** option button, type **ANI Dial-up** in the Policy name text box, and click **Next**.

11. Click **Add**, double-click **Authentication-Type** in the Select Attribute window, double-click **Unauthenticated**, and then click **OK**.

12. Click **Add**, double-click **NAS-Port-Type** in the Select Attribute window, double-click **Async (Modem)**, and then click **OK**.

13. Click **Add**, double-click **Windows-Groups** in the Select Attribute window, click **Add**, type **ANI Users**, and then click **OK**. Click **OK**, and then click **Next**.

14. Click **Grant remote access permission** option button, and then click **Next**.

15. Click **Edit Profile**.

16. On the Dial-In Constraints tab, check the **Minutes server can remain idle before it is disconnected (Idle-Timeout)** check box, and then type **10** in the text box.

17. Check the **Minutes client can be connected (Session-Timeout)** check box, and then type **60** in the text box.

18. Check the **Allow access only on these days and at these times** check box, and then click **Edit**.

19. Click and hold **Sunday 12 a.m.** and drag to Saturday 6 a.m. Click the **Denied** option button. The area turns white (as shown in Figure 11-12) to indicate that access will be denied at that time. Click **OK**.

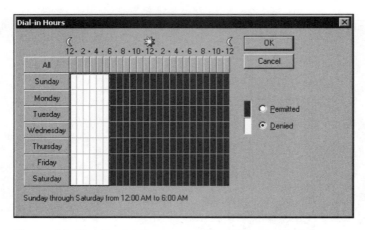

Figure 11-12 Restricting access based on time of day

20. Click the **IP** tab, click **Input Filters**, and then click **New**.

21. In the Add IP Filter window, click the **Protocol** drop-down list arrow, and select **ICMP**. Leave the Source and Destination port blank, and then click **OK**.

22. In the Inbound filters window, click the **Permit only the packets listed below** option button.

23. Click **New** and then, in the Add IP Filter window, click the **Protocol** drop-down list arrow, and select **TCP**. In the Destination port text box, type **80**. Click **OK**.

24. Repeat the previous step to permit the following ports: UDP/53. TCP/25. TCP/110. Figure 11-13 shows a configured inbound filter. This configuration will allow the students to send/receive e-mail and perform basic Web browsing but is restrictive enough that it should disable online games and file sharing applications.

 NOTE

To see a list of common ports and their applications, use Notepad to view the C:\WINDOWS\system32\drivers\etc\services file.

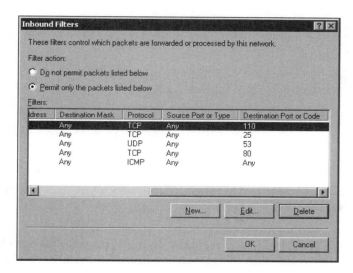

Figure 11-13   Inbound filter configuration

25. Click **OK** to close the Inbound Filters window.

26. Click the **Multilink** tab, and then click the **Do not allow Multilink connections** option button.

27. Click the **Authentication** tab, uncheck the **MS-CHAPv2** & **MS-CHAP** check boxes, and then check the **Allow clients to connect without negotiating an authentication method** check box.

28. Click **OK** to close the Edit Dial-in Profile window. Click **No** to acknowledge the warning.

29. Click **Next** to continue the wizard, and then click **Finish**.

30. A registry change is needed so that ANI data from the telephone company will be used as the user name. Click **Start**, click **Run**, type **regedt32**, and then click **OK**.

31. Navigate to the following registry key: HKEY_LOCAL_MACHINE\ System\CurrentControlSet\Services\RemoteAccess\Policy\.

32. Right-click **Policy**, point to **New**, and then click **DWORD Value**. Type **User Identity Attribute** as the value name, and then press **Enter**.

33. Double-click **User Identity Attribute**. In the Base section, click **Decimal**. In the Value data section, type **31** and click **OK**. The new value will be the same as that shown in Figure 11-14. Close the Registry Editor.

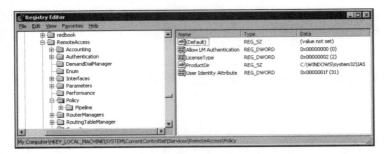

Figure 11-14   Registry entry sets dial-in user name to RADIUS value 31: ANI/CLI

34. The final step is to add users for the connection. Click **Start**, point to **Administrative Tools**, and then click **Computer Management**.

35. Double-click **Local Users and Groups**, click **Users**, right-click **Users**, and click **New User**.

36. In the New User window, you need to type a phone number as the user name. Type **5557654321**, uncheck the **User must change password at next logon** check box (as shown in Figure 11-15), click **Create**, and then click **Close**.

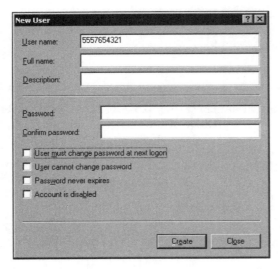

Figure 11-15   Creating an ANI user using a phone number as the user name

37. Double-click the newly created **5557654321** user. Click the **Member Of** tab, click **Add**, type **ANI Users**, and then click **OK**. Click **OK** to close the next window. This user could now dial in to your server from that specific phone number while entering no user name and no password in the dial-up connection. Close all windows.

38. Rejoin the domain in preparation for the next chapter. Click **Start**, right-click **My Computer**, click **Properties**, click the **Computer Name** tab, click **Change**, click **Domain** option button, type **Arctic.local** in the text box, and then click **OK**. Authenticate as **Administrator** with the **Password!** password, and then click **OK**. Click **OK** to acknowledge the confirmation, click **OK** to acknowledge the warning, click **OK** to restart and click **OK** to close System Properties, and then click **Yes** to restart your computer.

Certification Objectives

Objectives for Microsoft Exam #70-293: Planning a Microsoft Windows Server 2003 Network:

- Plan security for remote access users.

- Plan remote access policies.

- Plan authentication methods for remote access clients.

11

REVIEW QUESTIONS

1. RRAS can authenticate on the basis of which of the following?

    a. Automatic Number Identification (ANI)

    b. Calling Line Identification (CLI)

    c. Dialed Number Identification Service (DNIS)

    d. all of the above

2. Which of the following is not a protocol that you can filter?

    a. TCP

    b. FTP

    c. UDP

    d. ICMP

3. What is the common TCP port for HTTP (WWW)?

    a. 110

    b. 53

    c. 80

    d. 8080

4. Which authentication method must be allowed for ANI authentication to function?

    a. MS-CHAPv2

    b. PAP

    c. Unauthenticated

    d. Unauthorized

5. Where can a list of common port numbers be found?

    a. \Windows\System32\drivers\services

    b. \Windows\System32\drivers\etc\services

    c. \Windows\Ports\services

    d. \Windows\System32\Firewall\etc\services

PLANNING AND IMPLEMENTING SERVER AVAILABILITY AND SCALABILITY

Labs included in this chapter:

♦ 12.1 Implementing a Server Cluster for Server Consolidation

♦ 12.2 Creating a Virtual Server

♦ 12.3 Managing Resource Failure and Recovery

♦ 12.4 Managing Server Clusters with Cluster.exe

♦ 12.5 Installing and Managing an NLB Cluster

Microsoft MCSE Exam #70-293 Objectives	
Objective	Lab
Plan services for high availability.	12.1, 12.2, 12.3, 12.4
Plan a high availability solution that uses clustering services.	12.1, 12.2, 12.3, 12.4
Plan a high availability solution that uses Network Load Balancing.	12.5
Implement a cluster server.	12.1, 12.2, 12.3, 12.4
Recover from cluster node failure.	12.1, 12.2, 12.3, 12.4
Manage Network Load Balancing. Tools might include the Network Load Balancing Monitor Management Console (MMC) snap-in and the WLBS cluster control utility.	12.5

Lab 12.1 Implementing a Server Cluster for Server Consolidation

Objectives

The goal of this lab activity is to install a server cluster for the task of server consolidation.

Materials Required

This lab will require the following:

- Windows Server 2003 installed and configured according to the instructions at the beginning of this lab manual

Estimated completion time: **15 minutes**

Activity Background

Server clusters are used to provide highly available services on Windows servers using relatively inexpensive standardized hardware. Most forms of server clustering required shared storage to hold a quorum resource. The quorum resource is used to determine which node in the server cluster owns the server cluster, and to store configuration information for the cluster. A single node virtual server cluster does not use shared storage because there is only one server in the server cluster.

As part of installing a server cluster, you must define a cluster service account that the server logs on to perform its tasks. This account must be a member of the local Administrators group. Membership in the local Administrators group is performed automatically during the installation process.

ACTIVITY

Activity

1. Log on as **Administrator** to the Arctic.local domain with a password of **Password!**.

2. If necessary, disable the Network Load Balancing driver by doing the following:

    a. Click **Start**, point to **Control Panel**, point to **Network Connections**, right-click **Classroom**, and then click **Properties**.

    b. Uncheck the **Network Load Balancing** check box, if necessary, and then click **OK**.

3. If necessary, remove any secondary IP addresses by doing the following:

   a. Click **Start**, point to **Control Panel**, point to **Network Connections**, right-click **Classroom**, and then click **Properties**.

   b. Scroll down the This connection uses the following items list box, and then double-click **Internet Protocol (TCP/IP)**.

   c. Click **Advanced** to view all IP addresses bound to the Classroom connection.

   d. The only IP address that should be bound to this connection is 192.168.1.1*XX*, (where *XX* is your student number). If any other addresses are bound here they must be removed. To remove an IP address from the connection, click the IP address you want to remove, and then click **Remove**. Repeat this to remove all extra IP addresses, and then click **OK**. Close all remaining dialog boxes by clicking **OK**.

4. You next need to create a cluster service account. This is the user account that the cluster service will use to log on.

   a. Click **Start**, click **Run**, type **mmc**, and then click **OK**.

   b. Click the **File** menu, and then click **Add/Remove Snap-in**.

   c. Click **Add**, double-click **Active Directory Users and Computers**, click **Close**, and click **OK**. This adds the snap-in that allows you to manage users in Active Directory.

   d. Double-click **Active Directory Users and Computers** to expand it.

   e. Click **Arctic.local** to select it.

   f. Double-click **Arctic.local** to expand it.

   g. Right-click **Users**, point to **New**, and click **User**.

   h. In the First name text box, type **cluster*XX*** (where *XX* is your student number.)

   i. In the Last name text box, type **user**.

   j. In the User logon name text box, type **clusteruser*XX*** (where *XX* is your student number), and click **Next**.

   k. In the Password text box, type **Password!** and then in the Confirm password box, type **Password!**.

   l. Uncheck the **User must change password at next logon** check box, check the **Password never expires** check box, and then click **Next**. It is a good practice to stop service account passwords from expiring. Otherwise your services may stop working unexpectedly when they can no longer log on. When a password expires the service does not stop working immediately, only the next time the service logs on. Usually this is after a reboot.

   m. Click **Finish**.

   n. Close the MMC. If prompted to save changes, click **No**.

5. Click **Start**, click **Run**, type **cluadmin**, and then press **Enter**.

6. In the Action drop-down list box, select **Create new cluster** and click **OK**.

7. Click **Next** to begin the New Server Cluster Wizard.

8. In the Cluster name text box, type **clusterXX** (where *XX* is your student number), and click **Next**.

9. If necessary, in the Computer name text box, type **StudentXX** (where *XX* is your student number), and then click **Next**. The New Cluster Server Wizard now analyzes whether a cluster is possible.

10. The analysis of your server will generate warning messages. To read these messages, expand the section with error messages. The errors are because you do not have a shared storage system on your server. The error also indicates that a local quorum will be configured. This is normal for a single node virtual server cluster. Click **Next** to continue.

11. In the IP Address text box, type **192.168.1.2XX** (where *XX* is your student number), and then click **Next**.

12. In the User name text box, type **clusteruserXX** (where *XX* is your student number), in the Password text box type **Password!**, and click **Next**.

13. Click **Next** to accept the current configuration. The cluster then begins installation.

14. After the cluster node is installed, a log of the installation process is presented to you. Expand **Reanalyzing cluster**, expand **Finding common resources on nodes**, expand **StudentXX: The following disks will not be managed by the cluster:**, click **StudentXX: The physical disk \\.\PHYSICALDRIVE0 is not a SCSI disk and will not be managed by the cluster**, and then click **Details**.

15. Read the Additional information portion of the Task Details. This text indicates that non–SCSI disks cannot be managed by a cluster, as shown in Figure 12-1. Click **Close** to close the Task Details dialog box.

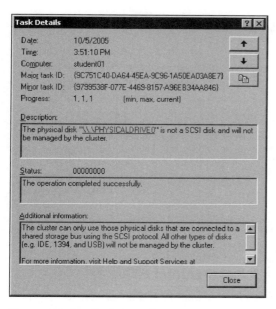

Figure 12-1 Task Details

16. Expand **Configure cluster services**, and then read the tasks in the list. One of these tasks indicates that the cluster service account has been added to the local Administrators group of the cluster node. This gives the cluster service account the necessary privileges to manage and operate the cluster.

17. Click **Next** to continue, and then click **Finish**.

18. Close Cluster Administrator.

19. Click **Start**, point to **Administrative Tools**, and then click **Local Security Policy**.

20. Expand **Local Policies** and click **User Rights Assignment**.

21. In the right pane, read through the list of policies to see which ones have the user ARCTIC\clusteruser*XX* listed. Specifically, view the following rights: Act as part of the operating system, Back up files and directories, Adjust memory quotas for a process, Increase scheduling priority, Log on as a service, and Restore files and directories. These six rights are granted to the cluster service account as part of the installation process.

22. Close the Local Security Settings window.

12

Certification Objectives

Objectives for Microsoft Exam #70-293: Planning a Microsoft Windows Server 2003 Network:

- Plan services for high availability.

- Plan a high availability solution that uses clustering services.

- Implement a cluster server.

- Recover from cluster node failure.

REVIEW QUESTIONS

1. In which group is the cluster service account required to be a member?

    a. Domain Admins

    b. Power Users

    c. Domain Users

    d. Local Users

    e. Local Administrators

2. Which of the following rights are required by the cluster service account? (Choose all that apply.)

    a. Log on locally

    b. Log on as a service

    c. Act as part of the operating system

    d. Increase scheduling priority

    e. Create a token object

3. What type of disk can be managed by the cluster service?

    a. SCSI

    b. IDE

    c. USB

    d. IEEE 1394 (FireWire)

4. As a best practice, which account option should be enabled for service account to prevent unexpected failures?

    a. User must change password at next logon

    b. User cannot change password

    c. Password never expires

    d. Account is disabled

5. If the password for a service account expires, when is the service most likely to experience problems?

    a. after a server reboot

    b. when a service fails over to a new node

    c. when a new node is added to the cluster

    d. when a node is removed from the cluster

LAB 12.2 CREATING A VIRTUAL SERVER

Objectives

The goal of this lab activity is to create a virtual server and resources on a single node virtual server.

Materials Required

This lab will require the following:

- Windows Server 2003 installed and configured according to the instructions at the beginning of this lab manual

- Successful completion of Lab 12.1

Estimated completion time: 15 minutes

Activity Background

When a service fails on a single node virtual server cluster, it does not failover to a new server because there is only one server in the server cluster. This type of server cluster does not provide high availability. A single node virtual server cluster is used when multiple older servers are consolidated onto one newer, more powerful server.

12

When this is done virtual servers are configured with the same name as each older server. File share and print resources are then created on the virtual servers that match the shares on the older servers. All of this is done so that client computers do not need to be reconfigured. They will continue to access resources through exactly the same share names.

Activity

1. Log on as **Administrator** to the Arctic.local domain with a password of **Password!**.

2. Click **Start**, click **Run**, type **cluadmin**, and press **Enter**.

3. Right-click **Groups**, point to **New**, and then click **Group**.

4. In the Name text box, type **OldNTServer**.

5. In the Description text box, type **Resources from NTServer** and click **Next**.

6. In the Available nodes list box, double-click your server, and then click **Finish**.

7. Click **OK** to close the dialog box confirming the successful creation of the cluster group OldNTServer.

8. To start the resource group OldNTServer, right-click **OldNTServer** and then click **Bring Online**.

9. Right-click **Resources**, point to **New**, and then click **Resource**.

10. In the Name text box, type **IP for NTServer**.

11. In the Resource type drop-down list box, select **IP Address**.

12. In the Group drop-down list box, select **OldNTServer** and then click **Next**.

13. Only one server is a possible owner for this resource, as shown in Figure 12-2. This is because there is only one node in a single node virtual server. If more nodes were available in the server cluster, then any node in the cluster could be chosen as a possible owner. Click **Next** to continue.

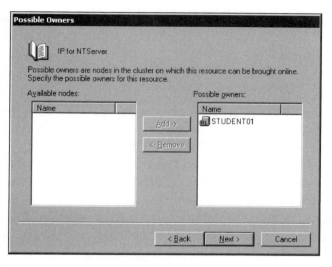

Figure 12-2   Possible owners

14. There are no other resources that can be chosen for dependencies, because this is the first resource being created. Click **Next**.

15. In the Address text box, type **192.168.1.*150+XX*** (where *XX* is your student number). For example, if your student number is 01, you would enter 192.168.1.151.

16. In the Subnet mask text box, type **255.255.255.0**.

17. In the Network drop-down list box, select **Classroom**.

18. If necessary, check the **Enable NetBIOS for this address** check box. If this check box is not enabled then you will not be able to browse the virtual server using this IP address in My Network Places. Click **Finish**.

19. Click **OK** to close the dialog box confirming the successful creation of the resource. Notice that the resource group OldNTServer has automatically been taken offline as the IP address resource was added.

20. Click **Groups** if necessary, right-click **OldNTServer**, and then click **Bring Online**. This brings the resource group and the resources in it online

21. Right-click **Resources**, point to **New**, and then click **Resource**.

22. In the Name text box, type **Cname NTServer**.

23. In the Resource type drop-down list box, select **Network Name**.

24. In the Group drop-down list box, select **OldNTServer** and then click **Next**.

25. Click **Next** to continue, because the only possible owner of the resource is already selected.

26. Network Name resources must be dependent on IP Address resources. Double-click **IP for NTServer** to add it as a resource dependency, and then click **Next**.

27. In the Name text box, type **NTServerXX** (where *XX* is your student number).

28. If necessary, uncheck the **DNS Registration must succeed** check box. If this is checked, the resource will fail if the Network Name is not successfully registered in DNS. This is appropriate if the Network Name is used by applications that rely on DNS name resolution.

29. Check the **Enable Kerberos Authentication** check box to allow Kerberos authentication on the virtual server using this Network Name. If this is not used, only NTLM authentication will be possible. Click **Finish**.

30. Click **OK** to close the dialog box confirming the successful creation of the resource. Notice that the resource group OldNTServer is showing an error state because the new Network Name resource is not online.

31. Right-click **Cname NTServer** and then click **Bring Online**. Notice that the error state for the resource group OldNTServer is gone.

32. Click **OldNTServer** to view the resources that are assigned to it.

33. Close Cluster Administrator.

34. Click **Start**, click **Run**, type **\\NTServerXX** (where *XX* is your student number), and then press **Enter**. A screen appears showing resources available, as shown in Figure 12-3. This confirms that your virtual server is available on the network. Note that the CertEnroll share may not be present on your system.

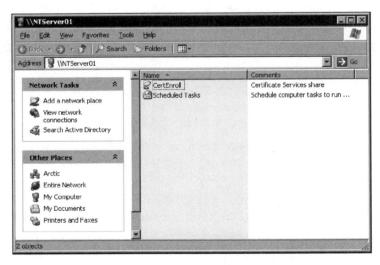

Figure 12-3   Confirming virtual server availability

35. Close the Explorer window.

Certification Objectives

Objectives for Microsoft Exam #70-293: Planning a Microsoft Windows Server 2003 Network:

- Plan services for high availability.

- Plan a high availability solution that uses clustering services.

- Implement a cluster server.

- Recover from cluster node failure.

REVIEW QUESTIONS

1. What is the main reason to create a single node virtual server cluster?

   a. Avoid client reconfiguration during server consolidation.

   b. Provide high availability for file resources.

   c. Scale out by spreading processing across multiple servers.

   d. Reduce service outages.

2. How can you test the availability of a virtual server? (Choose all that apply.)

   a. Access the virtual server via UNC path.

   b. Ping the virtual server.

   c. Access a resource on the virtual server.

   d. View the status of the resource group in Cluster Administrator.

3. Which IP Address resource option controls whether a service will be browsable in My Network Places?

   a. DNS registration must succeed

   b. Enable Kerberos Authentication

   c. Enable NetBIOS for this address

   d. Enable browsing for this address

4. Which type of authentication is enabled for server clusters by default?

   a. Kerberos

   b. NTLM

   c. smart cards

   d. certificates

12

    5. On what resource is a Network Name dependent?

      a. resource group

      b. quorum

      c. file share

      d. IP address

LAB 12.3 MANAGING RESOURCE FAILURE AND RECOVERY

Objectives

The goal of this lab activity is to manage the failure of a File Share resource.

Materials Required

This lab will require the following:

- Windows Server 2003 installed and configured according to the instructions at the beginning of this lab manual

- Successful completion of Lab 12.2

Estimated completion time: **15 minutes**

Activity Background

File shares are one of the most important resources available within an organization. Making file shares highly available on a cluster can contribute significantly to organizational performance. Imagine the wasted staff hours if your file shares were unavailable for an hour or two. For large organizations this can cost hundreds of thousands of dollars.

It is important to understand how clustered file shares work so that you understand what users will see if a clustered file share fails. In this lab you create a file share resource on your single node virtual server. This does not allow you to see failover from one node to another, but it will allow you to view the effect of failed resources.

ACTIVITY

Activity

1. Log on as **Administrator** to the Arctic.local domain with a password of **Password!**.

2. Click **Start**, click **Run**, type **cmd**, and then press **Enter**.

3. Type **md c:\datafiles**, press **Enter**, and then close the Command Prompt window.

4. Click **Start**, click **Run**, type **cluadmin**, and then press **Enter**.

5. Right-click **Resources**, point to **New**, and then click **Resource**.

6. In the Name text box, type **Datafiles for NTServer**.

7. In the Resource type drop-down list box, select **File Share**. You may have to scroll up to see the File Share resource type.

8. In the Group drop-down list box, select **OldNTServer** and then click **Next**.

9. Click **Next** to continue because the only possible owner of the resource is already selected.

10. To add it as a dependency, double-click **Cname for NTServer**. You could also add the IP resource as a resource dependency, but because the Network Name resource is dependent on it, adding the resource would be redundant. In a high availability situation, you would also add the physical disk holding the files as a dependent resource. A physical disk resource represents shared storage. Click **Next**.

11. In the Share name text box, type **Datafiles**.

12. In the Path text box, type **c:\datafiles**.

13. Click **Permissions** to view the default permissions. By default the Everyone group is assigned read permission. This is overly cautious. NTFS permissions should be used to control access to the files in the share.

14. Under Allow, check the **Full Control** check box. This is a more standard permission to apply for file system access. If preferred, you can use the Authenticated Users group instead of Everyone. The Authenticated Users group is all users that have logged on to the domain or a trusted domain. The Everyone group includes anyone, including anonymous users. Click **OK**.

15. Click **Advanced**. This shows three different ways that shares can be configured, as shown in Figure 12-4. Normal share is a standard file share like that which is created when you right-click on a directory and click Sharing. Dfs root is used when you would like the root of a stand-alone DFS (distributed file systems) structure to be fault tolerant. Share subdirectories specifies that each subdirectory should be configured as a separate file share. This is useful for user home directories or profiles directories. When Share subdirectories is selected, then you also have the option to specify that all of the shares created for the subdirectories are hidden shares with "$" appended to the end of the share name. Click **Cancel**.

Figure 12-4   File share parameters

16. Click **Caching**. This allows you to set the same file caching options available with a regular Windows file share. The default setting allows caching of files, but users must manually choose which files to cache. When failover of a file share occurs, users are disconnected from the file. They must then reconnect when the file share becomes available on the new server. This could result in lost data. If the file is cached, users can continue working on the cached copy of the file and no data will be lost. Click **Cancel**.

17. Click **Finish** and click **OK**.

18. Right-click **Datafiles for NTServer** and click **Bring Online**.

19. Right-click **IP for NTServer**, and click **Properties**.

20. Click the **Dependencies** tab. Notice that there are no dependencies for this resource.

21. Click the **Advanced** tab. Notice that by default when this resource fails it will attempt to restart. In addition, if this resource fails then the group will fail. Finally, if this resource fails three times within 900 seconds (15 minutes), then it will not restart. Click **Cancel**.

22. Click **OldNTServer** in the left pane to select it, right-click **IP for NTServer**, and then click **Initiate Failure**. Notice that all three resources change to the state Online Pending and then Online. This is because they are automatically recovering from the failure. All three resources are affected because Datafiles for NTServer is dependent on Cname for NTServer, and Cname for NTServer is dependent on IP for NTServer.

23. Repeat Step 22 two more times or until the status of IP for NTServer remains failed. Notice that the status of both Cname for NTServer and Datafiles for NTServer are now Offline. If this were a multinode server cluster the OldNTServer resource group would not failover to another server.

24. Right-click **IP for NTServer** and then click **Bring Online**. Notice that this resource comes online, but other resources that depend on it do not come online automatically.

25. Right-click **OldNTServer** and then click **Bring Online**. Notice that bringing the resource group online brings all of the resources in that resource group online. Close Cluster Administrator.

Certification Objectives

Objectives for Microsoft Exam #70-293: Planning a Microsoft Windows Server 2003 Network:

- Plan services for high availability.

- Plan a high availability solution that uses clustering services.

- Implement a cluster server.

- Recover from cluster node failure.

REVIEW QUESTIONS

1. How can you allow users uninterrupted access to file shares?

   a. Create a file share resource.

   b. Create a file share resource and cache the files.

   c. Create a disk resource.

   d. Enable connection retention.

2. In what situations might you want to share all of the subfolders in a directory being used for a file share resource? (Choose all that apply.)

   a. user home directories

   b. data directories

   c. directories holding printer drivers

   d. user profile directories

3. What Advanced File Share property would you select for data files?

   a. Normal share

   b. Dfs root

   c. Share subdirectories

   d. Hide subdirectory shares

4. What happens the first time a resource fails?

   a. The cluster service attempts to restart it.

   b. All dependent resources fail.

   c. The resource migrates to another node.

   d. The resource group migrates to another node.

12

5. For a highly available file share, what should be configured as dependencies? (Choose all that apply.)

   a. a Network Name resource

   b. an IP Address resource

   c. a Physical Disk resource

   d. a Local Quorum resource

LAB 12.4 MANAGING SERVER CLUSTERS WITH CLUSTER.EXE

Objectives

The goal of this lab activity is to manage a server cluster using cluster.exe.

Materials Required

This lab will require the following:

- Windows Server 2003 installed and configured according to the instructions at the beginning of this lab manual

- Successful completion of Lab 12.3

Estimated completion time: **10 minutes**

Activity Background

In most cases you will want to perform cluster management with the GUI utility Cluster Administrator (cluadmin.exe). However, there may be times when a GUI utility is not appropriate. For example, using scripts to perform configuration, or very slow WAN links, may require a non-GUI utility.

Cluster.exe is a command-line utility that can be used to create, configure, and administer server clusters. It is available on all computers running Windows Server 2003. You can use it to manage local and remote cluster nodes running Windows NT 4 Server, Windows 2000 Server, and Windows Server 2003.

When performing remote management using cluster.exe, the default locale on the remote computer must be the same as on the local computer. In addition, NetBIOS over TCP/IP (NetBT) must be enabled on the client running cluster.exe.

Activity

1. Log on as **Administrator** to the Arctic.local domain with a password of **Password!**.

2. Click **Start**, click **Run**, type **cmd**, and press **Enter**.

3. Type **cluster /?** and press **Enter** to view the list of options available for the cluster command. You need to scroll up in the command prompt window to see all of the options.

4. Type **cluster /prop** and press **Enter** to view the properties of the cluster.

5. Type **cluster node /?** and press **Enter** to view the list of options available to manage a node.

6. Type **cluster node /stat** and press **Enter** to view the status of the node.

7. Type **cluster node /prop** and press **Enter** to view the properties of the node.

8. Type **cluster node /pause** and press **Enter** to pause your node in your server cluster. This can be useful for maintenance on the node.

9. Type **cluster node /resume** and press **Enter** to start your node again after pausing it.

10. Type **cluster group /?** and press **Enter** to view the cluster resource group options.

11. Type **cluster group OldNTServer /stat** and press **Enter** to view the status of the resource group.

12. Type **cluster group OldNTServer /prop** and press **Enter** to view the properties of the resource group.

13. Type **cluster group OldNTServer /off** and press **Enter** to take the resource group offline.

14. Type **cluster group OldNTServer /on** and press **Enter** to put the resource group online.

15. Type **cluster node StudentXX /evict** (where *XX* is your student number) and press **Enter** to remove the cluster from your server.

16. Type **cluster /prop** and press **Enter** to view the properties of the cluster. You receive an error message because Cluster Services is no longer configured on your server.

17. Close the Command Prompt window.

Certification Objectives

Objectives for Microsoft Exam #70-293: Planning a Microsoft Windows Server 2003 Network:

- Plan services for high availability.

- Plan a high availability solution that uses clustering services.

- Implement a cluster server.

■ Recover from cluster node failure.

REVIEW QUESTIONS

1. What must be configured to allow remote management of a cluster using cluster.exe? (Choose all that apply.)

   a. The default locale must be the same on the local and remote computer..

   b. NetBIOS over TCP/IP must be configured on the computer running cluster.exe.

   c. NetBIOS over TCP/IP must be configured on the cluster node being managed.

   d. A secondary IP address must be added to the cluster for remote management.

2. On what operating systems can cluster.exe manage clusters? (Choose all that apply.)

   a. Windows NT 3.5 Server

   b. Windows NT 4.0 Server

   c. Windows 2000 Server

   d. Windows Server 2003

3. Which of the following might be a reason you would choose to use cluster.exe rather than Cluster Administrator to manage a server cluster? (Choose all that apply.)

   a. You are accessing the cluster across very slow WAN links.

   b. You are running the cluster node in safe mode.

   c. You are using scripts to perform cluster maintenance.

   d. You are performing maintenance while in the recovery console.

4. Which command makes all of the resources in a resource group available if they are offline?

   a. cluster group *resourcegroup* /on

   b. cluster resourcegroup *resourcegroup* /on

   c. cluster group *resourcegroup* /online

   d. cluster resource group *resourcegroup* /online

    5. Which command removes a node from the server cluster?

       a. cluster *nodename* /evict

       b. cluster node *nodename* /evict

       c. cluster *nodename* /remove

       d. cluster node *nodename* /eject

LAB 12.5 INSTALLING AND MANAGING AN NLB CLUSTER

Objectives

The goal of this lab activity is to install and manage a Network Load Balancing (NLB) cluster.

Materials Required

This lab will require the following:

- Windows Server 2003 installed and configured according to the instructions at the beginning of this lab manual

- A server cluster is not configured on your server

- A partner to complete the exercise with. If a partner is not available you can play the role of both partners by using two student servers

12

Estimated completion time: **15 minutes**

Activity Background

A variety of different tools can be used to manage a NLB cluster. Network Load Balancing Manger is a GUI utility that can create and manage NLB clusters. In most cases this is the most appropriate and easiest tool to use. However, there is also a command-line program called nlb.exe that can be used to manage NLB clusters.

When nlb.exe is used to manage the NLB cluster from a computer that is not a host in the NLB cluster, then the NLB cluster must be configured for remote control. Enabling remote control is a potential security risk. Microsoft recommends that you use Network Load Balancing Manager to manager your NLB cluster rather than nlb.exe. Nlb.exe is a replacement for wlbs.exe, which was found in Windows NT.

Activity

1. Both partners complete the steps in this lab unless otherwise noted. Log on as **Administrator** to the Arctic.local domain with a password of **Password!**.

To be completed by Partner One only:

1. Click **Start**, click **Run**, type **nlbmgr**, and press **Enter**.

2. Click the **Cluster** menu and then click **New**.

3. In the IP address text box, type **192.168.1.2YY** (where *YY* is the group number assigned to you and your partner by your instructor).

4. In the Subnet mask text box, type **255.255.255.0**.

5. In the Full Internet name text box, type **nlbYY.arctic.local** (where *YY* is the group number assigned to you and your partner by your instructor).

6. Select the **Multicast** option button, and then click **Next**.

7. You do not need to add any additional IP addresses to the cluster at this time. Click **Next** to continue.

8. Click **Add** to create a new port rule, as shown in Figure 12-5.

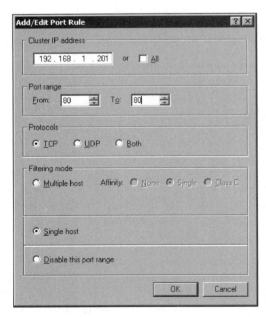

Figure 12-5   Add/Edit Port Rule dialog box

9. To assign this port rule to a single IP address, uncheck the **All** check box, and in the IP address text box, type **192.168.1.2YY** (where *YY* is the group number assigned to you and your partner by your instructor). This is appropriate if the service you are load balancing is available on only one IP address.

10. In the Port range From text box, type **80**, and then in the Port range To text box, type **80**. This setting is appropriate if you are load balancing a Web application that uses port 80.

11. In the Protocols section, select the **TCP** option button. Notice that UDP and Both are other available options. Applications must support TCP or UDP to be load balanced.

12. In the Filtering mode section, select the **Single host** option button. This would be appropriate if you wanted client requests to the NLB cluster directed only to the host with the highest priority. When this is selected, high availability is achieved but the load is not spread among multiple hosts.

13. Click **OK**.

14. Click **Next**.

15. In the Host text box, type **192.168.1.1XX** (where *XX* is your student number), and click **Connect**.

16. After connecting, both interfaces in your server will be listed. Click **Classroom** and then click **Next**. If you receive a message indicating that the interface is already configured as part of another cluster, click **OK** to reconfigure it.

17. In the Priority (unique host identifier) drop-down list box, select **10**. This allows you to add additional hosts with a higher priority later if necessary. If you accepted the default of 1, then this host would always be the one accepting client connections for TCP port 80 on the IP address 192.168.1.2*YY* (where *YY* is your group number).

18. Click **Finish**.

To be completed by Partner Two only:

1. Click **Start**, click **Run**, type **cmd**, and then press **Enter**.

2. Type **nlb query 192.168.1.2YY** (where *YY* is your group number), and press **Enter**. You get an error indicating there is no response. This is because remote control has not been enabled.

To be completed by Partner One only:

1. Right-click your cluster and click **Cluster Properties**.

2. Check the **Allow remote control** check box, and then click **Yes** to acknowledge the warning about security.

3. In both the Remote password and Confirm password text boxes, type **Password!** and then click **OK**.

4. Click **Yes** to confirm the changes.

To be completed by Partner Two only:

1. Type **nlb query 192.168.1.2*YY* /passw Password!** (where *YY* is your group number), and press **Enter**. This time you will get a status response back from the cluster.

To be completed by Partner One only:

1. Right-click your cluster and click **Cluster Properties**.

2. Uncheck the **Allow remote control** check box, and then click **OK**.

3. Click **Yes** to confirm the changes.

To be completed by Partner One only:

1. Right-click the cluster and click **Add Host to Cluster**.

2. In the Host text box, type **192.168.1.1*ZZ*** (where *ZZ* is your partner's student number), and then click **Connect**.

3. Click the **Classroom** interface, and the click **Next**. If you receive a message indicating that the interface is already configured as part of another cluster, click **OK** to reconfigure it.

4. In the Priority (unique host identifier) drop-down list box, select **5**. Notice that the Priority (unique host identifier) drop-down list box does not allow you to select the value 10 because it is already used by your server. Click **Finish**. When both hosts show a status of converged, the addition is complete. You may need to refresh the screen in order to see the updated status.

5. Close Network Load Balancing Manager.

To be completed by both partners:

1. If necessary, open a Command Prompt window. Click **Start**, click **Run**, type **cmd**, and then press **Enter**.

2. Type **nlb query** and press **Enter**. This shows the current status of the local host in the cluster.

3. Type **nlb drainstop** and press **Enter**. This stops servicing new client connections on the local host and after all client requests are finished, the host stops. This is the best way to stop a host in a cluster so that client connections are not affected.

4. Type **nlb start** and press **Enter**. This restarts NLB on the local host.

5. Type **nlb stop** and press **Enter**. This stops NLB with no regard to existing client connections.

6. Type **nlb start** and press **Enter**. This restarts NLB on the local host.

7. Type **nlb display** and press **Enter**. This displays configuration information about the cluster including the cluster IP address, cluster MAC address, and port rules. This information is queried from the registry and may not reflect the current configuration if the cluster service needs to be restarted for a setting to take effect.

8. Type **nlb params** and press **Enter**. This displays configuration information about the cluster but queries the information directly from the NLB driver.

9. Type **nlb ip2mac 192.168.1.2***YY* (where *YY* is your group number), and press **Enter**. This displays the MAC addresses that are used for the cluster when various cluster operation modes are used.

10. Close the Command Prompt window.

To be completed by Partner Two only:

1. Click **Start**, click **Run**, type **nlbmgr**, and press **Enter**.

2. Click the **Cluster** menu, and then click **Connect to Existing**.

3. In the Host text box, type **192.168.0.1***XX* (where *XX* is your student number), click **Connect**, and then click **Finish**.

4. Right-click your cluster and click **Delete Cluster**.

5. Click **Yes** to confirm removing Network Load Balancing.

6. Close Network Load Balancing Manager.

Certification Objectives

Objectives for Microsoft Exam #70-293: Planning a Microsoft Windows Server 2003 Network:

- Plan a high availability solution that uses Network Load Balancing.

- Manage Network Load Balancing. Tools might include the Network Load Balancing Monitor MS Management Console (MMC) snap-in and the WLBS cluster control utility.

REVIEW QUESTIONS

1. Which of the following does nlb.exe replace?

    a. wlbs.exe

    b. wnlb.exe

    c. nlbmgr.exe

    d. lbs.exe

2. What parameter controls which cluster host receives packets addressed to the cluster when an NLB cluster operates in Single host filtering mode?

   a. weight

   b. affinity

   c. priority

   d. port number

3. Which nlb.exe command stops new client connections from being accepted, but allows existing client connections to finish?

   a. nlb stop

   b. nlb pause

   c. nlb drainstop

   d. nlb finish

4. Which nlb.exe command is used to view NLB cluster configuration information directly from the NLB driver rather than the registry?

   a. nlb query direct

   b. nlb display

   c. nlb query driver

   d. nlb params

5. A port rule is configured with the filtering mode single. Server1 is configured with a priority of 10, Server2 is configured with a priority of 20, and Server3 is configured with a priority of 30. What percentage of client requests will Server3 receive?

   a. 0%

   b. 30%

   c. 50%

   d. 100%

13

PLANNING SERVER AND NETWORK SECURITY

Labs included in this chapter:

♦ 13.1 Auditing Logons and File Access

♦ 13.2 Security Templates and Group Policy

♦ 13.3 Implementing SSL on a Web Server

♦ 13.4 Software Update Service

♦ 13.5 Microsoft Baseline Security Analyzer

Microsoft MCSE Exam #70-293 Objectives	
Objective	**Lab**
Plan a secure baseline installation.	13.2, 13.4
Plan security for servers that are assigned specific roles. Roles might include domain controllers, Web servers, database servers, and mail servers.	13.1, 13.2, 13.3
Configure network protocol security.	13.2, 13.3
Plan security for data transmission.	13.2, 13.3
Plan a framework for planning and implementing security.	13.1, 13.2, 13.4, 13.5
Plan a security update infrastructure. Tools might include Microsoft Baseline Security Analyzer and Microsoft Software Update Services.	13.4, 13.5

LAB 13.1 AUDITING LOGONS AND FILE ACCESS

Objectives

The goal of this lab activity is to audit user logons and file access.

Materials Required

This lab will require the following:

- Windows Server 2003 installed and configured according to the instructions at the beginning of this manual

Estimated completion time: **15 minutes**

Activity Background

Auditing is a valuable source of information about the activity on a computer system. A wide variety of information can be monitored, including successful and failed attempts to access files, log on, and access Active Directory objects.

The events generated by auditing are stored in the security log. The default size of the security log is only 16 MB for Windows Server 2003 servers. However, this may be too small for busy servers and can be expanded.

Select only very specific information to audit. If too much information is collected, then it is difficult to find the events you are concerned about. In addition, excessive auditing can place a load on the server and reduce server performance.

Activity

1. Log on as **Administrator** to the Arctic.local domain with a password of **Password!**.

2. Click **Start**, right-click **My Computer**, and then click **Manage**.

3. In the left pane, double-click **Local Users and Groups** to expand it, and then click **Users**.

4. Right-click **Users** and click **New User**.

5. In the User name text box, type **Audit**, type **Password!** in the Password text box, type **Password!** in the Confirm password text box, uncheck the **User must change password at next logon** check box, click **Create**, and then click **Close**.

6. In the left pane, click **Event Viewer**. The event logs available on your server are displayed. All Windows Server 2003 servers have at least three logs: Application, Security, and System. DNS servers have a DNS Server log, and domain controllers have a File Replication Service log and Directory Service log. Auditing events are written to the Security log.

7. Right-click the Security log, and then click **Properties**.

8. On the General tab, type **32000** in the Maximum log size text box to change the maximum size of the security log to 32 MB.

9. Click the **Do not overwrite events (clear log manually)** option button. When a security breach occurs, it is important that all records of the attack are retained. Configuring the log to be cleared manually ensures that a hacker cannot generate a high number of security events and push the events that record his attack out of the log.

10. Click **Clear Log** and click **No** to uncheck the log without saving it. Clearing the Security log will make it easier to see the event generated later in the lab. Click **OK**.

11. Click **Start**, point to **Administrative Tools**, and then click **Local Security Policy**.

12. If necessary, double-click **Local Policies** in the left pane to expand it, and then click **Audit Policy**. Notice that by default both successful account logon events and successful logon events are audited, as shown in Figure 13-1. Account logon events are only relevant to domain controllers and track domain logon events. Logon events track authentication events each time a user connects to a server. This is independent of logging on to the domain. Each time you access a server a logon event occurs even if you are already authenticated to the domain.

13

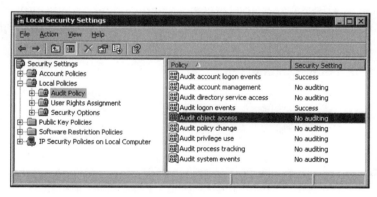

Figure 13-1   Audit configuration

13. Double-click **Audit object access**. Object access is used to track file system and printing access. The file system must be formatted as NTFS (NT file system) to perform auditing.

14. Check the **Failure** check box, and then click **OK**. This option enables the tracking of unsuccessful attempts to access files.

15. Close the Local Security Settings window.

16. Click **Start**, right-click **My Computer**, and then click **Explore**.

17. Click **Local Disk (C:)** in the left pane, right-click an empty area in the right pane (anywhere that you see white), point to **New**, and then click **Text Document**.

18. Type **audit.txt** and press **Enter** to rename the file.

19. Right-click **audit.txt** and then click **Properties**.

20. Click the **Security** tab and then click **Advanced**.

21. On the Permissions tab, uncheck the **Allow inheritable permissions from the parent to propagate to this object and all child object. Include these with entries explicitly defined here** check box, and then click **Remove**. This option removes all permissions except Full Control for the local Administrators group.

22. Click the **Auditing** tab, click **Add**, type **Everyone**, click **Check Names**, and then click **OK**.

23. In the Auditing Entry for audit.txt dialog box, check the **Failed** check box for Read Permissions, and then click **OK** three times.

24. Close the Explorer window, and then log off as Administrator.

25. Log on as the local user **Audit** using the password of **Password!**.

26. Click **Start**, right-click **My Computer**, and then click **Explore**.

27. Click **Local Disk (C :)** in the left pane, and then double-click **audit.txt** in the right pane.

28. Click **OK** to close the error message, and then close Notepad.

29. Close the Explorer window, and log off as Audit.

30. Log on as **Administrator** to the Arctic.local domain with a password of **Password!**.

31. Click **Start**, right-click **My Computer**, and then click **Manage**.

32. Click **Event Viewer** in the left pane, and then in the right pane, double-click **Security**. Notice that even though only one file open attempt was made, there are several Failure Audit events in the security log. Several audit events are created because the system actually performs several tasks in the background as part of opening a file. Also notice that the category for these events is Object Access.

33. Double-click the most recent Failure Audit event. Read the description of the event. The Object Name is C:\audit.txt, indicating the file that it applies to. The primary user name is Audit, indicating the user that attempted to access the file.

34. Click **Cancel** to close the event.

35. Close Computer Management.

Certification Objectives

Objectives for Microsoft Exam #70-293: Planning a Microsoft Windows Server 2003 Network:

- Plan security for servers that are assigned specific roles. Roles might include domain controllers, Web servers, database servers, and mail servers.

- Plan a framework for planning and implementing security.

REVIEW QUESTIONS

1. What audit category logs user authentication attempts only to domain controllers?

   a. object access

   b. system events

   c. logon events

   d. account logon events

2. Which event log records the events generated by auditing?

   a. Active Directory

   b. Security

   c. Audit

   d. System

3. Which audit category is enabled by default?

   a. failure account logon events

   b. success logon events

   c. success privileged use

   d. failure system events

13

4. What is the default size of a member server event log?

   a. 512 KB

   b. 2 MB

   c. 4 MB

   d. 8 MB

   e. 16 MB

5. Which utility can be used to configure auditing on a member server?

   a. Computer Management

   b. Active Directory Users and Computers

   c. Local Security Policy

   d. Active Directory Sites and Services

Lab 13.2 Security Templates and Group Policy

Objectives

The goal of this lab activity is to apply security templates using Group Policy.

Materials Required

This lab will require the following:

- Windows Server 2003 installed and configured according to the instructions at the beginning of this manual

- An organizational unit with your server as the only computer object in it

Estimated completion time: **15 minutes**

Activity Background

Security templates are an excellent tool for defining, analyzing, and configuring security settings. Using a security policy, you can define what security settings are required for your servers and workstations in a security template.

After the security settings are stored in a security template, they can be compared to existing settings on a workstation or server by using the Security Configuration and Analysis snap-in or the Secedit.exe command-line utility.

If the results of the comparison indicate that the security settings on a workstation or server are inadequate, then the settings from the security template can be imported. To make the application of security templates easier, they can be applied to hundreds or thousands of computers at a time using Group Policy.

Activity

1. Log on as **Administrator** to the Arctic.local domain with a password of **Password!**.

2. Click **Start**, click **Run**, type **mmc**, and then press **Enter**.

3. Click **File**, click **Add/Remove Snap-in**, click **Add**, double-click **Security Templates**, click **Close**, and then click **OK**.

4. In the left pane, double-click **Security Templates** to expand it, and then double-click **C:\WINDOWS\security\templates**. This shows the security templates that exist by default on Windows Server 2003, as shown in Figure 13-2. The templates with names ending in "dc" are designed for domain controllers. The templates with names ending in "ws" are designed for workstations and member servers.

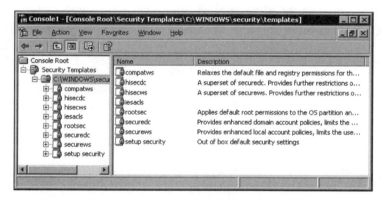

Figure 13-2   Default security templates

5. Right-click **C:\WINDOWS\security\templates**, and then click **New Template**.

6. In the Template name text box, type **Restrict Administrators** and then click **OK**.

7. In the right pane, double-click **Restrict Administrators**, and then double-click **Restricted Groups**. Restricted groups are used to control the membership of groups. When a security template is applied, all members of the group that are not listed in the restricted group are removed.

8. Right-click **Restricted Groups** and then click **Add Group**.

9. In the Group text box, type **Administrators** and then click **OK**.

13

10. Click **Add Members**.

11. In the Members of this group text box, type **Domain Admins** and then click **OK**.

12. Click **Add Members**.

13. In the Members of this group text box, type **StudentXX\Administrator** (where *XX* is your student number), and then click **OK**.

14. Click **OK** to close the Administrators Properties dialog box.

15. Close the MMC. If asked to save the console settings, click **No**.

16. Click **Yes** to save your new security template.

17. Click **Start**, right-click **My Computer**, and then click **Manage**.

18. In the left pane, double-click **Local Users and Groups** and then click **Groups**.

19. In the right pane, double-click **Administrators**.

20. Click **Add**, type **Guest**, click **Check Names**, click **OK**, and then click **OK**. This adds the user guest to the local Administrators group. Guest will be removed from the membership by the restricted group security option later in this lab.

21. Close the Computer Management window.

22. Click **Start**, click **Run**, type **cmd**, and then press **Enter**.

23. Type **secedit /?** and then press **Enter**. This lists the options available when using the Secedit utility, as shown in Figure 13-3. The /configure option is used to apply the security settings in a database. The /analyze option is used to compare the local security settings with the settings in a database. The /import options is used to import settings from a security template into a database. The /export option is used to export settings from a database to a security template. The /validate option is used to verify the syntax of a security template. The /generaterollback option is used to generate a security template that can roll back the settings of a specified template.

Figure 13-3   Secedit help

24. Type **secedit /analyze /db c:\security.sdb /cfg "c:\windows\security \templates\Restrict Administrators.inf" /overwrite /log c:\security.log** and then press **Enter**. The /db option specifies the name of the database to be used during the analysis. The /cfg option specifies a security template to be imported into the database. The /overwrite option specifies that old information in the database should be overwritten. The /log option specifies the name of a log file.

25. Type **notepad c:\security.log** and press **Enter**. This opens the security.log file in Notepad.

26. Scroll down the Notepad window to the section Analyze Group Membership. Notice that below the Analyze Administrators line, a mismatch is indicated.

27. Close Notepad and then close the Command Prompt window.

28. Click **Start**, click **Run**, type **mmc**, and then press **Enter**.

29. Click **File**, click **Add/Remove Snap-in**, click **Add**, double-click **Active Directory Users and Computers**, click **Close**, and then click **OK**.

30. Expand **Active Directory Users and Computers**, expand **Arctic.local**, and then click **OU*XX*** (where *XX* is your student number). This is the organizational unit (OU) that contains the computer object for your server.

31. Right-click **OU*XX***, click **Properties**, and then click the **Group Policy** tab.

32. Click **New**, type **Restricted*XX*** (where *XX* is your student number), and then press **Enter**.

33. Click **Edit**.

34. In the left pane, expand **Windows Settings** under Computer Configuration, right-click **Security Settings**, and then click **Import Policy**.

35. Double-click **Restrict Administrators.inf**.

36. Close the Group Policy Object Editor window, and then click **Close**.

37. Close MMC. If prompted to save the console settings, click **No**.

38. Click **Start**, click **Run**, type **gpupdate /force**, and press **Enter**. The /force option reapplies all policy settings rather than only the settings that have changed.

39. Click **Start**, right-click **My Computer**, and then click **Manage**.

40. In the left pane, double-click **Local Users and Groups** and then click **Groups**.

41. In the right pane, double-click **Administrators**. Notice that the group membership now matches what you specified in the restricted group.

42. Click **OK** and then close the Computer Management window.

13

Certification Objectives

Objectives for Microsoft Exam #70-293: Planning a Microsoft Windows Server 2003 Network:

- Plan a secure baseline installation.

- Plan security for servers that are assigned specific roles. Roles might include domain controllers, Web servers, database servers, and mail servers.

- Configure network protocol security.

- Plan security for data transmission.

- Plan a framework for planning and implementing security.

REVIEW QUESTIONS

1. Which option can be used with the Gpupdate utility to reapply all policy settings rather than only the changed settings?

   a. /all

   b. /enforce

   c. /force

   d. /complete

2. Which option can be used with the Secedit utility to compare the settings in a security template with the local computer?

   a. /analyze

   b. /compare

   c. /validate

   d. /export

3. What must be done with a security template before Secedit and the Security Configuration and Analysis snap-in can perform an analysis?

   a. It must be copied to C:\WINDOWS\security\templates.

   b. It must be validated.

   c. The Everyone group must be given Read NTFS permission.

   d. It must be imported into a database.

4. Which method is the best to use when distributing security settings to many computers?

   a. editing the registry with Regedit

   b. importing a security template into Group Policy

   c. applying a security template using Secedit

   d. applying a security template using the Security Configuration and Analysis snap-in

5. What file extension is used for security templates?

   a. .dc

   b. .ws

   c. .sec

   d. .inf

LAB 13.3 IMPLEMENTING SSL ON A WEB SERVER

Objectives

The goal of this lab activity is to implement SSL on a Web server to secure communication.

Materials Required

This lab will require the following:

- Windows Server 2003 installed and configured according to the instructions at the beginning of this manual

- IIS installed

Estimated completion time: **15 minutes**

Activity Background

Many companies are starting to use Web servers to implement complex applications that are available to internal and external users. Web servers support several authentication methods, but only basic authentication is guaranteed to work with all Web browsers. The problem with basic authentication is that it transmits both the user name (or ID) and password in clear text. This format makes this information susceptible to hackers with packet sniffers.

To secure basic authentication, you can use Secure Sockets Layer (SSL). SSL encrypts all network traffic between the Web browser and Web server. However, the Web server must have a certificate installed to use SSL.

13

The certificate used by the Web server can be issued by an internal certification authority (CA) or a third party CA. An internal CA offers the advantage of being free to use. Certificate Services can be installed on Windows Server 2003 to make it a CA. However, an internal CA is not automatically trusted by Web browsers. For internal workstations, this can be fixed by installing the internal CA's certificate as a trusted CA on all of the workstations. However, this is not feasible for anonymous Internet users. If your Web server is accessed by Internet users, you should use a third party CA that is trusted automatically by Web browsers.

On a Web server with SSL enabled, you can add an additional layer of security using client certificates. User certificates can be installed on client computers, and those certificates mapped to user accounts. Then, when users access the Web site, they are authenticated based on the certificate rather than a user name and password.

ACTIVITY

Activity

1. Log on as **Administrator** to the Arctic.local domain with a password of **Password!**.

2. If necessary, remove Certificate Services by doing the following:

   a. Click **Start**, point to **Control Panel**, and then click **Add or Remove Programs**.

   b. Click **Add/Remove Windows Components**.

   c. Uncheck the **Certificate Services** check box, and then click **Next**.

   d. Click **Finish** and close Add or Remove Programs.

3. Install Certificate Services by doing the following:

   a. Click **Start**, point to **Control Panel**, and then click **Add or Remove Programs**.

   b. Click **Add/Remove Windows Components**.

   c. Check the **Certificate Services** check box, click **Yes**, and then click **Next**.

   d. Click the **Stand-alone root CA** option button, and then click **Next**. This type of CA can issue certificates only through the Certificate Services Web pages.

   e. In the Common name for this CA text box, type **SSLXX** (where *XX* is your student number), and then click **Next**.

   f. Click **Next** to accept the default locations for the certificate database and certificate database log.

   g. Click **Yes** to acknowledge stopping IIS.

   h. If prompted for the Windows Server 2003 CD-ROM, click **OK**, click **Browse**, select the **C:\I386 folder**, and then click **Open**. click **OK** in the Files needed dialog box.

   i. If prompted to enable Active Server Pages (ASPs), click **Yes**.

   j. Click **Finish** and then close Add or Remove Programs.

4. Click **Start**, point to **Administrative Tools**, and then click **Internet Information Services (IIS) Manager**.

5. In the left pane, double-click your server to expand it, and click **Web Sites** to select it.

6. Right-click **Default Web Site** and click **Properties**.

7. Click the **Directory Security** tab, and then click **Server Certificate**.

8. Click **Next** to start the Web Server Certificate Wizard.

13

9. If necessary, click the **Create a new certificate** option button, as shown in Figure 13-4, and then click **Next**. This option is used to generate a certificate signing request (CSR) that is given to a CA. The CA then processes the CSR and returns a signed certificate. This process can be used with external CAs or internal CAs. The Assign an existing certificate option is used when a certificate already exists on the server and should be used for SSL. You can also import existing certificates from a Key Manager backup file or a .pfx file, or you can install a certificate on this server from another server.

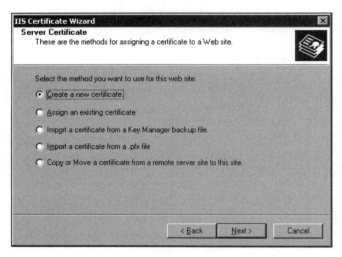

Figure 13-4   Selecting a certificate method

10. Click **Next** to accept the default to prepare the request now, but send it later. The option to send the request immediately to an online certification authority is available only if there is an Enterprise CA available.

11. Click **Next** to accept the default settings for certificate creation. By default the certificate name is the same as the Web site, and the bit length is 1024. Stronger bit lengths up to 16384 can be selected. A greater bit length generates a more secure certificate, but will decrease server performance.

12. In the Organization text box, type **Arctic University**, type **IT** in the Organization unit text box, and then click **Next**.

13. In the Common name text box, type **studentXX.arctic.local** (where *XX* is your student number) and then click **Next**. The common name of the certificate should match the DNS name of the Web server. If the Web server is hosting multiple Web sites using host headers, then the common name of the certificate should match the DNS name of the Web site. If the common name of the certificate does not match the DNS name of the Web site being accessed, then a warning message will pop up for users indicating that the name of the certificate does not match the Web site being accessed. You can also use the IP address of the Web site for the common name to avoid errors.

14. If necessary, select **US (United States)** in the Country/Region drop-down list.

15. In the State/province text box, type **Alaska**, type **Ice Town** in the City/locality text box, and then click **Next**.

16. If necessary, type **c:\certreq.txt** in the File name text box, and click **Next**. This is the file that contains the CSR. The contents of this file are given to a CA, which creates a certificate based on it.

17. Click **Next** to generate the CSR, and then click **Finish**.

18. Click **OK** to close the Default Web Site Properties dialog box. If necessary, start the Default Web Site.

19. Click **Start**, point to **All Programs**, and then click **Internet Explorer**.

20. Enable scripting in your browser if you have not already done so by completing the following steps:

    a. Click the **Tools** menu, and then click **Internet Options**.

    b. Click the **Security** tab, and then click the **Internet** icon.

    c. Click **Custom Level**.

    d. In the Reset to drop-down list box, select **Medium–low**.

    e. Click **Reset** and then click **Yes** to confirm.

    f. Click **OK**, and then click **OK**.

21. In the Address bar, type **http://studentXX.arctic.local/certsrv** (where *XX* is your student number), and then press **Enter**.

22. Click **Request a certificate**.

23. Click **advanced certificate request**.

24. Click **Submit a certificate request by using a base-64-encoded CMC or PKCS #10 file, or submit a renewal request by using a base-64-encoded PKCS #7 file**. This option is used when a CSR has already been created by an application like IIS. If a CSR did not already exist, you would choose the Create and submit a request to the CA option instead.

25. Click **Start**, click **Run**, type **c:\certreq.txt**, and then press **Enter**. This will open certreq.txt in Notepad.

13

26. Copy the data from the contents of the file in Notepad, and paste the data into the Saved Request text box on the Submit a Certificate Request or Renewal Request Web page, as shown in Figure 13-5.

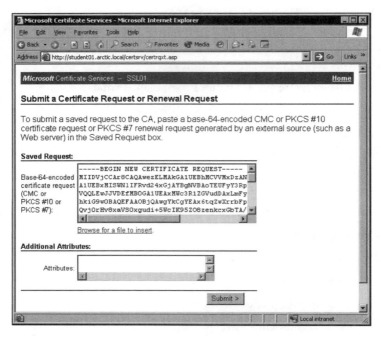

Figure 13-5   Submitting a CSR

27. Close Notepad and then click the **Submit** button on the Submit a Certificate Request or Renewal Request Web page. If necessary, click **OK** to continue. The request must now be manually approved by an Administrator.

28. Close Internet Explorer.

29. Click **Start**, point to **Administrative Tools**, and then click **Certification Authority**.

30. In the left pane, double-click your CA to expand it, and then click **Pending Requests**.

31. Right-click the waiting request, point to **All Tasks**, and then click **Issue**.

32. Click **Issued Certificates**. Notice that the certificate request now appears here.

33. Close the Certification Authority window.

34. Click **Start**, point to **All Programs**, and then click **Internet Explorer**.

35. In the Address bar, type **http://studentXX.arctic.local/certsrv** (where *XX* is your student number), and then press **Enter**.

36. Click **View the status of a pending certificate request**. This is where you must go to retrieve your new certificate.

37. Click **Saved–Request Certificate** (*today's date*).

38. Click **Download certificate** to accept the default setting of DER encoded. Notice that the certificate can be downloaded as DER encoded or Base 64 encoded. Either option is supported by most certificate-based applications.

39. Click **Save**, type **c:\certnew.cer** in the File name text box, click **Save**, and then click **Close**.

40. Close Internet Explorer.

41. In the Internet Information Services (IIS) Manager window, right-click **Default Web Site** and then click **Properties**.

42. Click the **Directory Security** tab, and then click **Server Certificate**. Notice that the Welcome screen for the Web Server Certificate Wizard indicates that there is a pending certificate request.

43. Click **Next** to begin processing the response from the CA.

44. If necessary, click the **process the pending request and install the certficate** option button, and click **Next**.

45. If necessary, type **c:\certnew.cer** in the Path and file name text box, and click **Next**.

46. Click **Next** to accept the default SSL port of 443 for this Web site.

47. Click **Next** to install the certificate, and then click **Finish**.

48. Click **OK** to close the Default Web Site Properties dialog box, and then close Internet Information Services (IIS) Manager.

49. Click **Start**, point to **All Programs**, and then click **Internet Explorer**.

50. In the Address bar, type **https://studentXX.arctic.local** (where XX is your student number), and press **Enter**.

51. If you receive a Security Alert dialog box, check the **In the future, do not show this warning** check box, and then click **OK**.

52. Read the URL in the Address bar. Notice it is using https for the protocol, which means that the Web site is using SSL. You should be viewing an Under Construction Web page. This appears because you have not configured any other Web pages for this site.

53. Close Internet Explorer.

Certification Objectives

Objectives for Microsoft Exam #70-293: Planning a Microsoft Windows Server 2003 Network:

- Plan security for servers that are assigned specific roles. Roles might include domain controllers, Web servers, database servers, and mail servers.

■ Configure network protocol security.

■ Plan security for data transmission.

REVIEW QUESTIONS

1. What is required to enable SSL on a Web server?

    a. a certificate

    b. a registered domain name

    c. an internal certificate authority

    d. IPSec being enabled first

2. Which protocol is used to access Web sites using SSL?

    a. http

    b. https

    c. ssl

    d. secureweb

3. What utility is used to approve certificate requests made on a stand-alone CA?

    a. Certificate Services Web pages

    b. Certificates snap-in

    c. Certification Authority snap-in

    d. Internet Information Services (IIS) Manager

4. What utility is used to configure SSL on a Web site?

    a. Certificate Services Web pages

    b. Security Manager

    c. Certification Authority snap-in

    d. Internet Information Services (IIS) Manager

5. What type of CA should be used when users from the Internet are accessing your secure Web site?

    a. Internal

    b. External

    c. Stand-alone

    d. Enterprise

LAB 13.4 SOFTWARE UPDATE SERVICE

Objectives

The goal of this lab activity is to use Software Update Service (SUS) to help you centralize and control software updates for your servers and workstations. It can be installed on Windows 2000 Server and Windows Server 2003. SUS must be downloaded from Microsoft's Web site.

Materials Required

This lab will require the following:

- Windows Server 2003 installed and configured according to the instructions at the beginning of this manual

- IIS installed

- An organizational unit with your server as the only computer object in it

- Approximately 3 GB of free disk space.

Estimated completion time: **90 minutes**

Activity Background

Be aware that this is a very long lab that takes significant network and hard disk resources. Approximately 3 GB of files are downloaded from the Internet for each student computer.

SUS is used in conjunction with automatic updates. Automatic updates can be configured to obtain updates from a SUS server rather than Windows Update. This lets you to control which updates are available to your servers and computers. SUS can be configured so that each update must be approved by an administrator.

13

Activity

ACTIVITY

1. Log on as **Administrator** to the Arctic.local domain with a password of **Password!**.

2. Click **Start**, point to **All Programs**, and then click **Internet Explorer**.

3. In the Address bar, type **http://www.microsoft.com/sus** and press **Enter**.

4. Under the downloads heading, click **Download SUS with Service Pack 1 (SP1)**. Note that this link may change over time. If this exact link is not available, look for another link that will allow you to download SUS.

5. On the right side of the page, click **Download**, click **Save**, click **Desktop**, and then click **Save**. This file is 32 MB. The time to download will vary depending on your Internet speed. If you are using a high speed Internet connection, it only takes about five minutes.

6. After the download is complete, click **Close** and then close Internet Explorer.

7. On the desktop, double-click **SUS10SP1.exe**.

8. Click **Next** to start the Software Update Services Setup Wizard.

9. Click the **I accept the terms in the License Agreement** option button, and then click **Next**.

10. Click **Custom**.

11. The first screen gives you the option to set the location where the Web pages for SUS are stored, as well as the location of the updates. The default location for the Web pages is C:\SUS\. The default location for the updates is C:\SUS\content. You have the option to change either of these locations, and the option to redirect clients to another Windows Update server instead of storing the updates locally. Most of the time, updates are stored locally. When updates are stored locally, they should not be stored on the same volume as the operating system because the updates are downloaded automatically and could cause the disk to run out of space, which would crash the server. Click **Next** to continue and accept the default location.

12. Click the **English only** option button, and then click **Next**. This will reduce the time needed to download all of the updates if support for other languages is not required.

13. If necessary, click the **I will manually approve new version of approved updates** option button, and then click **Next**. This option allows you to test and approve each update before it is available to users. Alternatively you can select the Automatically approve new versions of previously approved updates option to make the process more automated.

14. Click **Install**.

15. Click **Finish** to complete the installation of SUS. The Web page to administer SUS on your server is automatically opened. This Web page is accessed through http://*servername*/SUSAdmin (where *servername* is the name of your server).

16. In the left pane of the Web page, click **Synchronize server**. Before the server can be used by Automatic Update clients, the server must download the available updates. This is referred to as synchronizing the server. You should schedule when synchronization happens to ensure that updates are available automatically.

17. Click **Synchronize Now** to download the available updates. Depending on the speed of your Internet connection, this process may take 30 minutes to several hours. The status bar shows the synchronization progress.

18. When synchronization is complete, click **OK** to close the dialog box. This will automatically open the Approve Updates Web page.

19. Scroll through the list of updates and read some of the information. Notice that each of the updates has a short description with a link to more details and a list of the operating systems to which it applies.

20. Find an update that applies to Windows Server 2003, check the check box to the left of it, and then click **Approve** to approve the update for download.

21. Click **Yes** to continue.

22. If prompted to accept a license agreement, click **Accept**.

23. Click **OK** to close the Successful dialog box.

24. Close Internet Explorer.

25. Click **Start**, click **Run**, type **mmc**, and then press **Enter**.

26. Click **File**, click **Add/Remove Snap-in**, click **Add**, double-click **Active Directory Users and Computers**, click **Close**, and then click **OK**.

27. Expand **Active Directory Users and Computers**, expand **Arctic.local**, and click **OUXX** (where *XX* is your student number). This is the organizational unit that contains the computer object for your server.

28. Right-click **OUXX**, click **Properties**, and then click the **Group Policy** tab.

29. Click **New**, type **UpdateXX** (where *XX* is your student number), and then press **Enter**.

30. Click **Edit**.

31. In the left pane under Computer Configuration, expand **Administrative Templates**, expand **Windows Components**, and then click **Windows Update**.

32. Double-click **Configure Automatic Updates**, and then click the **Enabled** option button.

33. In the Configure automatic updating drop-down list, select **4 – Auto download and schedule the install**, and then click **OK**.

34. Double-click **Specify intranet Microsoft update service location**, and then click the **Enabled** option button.

35. In the Set the intranet update service for detecting updates text box, type **http://studentXX.arctic.local** (where *XX* is your student number). This specifies the server from which updates are downloaded.

36. In the Set the intranet statistics server text box, type **http://studentXX.arctic.local** (where *XX* is your student number). This specifies the server to which statistics about updates are sent.

37. Click **OK** and then close the Group Policy Object Editor window.

38. Click **Close**, close the MMC, and click **No** if prompted to save the console settings.

13

Certification Objectives

Objectives for Microsoft Exam #70-293: Planning a Microsoft Windows Server 2003 Network:

- Plan a secure baseline installation.

- Plan a framework for planning and implementing security.

- Plan a security update infrastructure. Tools might include Microsoft Baseline Security Analyzer and Microsoft Software Update Services.

REVIEW QUESTIONS

1. Through what is SUS administered?

    a. SUS Administration snap-in

    b. http://*servername*/SUSAdmin

    c. Active Directory Sites and Services

    d. Computer Management

2. What must be done before SUS can begin delivering updates to servers and workstations? (Choose all that apply.)

    a. Each update must be approved.

    b. A synchronization schedule must be configured.

    c. The SUS server must be synchronized.

    d. You must activate your installation of SUS.

3. What is the default file system location that SUS uses to store updates?

    a. C:\SUS

    b. C:\SUSAdmin

    c. C:\SUS\content

    d. C:\SUS\updates

4. How can you configure automatic updates to download from a SUS server instead of Windows Update? (Choose all that apply.)

    a. Edit the Registry with Regedit.

    b. Edit Autoupdate.ini.

    c. Apply a security template.

    d. Use a Group Policy.

5. From which URL can you download SUS?

    a. http://sus.microsoft.com/

    b. http://www.microsoft.com/sus

    c. http://www.microsoft.com/windowstools/sus

    d. http://www.microsoft.com/windowsupdate

LAB 13.5 MICROSOFT BASELINE SECURITY ANALYZER

Objectives

The goal of this lab activity is to use Microsoft Baseline Security Analyzer (MBSA) to secure workstations and server. MBSA is a tool that scans computers on your network for missing security patches and insecure configurations. It has both graphical and command-line interfaces. This tool can be run from Windows 2000, Windows XP, and Windows Server 2003.

Materials Required

This lab will require the following:

- Windows Server 2003 installed and configured according to the instructions at the beginning of this manual

- IIS installed

Estimated completion time: **20 minutes**

13

Activity Background

MBSA is a more comprehensive security tool than SUS because it looks for more than just missing operating system updates. It also scans a wider variety of operating systems. MBSA can scan Windows NT, Windows 2000, Windows XP, and Windows Server 2003. The applications scanned for updates by MBSA are IIS versions 4.0 and 5.0, SQL Server 7.0 and SQL Server 2000, Internet Explorer 5.01 and later, Exchange 5.5 and Exchange 2000, and Windows Media Player 6.4 and later.

Beyond looking for missing updates, MBSA also looks for security configuration errors. It scans for configuration errors in Windows NT 4.0, Windows 2000, Windows XP, Windows Server 2003, IIS versions 4.0 and 5.0, SQL Server 7.0 and SQL Server 2000, Internet Explorer 5.01 and later, and Office 2000 and Office 2002.

MBSA is not included with Windows Server 2003 and must be downloaded from the Microsoft Web site. The URL to download MBSA is *www.microsoft.com/mbsa*.

ACTIVITY

Activity

1. Log on as **Administrator** to the Arctic.local domain with a password of **Password!**.

2. Click **Start**, point to **All Programs**, and then click **Internet Explorer**.

3. In the Address bar, type **http://www.microsoft.com/mbsa** and then press **Enter**.

4. At the top of the Web page, click **Download Now**.

5. Under the Download Now heading, click the link to download MBSA, click **Save**, click **Desktop**, and then click **Save**. This download is about 4 MB and takes less than one minute on high-speed Internet.

6. Click **Close** and close Internet Explorer.

7. On the desktop, double-click **MBSASetup-en.msi**.

8. Click **Next** to begin the Microsoft Baseline Security Analyzer Setup Wizard.

9. Click the **I accept the license agreement** option button, and then click **Next**.

10. Click **Next** to accept the default installation location of C:\Program Files\Microsoft Baseline Security Analyzer\.

11. In the Microsoft Baseline Security Analyzer Setup dialog box, click **Install**. After the installation has finished, click **OK**.

12. Double-click the **Microsoft Baseline Security Analyzer 1.2** shortcut on the desktop and then click **Scan a computer**. This brings up a screen of MBSA scanning options as shown in Figure 13-6. Notice that you can choose a variety of security issues to scan for, including the following: Windows vulnerabilities, weak passwords, IIS vulnerabilities, SQL vulnerabilities, and security updates. The default location to check for security updates is the Windows Update Web site. However, you can reconfigure it to use a local SUS server instead.

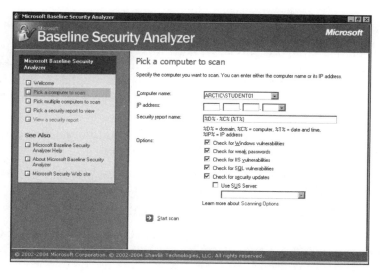

Figure 13-6   MBSA scanning options

13. Click the **Start scan** link to perform a complete scan using the default options. For MBSA to properly scan remote systems for SQL server issues, SQL server must be installed locally on the computer running MBSA. This also applies for IIS issues. However, the remaining portions of the MBSA scan are performed.

14. After the scan is complete, a security report is displayed. By default the worst security risks are displayed first. However, you can change this default to display the best results first or simply by issue name. In most cases you want to see the greatest concerns first. If necessary, select **Score (worst first)** in the Sort Order drop-down list box.

15. Several icons are used to display information in the security report. A red x indicates a critical error, a yellow x indicates a noncritical error, and a green check mark indicates that a check was successful. A blue asterisk indicates a best practice that should be implemented, and a blue i in a circle is additional information. Scroll through the list and find an issue with a red x.

16. At the issue with a red x you have found, click **What was scanned**. This opens an additional window with more information about the scan option that found this issue.

17. Close the Internet Explorer window with the check description.

13

18. At the issue with a red x you have found, click **Result details**. This opens an additional window with detailed information about the critical error that was encountered.

19. Close the Internet Explorer window with the result details.

20. At the issue with a red x you have found, click **How to correct this**. This opens an additional window with information about how to fix the critical error.

21. Close the Internet Explorer window with the critical error information.

22. To scan another computer across the network, NetBIOS over TCP/IP must be enabled on the local and remote computers. In addition, remote computers must have the Server service, Remote Registry service, and File & Print Sharing enabled. Confirm that NetBIOS over TCP/IP is enabled on your server by doing the following:

   a. Click **Start**, point to **Control Panel**, point to **Network Connections**, right-click **Classroom**, and then click **Properties**.

   b. In the This connection uses the following items list box, select **Internet Protocol (TCP/IP)**, and then click **Properties**.

   c. Click the **Advanced** button, and then click the **WINS** tab.

   d. In the NetBIOS setting section, click the **Enable NetBIOS over TCP/IP** option button. Under normal conditions, the default setting is sufficient to enable NetBIOS over TCP/IP. However, choosing this option ensures that NetBIOS over TCP/IP is enabled.

   e. Click **OK** twice and then click **Close**.

23. In the left pane of the MBSA window, click **Pick multiple computers to scan**. Using this option, you can select a domain and scan all the computers in it, or you can specify a range of IP addresses to scan.

24. In the IP address range text box, type **192.168.1.2 to 192.168.1.20**. This setting looks for computers in this IP range and scans them all.

25. Click **Start scan** to begin scanning.

26. Read the scan of the Instructor server and view information about some of the results.

27. Close MBSA.

Certification Objectives

Objectives for Microsoft Exam #70-293: Planning a Microsoft Windows Server 2003 Network:

- Plan a framework for planning and implementing security.

- Plan a security update infrastructure. Tools might include Microsoft Baseline Security Analyzer and Microsoft Software Update Services.

REVIEW QUESTIONS

1. Which of the following operating systems can be scanned for vulnerabilities by MBSA? (Choose all that apply.)

   a. Windows 98

   b. Windows NT

   c. Windows 2000

   d. Windows XP Home

   e. Windows Server 2003

2. Which of the following applications can be scanned for vulnerabilities by MBSA? (Choose all that apply.)

   a. Internet Explorer

   b. Microsoft SQL Server

   c. Microsoft Exchange

   d. IIS

   e. Microsoft Office 2000

3. Which icon indicates a best practice is not being met in an MBSA security report?

   a. red x

   b. yellow x

   c. blue asterisk

   d. blue i in a white circle

13

4. Which icon indicates a critical error in an MBSA security report?

   a. red x

   b. yellow x

   c. blue asterisk

   d. blue i in a white circle

5. Which of the following must be enabled on a computer being scanned remotely? (Choose all that apply.)

   a. NetBIOS over TCP/IP

   b. Remote Registry service

   c. File & Printer Sharing

   d. Active Server Pages

   e. Server service

CHAPTER 14

PROBLEM RECOVERY

Labs included in this chapter:

◆ Lab 14.1 Using the Remote Desktops MMC Snap-in

◆ Lab 14.2 Using Terminal Services Command-line Utilities

◆ Lab 14.3 Installing and Using the Remote Desktop Web Connection

◆ Lab 14.4 Configuring a Backup Schedule

◆ Lab 14.5 Preparing for Automated System Recovery

Microsoft MCSE Exam #70-293 Objectives	
Objective	Lab
Plan for remote administration by using Terminal Services.	14.1, 14.2, 14.3
Plan a backup and recovery strategy.	14.4, 14.5
Plan system recovery that uses Automated System Recovery (ASR)	14.5

Lab 14.1 Using the Remote Desktops MMC Snap-in

Objectives

The goal of this lab activity is to learn how to configure and use the Remote Desktops MMC snap-in to connect to and administer your server.

Materials Required:

This lab will require the following:

- Two Windows Server 2003 systems

- A lab partner

Estimated completion time: **15 minutes**

Activity Background

Implementations of Terminal services in Windows NT and Windows 2000 had one great deficiency: they did not allow you to connect to the console session of the remote server. Accessing the console is important because there are many third party applications, such as print monitors and backup software, which will only deliver their messages to the console session. This forced many administrators into using third party applications for remote control of their computers. Windows Server 2003 offers several tools to access the console session remotely.

The Remote Desktops administrative tool allows you to create a connection to a remote terminal session. It has the additional advantage of enabling you to connect to multiple servers in one window. In this lab you will connect to the console of your partner's server and to a new terminal session of your own server.

ACTIVITY

Activity

To be completed by both partners:

1. If necessary, log on as **Administrator** to the Arctic.local domain with a password of **Password!**. Close any open windows.

2. Click **Start**, click **Run**, type **mmc**, and then click **OK**.

3. If necessary, maximize the Console Root window and then maximize the Console1 window. The remote desktop will be only as large as your open window.

4. Click **File**, click **Add/Remove Snap-in**, click **Add**, and then scroll down and click **Remote Desktops**. Click **Add**. Click **Close** and then click **OK**.

5. Click the **Remote Desktops** folder. Right-click the **Remote Desktops** folder and click **Add new connection**.

6. In the Server name or IP address text box, type **StudentXX** (where *XX* is your student number). Uncheck the **Connect to console** check box. In the Logon information section, type **Administrator** in the User name text box, and type **Arctic.local** in the Domain text box (as shown in Figure 14–1). Click **OK**.

Figure 14-1   Connection to your server

7. Click the **plus sign [+]** next to Remote Desktops. Click **StudentXX**. Type your password and then click **OK** to log on to a terminal session to your server.

14

8. In the remote session, right–click the taskbar and click **Task Manager**. Click the **Users** tab. You see two sessions, similar to Figure 14-2. Close Task Manager.

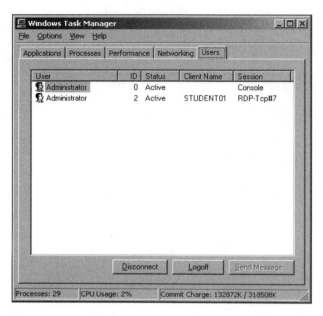

Figure 14-2   Task Manager with one console session and one remote session

9. In the Remote Desktop session, click **Start**. Click **Log Off** and again click **Log Off**. Once your MMC window displays the message "Disconnected from server," click the **Remote Desktops** folder in the left pane of your MMC.

10. Click **Start**, click **Run**, type **dsa.msc**, and then click **OK**.

11. Expand **Arctic.local**, click **Users**, right-click **Administrator**, and then click **Copy**.

12. In the Copy Object – User window, type **rdtestXX** in the Full name text box (where *XX* is your student number). Type **rdtestXX** in the User logon name text box. Click **Next**, type and confirm the password **Password!**, click **Next**, and then click **Finish**. Close Active Directory Users and Computers.

To be completed by Partner One only:

1. Right-click **Remote Desktops** and click **Add new connection**.

2. In the Server name or IP address box, type **StudentYY** (where YY is your partner's student number). Confirm that the **Connect to console** check box is checked. In the Logon information section, type **Administrator** in the User name text box, and type **Arctic.local** in the Domain text box (as shown in Figure 14-3). Click **OK**.

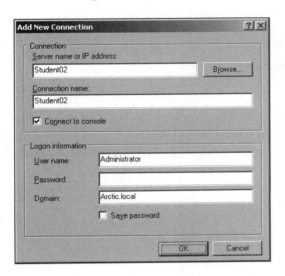

Figure 14-3 Console connection to partner server

3. Do not continue until your partner has completed the preceding step sequence. Click **StudentYY** (where YY is your partner's student number) in your MMC. Type the administrator password. When the connection is complete, your window will be exactly as your partner left it. When you connected using the same account name, your partner's screen was locked. Only one person may be on the console session at one time. If your partner unlocks the computer, you will be disconnected.

14

4. In the remote session, right-click the taskbar and click **Task Manager**. Click the **Users** tab. Note that only one user session exists, and even though you are effectively at the console, you are still listed as an RDP-TCP session (as shown in Figure 14-4). Close Task Manager.

Figure 14-4   Users tab of Task Manager with one remote session to console

5. In the left pane of your MMC, right-click **Student YY** (where *YY* is your partner's student number) and click **Disconnect**. Close MMC and then click **No**.

To be completed by Partner Two only:

1. Do not continue until your partner has completed the preceding step sequence. Unlock your computer. Press **Ctrl+Alt+Del**, type **Password!**, and then press **Enter**.

2. In your MMC, right-click **Remote Desktops** and click **Add new connection**.

3. In the Server name or IP address text box, type **StudentYY** (where *YY* is your partner's student number). Confirm that the **Connect to console** check box is checked. You will log on as a different user than your partner. In the Logon information section, type **rdtestYY** in the User name text box. Type **Password!** in the Password text box, type **Arctic.local** in the Domain text box, and then check the **Save password** check box (as shown in Figure 14-5). Click **OK**.

Figure 14-5   Remote Desktops console connection using Administrator account

4. Click **StudentYY** (where *YY* is your partner's student number) in your MMC. Read the dialog box that appears. Only one user can use the console at one time and you are logging in with a different user name, so your partner will be forced to log off before you can continue. Click **Yes**.

5. Once connected, click **Start**, click **Log Off**, and again click **Log Off**. Close MMC and then click **No**.

Certification Objectives

Objectives for Microsoft Exam #70-293: Planning a Microsoft Windows Server 2003 Network:

■ Plan for remote administration by using Terminal Services.

REVIEW QUESTIONS

1. What advantage does the Remote Desktops MMC snap-in have that the Remote Desktop Connection tool does not?

   a. allows multiple active remote sessions in one window

   b. allows two users to connect to the console session simultaneously

   c. provides ability to access the console session

   d. does not require anyone to be at the remote server

2. What advantages does the Remote Desktops MMC snap-in have that Remote Assistance does not? (Choose all that apply.)

   a. allows multiple active remote sessions in one window

   b. allows two users to connect to the console session simultaneously

   c. provides ability to access the console session

   d. does not require anyone to be at the remote server

3. What will happen to a user who is logged on to the console session when you log on to the console session with the same account using the Remote Desktops MMC snap-in?

   a. The user will be forced to log off.

   b. The user will be locked.

   c. Nothing, it will not affect the console user.

   d. The user will be asked to accept the connection.

4. What will happen to a user who is logged on to the console session when you log on to the console session with a different account using the Remote Desktops MMC snap-in?

   a. The user will be forced to log off.

   b. The computer will be locked.

   c. Nothing, it will not affect the console user.

   d. The user will be asked to accept the connection.

5. Which of the following statements about the Remote Desktops MMC snap-in is false?

   a. If you disconnect from an active remote session, the session will continue on the remote server.

   b. If you log off in an active remote session, the session will close on the remote server.

   c. If you close MMC while an active remote session exists, the session will continue on the remote server.

   d. You cannot return to a disconnected session; you must start a new session.

LAB 14.2 USING TERMINAL SERVICES COMMAND-LINE UTILITIES

Objectives

The goal of this lab activity is to learn how to use some of the command-line utilities to manage terminal server connections.

Materials Required:

This lab will require the following:

- Two Windows Server 2003 systems

- A lab partner

Estimated completion time: **15 minutes**

14

Activity Background

Your server includes several useful command-line utilities to manage connections to your terminal server. As an administrator you can disconnect, log off, or join other users' sessions from the command line. You can also initiate your own connections from the command line.

Activity

To be completed by both partners:

1. If necessary, log on as **Administrator** to the Arctic.local domain with a password of **Password!**. Close any open windows.

2. Click **Start** and then click **Help and Support**. In the Search text box, type **Managing terminal services from the command line** and then press **Enter**. In the Search Results pane, click **Help Topics**, if necessary, and then click the entry that reads **Managing Terminal Services from the command line : Terminal Services** (as shown in Figure 14-6). The Help page lists all of the commands available. As time permits, read through this information. Close the Help and Support Center.

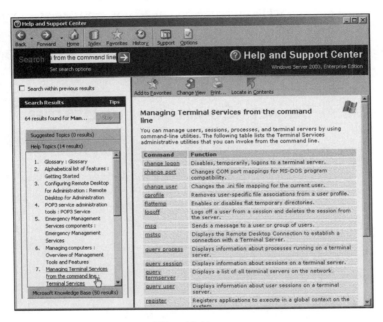

Figure 14-6   Command-line Help page

3. Click **Start**, click **Run**, type **dsa.msc**, and then click **OK**. If necessary, click the **plus sign [+]** next to Arctic.local, and then click the **Users** container. Right-click the **rdtestXX** account (where *XX* is your student number) and click **Properties**. Click the **Remote control** tab, check the **Require user's permission** check box, click **OK**, and then close the Active Directory Users and Computers window.

4. Click **Start**, click **Run**, type **mstsc**, and then click **OK**.

5. In the Computer text box, type **StudentYY** (where *YY* is your partner's student number). Click **Options**, type **rdtestXX** in the User name text box (where *XX* is your student number), and type **Password!** in the Password text box. Type **Arctic.local** in the Domain text box, check the **Save my password** check box to select it, and then click **Save As**. Type **StudentYY** in the File name text box (where *YY* is your partner's student number), click **Save**, and then click **Connect**.

6. In the remote session to your partner's server, click **Start**, click **Run**, type **notepad**, and then press **Enter**. Leave the connection open in the background.

7. Do not continue until your partner has a session open to your server. At your console, click **Start**, click **Run**, type **cmd**, and then press **Enter**.

8. Type **query session** and then press **Enter**. You will see the following three sessions, similar to what is shown in Figure 14-7.

- The console session has a greater than symbol (>) before it. This indicates that it is the session you are currently in.

- The session that has a state of Listen is not a real session. This indicates that your server is listening for connections.

- The third session is your partner's remote session. Make a note of the session name; it will be rdp-tcp# followed by a number. The session ID can also be used to identify the session; it is a whole number. In Figure 14-7, the session name is rdp-tcp#11, and the session ID of the remote connection is 1.

Figure 14-7   Results of the query session command

9. Type **query process** *SessionName* (where *SessionName* is the name recorded in Step 8). Press **Enter**. Your results will look similar to Figure 14-8. Make a note of the session ID and the PID for notepad.exe.

Figure 14-8   Results of the query process command

10. Type **tskill** *PID* **/id:***SessionID* **/v** (where *PID* and *SessionID* are the numbers recorded in Step 9). Press **Enter**.

To kill the notepad.exe process shown in Figure 14-8, you would type the command shown in Figure 14-9. Note that in your partner's remote connection to your server, Notepad has been terminated.

NOTE

Figure 14-9   Ending the notepad.exe process with the tskill command

14

11. Type **query process** *SessionName* (where *SessionName* is the name recorded in Step 8) to confirm that notepad.exe is no longer present.

12. Type **msg** *SessionName* **Testing message function** (where *SessionName* is the name recorded in Step 8). Press **Enter**. Your message appears in your partner's remote connection to your server. By default it will disappear in 60 seconds if your partner does not click OK.

13. In order to use the Shadow command, you must open a terminal session to your own server. The Shadow command cannot be completed from the console session. Click **Start**, click **Run**, type **mstsc**, and then press **Enter**.

14. In the Computer text box, type **StudentXX** (where *XX* is your student number). Click **Options**, type **Administrator** in the User name text box, and type **Password!** in the Password text box. Type **Arctic.local** in the Domain text box, check the **Save my password** check box to select it, and then click **Save As**. Type the file name **StudentXX** (where *XX* is your student number), and click **Save**. Click **Cancel**.

15. In your Command Prompt window, type **cd My Documents** and then press **Enter**. Type **mstsc StudentXX.rdp** (where *XX* is your student number), and then press **Enter**.

16. In your remote session to your own server, click **Start**, click **Run**, type **cmd**, and then press **Enter**.

17. Type **shadow** *SessionName* (where *SessionName* is the name recorded in Step 8), as shown in Figure 14-10. Press **Enter**. You connect to your partner's remote session with your server. While in shadowing mode, you both share control of the mouse and keyboard in this session.

Figure 14-10 Launching a remote desktop connection using the Shadow command

18. In this session, click **Start**, click **Run**, type **cmd**, and then press **Enter**.

19. Type **query session** and then press **Enter**. Your result will be similar to Figure 14-11. The active session, which is your partner's session that you are shadowing, will be indicated by the greater than symbol (>). Your session will now have a state of RCtrl. Type **Exit**, and then press **Enter**.

Figure 14-11   Results of a query session command while shadowing

20. Right-click the taskbar and click **Task Manager**. Click the **Users** tab. Your result will be similar to Figure 14-12. Your session has a status of Shadowing. Close Task Manager.

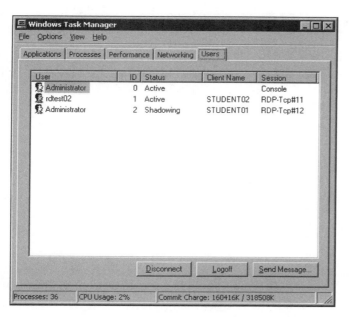

Figure 14-12   Users tab of the Task Manager while shadowing

21. Press **Ctrl+*** (asterisk) to stop shadowing your partner's session. You will return to your session with your server. Click **Start**, click **Log Off**, and again click **Log Off**.

22. Back in your console, return to your command prompt. Type **query session** and then press **Enter**. The greater than symbol (>) will be beside the console session, which is your active session. Your partner will still be connected with the same session name as before.

23. Type **tsdiscon** *SessionName* (where *SessionName* is the name recorded in Step 8). Press **Enter**. A dialog box, as shown in Figure 14-13, will appear on your partner's console. The same dialog box will appear on your console when your partner completes this step. Click **OK** to close the Remote Desktop Disconnected dialog box when it appears.

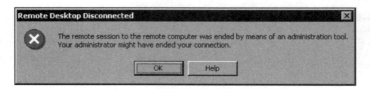

Figure 14-13   Remote Desktop Disconnected dialog box

24. At the command prompt, type **query session** and then press **Enter**. Notice that your partner's session still exists, but that the session name is blank. Anyone with the correct password for that account could reconnect to the session, and the applications would still be running.

25. You need the numerical Session ID of your partner's disconnected session to log off the session. Type **logoff** *SessionID* (for example, logoff 2), press **Enter**, type **query session**, and then press **Enter** to confirm that the session is deleted. Note that, if the session hangs, you can use the "reset session *SessionID*" command to force it to delete.

26. Close all open windows.

Certification Objectives

Objectives for Microsoft Exam #70-293: Planning a Microsoft Windows Server 2003 Network:

- Plan for remote administration by using Terminal Services.

REVIEW QUESTIONS

1. Which command can be used from the command line to disconnect a remote session but leave it active?

   a. logoff

   b. tsdiscon

   c. tskill

   d. reset session

2. Which command can be used from the command line to end a process in a remote session?

   a. logoff

   b. tsdiscon

   c. tskill

   d. reset session

3. Which command-line utility allows you to share control of a session if the appropriate permissions are configured?

   a. RCtrl

   b. Mstsc

   c. Change logon

   d. Shadow

4. In the Active Directory Users and Computers MMC, which tab of the User Properties window must be properly configured to allow you to shadow and interact with a user's active session?

   a. Terminal Services Profile

   b. Remote Control

   c. Sessions

   d. Environment

5. Which of the following commands can show you the session name and Session ID of a remote session? (Choose all that apply.)

   a. query session

   b. query user

   c. query process

   d. query termserver

14

LAB 14.3 INSTALLING AND USING THE REMOTE DESKTOP WEB CONNECTION

Objectives

The goal of this lab activity is to learn how to Install the Remote Desktop Web Connection utility and access your server from Internet Explorer.

Materials Required:

This lab will require the following:

- A Windows Server 2003 system installed and configured according to the instructions at the beginning of this lab manual

Estimated completion time:**20 minutes**

Activity Background

The Remote Desktop Web Connection is another useful tool that enables remote administration of your server. It is an ActiveX plug-in that is downloaded to a connecting Web browser. It allows you to connect from any computer with Microsoft Internet Explorer 5 (MSIE) or later without requiring installation of a special client application. It does not allow remote access to the console session. Note that you do not need to install the utility on all of the servers you want to access; one installation is enough for a single network. The utility is a component of Internet Information Server 6 (IIS), so that must also be installed in this lab.

ACTIVITY

Activity

1. If necessary, log on as **Administrator** to the Arctic.local domain with a password of **Password!**. Close any open windows.

2. Click **Start**, click **Control Panel**, and then click **Add or Remove Programs**.

3. Click **Add/Remove Windows Components**.

4. In the Windows Components window, double-click **Application Server**.

5. In the Application Server window, double-click **Internet Information Services (IIS)**.

6. In the Internet Information Services (IIS) window, scroll down and double-click **World Wide Web Service**.

7. In the World Wide Web Service window, check the **Remote Desktop Web Connection** checkbox. Additional components that are required are automatically selected, as shown in Figure 14-14. Click **OK** three times until you are back at the Windows Components window. Click **Next**. When prompted for the Windows Server 2003 CD, type the path to the i386 folder (**D:\i386**), click **OK**, and then click **OK** again.

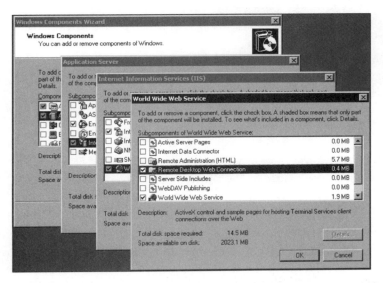

Figure 14-14   Dependencies to be installed when Remote Desktop Web Connection is selected

8. In the Completing the Windows Components Wizard screen, click **Finish**. Close the Add or Remove Programs window.

9. Click **Start**, click **Control Panel**, and then click **Internet Options**. Click the **Security** tab, and then click the **Trusted sites** icon. Click **Sites**. In the Trusted sites window, type **http://StudentXX** (where *XX* is your student number) in the Add this Web site to the zone text box, click **Add**, click **Close**, and then click **OK** to close the Internet Properties window.

14

10. Click **Start**, click **Run**, and then type **http://studentXX/tsweb** (where *XX* is your student number). Click **OK**. A Security Warning message appears, as shown in Figure 14-15. Click **Yes** to install the Remote Desktop ActiveX Control.

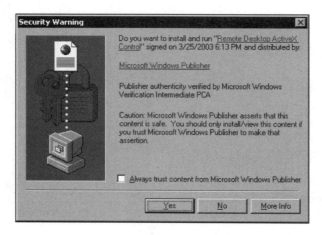

Figure 14-15   Security warning regarding the installation of the ActiveX control

11. Read the Remote Desktop Web Connection page. In the Server text box, type **StudentXX** (where *XX* is your student number). Check the **Size** drop-down list arrow, and select **800 by 600**. Check the **Send logon information for this connection** check box to select it. Type **Administrator** in the User name text box and **Arctic.local** in the Domain text box (as shown in Figure 14-16). Click **Connect**.

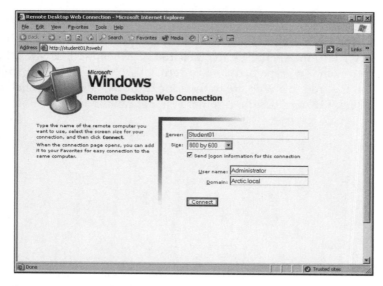

Figure 14-16   Configuring a Web connection

12. In the Log On to Windows screen, type **Password!** in the Password text box, and click **OK**.

13. Once logged on to the terminal session, you can administer your server like any other terminal session. Click **Start**, click **Log Off**, and again click **Log Off**. Close the Remote Desktop Web Connection window.

Certification Objectives

Objectives for Microsoft Exam #70-293: Planning a Microsoft Windows Server 2003 Network:

- Plan for remote administration by using Terminal Services.

REVIEW QUESTIONS

1. Which of the following remote administration utilities allows you to access the console session? (Choose all that apply.)

   a. Remote Desktop Connection

   b. Remote Assistance

   c. Remote Desktops MMC snap-in

   d. Remote Desktop Web Connection

2. What kind of Web component is installed at the client to use Remote Desktop Web Connection?

   a. Javascript

   b. ActiveX

   c. Flash

   d. XML

3. Which of the following IIS services requires installation to run the Remote Desktop Web Connection utility?

   a. World Wide Web Service

   b. File Transfer Protocol (FTP) Service

   c. SMTP Service

   d. NNTP Service

14

4. What advantage does the Remote Desktop Web Connection utility have over the Remote Desktop Connection tool?

   a. Multiple active remote sessions can be in one window.

   b. Installation of a client application is not required.

   c. It provides the ability to access the console session.

   d. No one needs to be at the remote server.

5. Which of the following systems can be used to access a Microsoft Terminal Server? (Choose all that apply.)

   a. Windows XP desktop system

   b. Macintosh OS X desktop system

   c. PDA running Windows Pocket PC 2002

   d. Windows 95

LAB 14.4 CONFIGURING A BACKUP SCHEDULE

Objectives

The goal of this lab activity is to learn how to use the task scheduler portion of Ntbackup to set a typical ongoing backup schedule.

Materials Required:

This lab will require the following:

- A Windows Server 2003 system installed and configured according to the instructions at the beginning of this lab manual

Estimated completion time: **15 minutes**

Activity Background

Most servers back up to tape or other removable media. To balance efficiency of storage size/speed of completion versus ease of restoration, you would typically mix differential and incremental backups to follow up on a weekly normal backup. In this scenario, we will be backing up to disk but planning as if the backup was to be implemented on removable media changed daily. An eight-tape schedule would have four tapes for Mon-Thurs and four tapes for a Friday normal backup, one tape per week rotated monthly. Plan to use differential backups the first couple of days following the normal backup when there are fewer changed files. Incremental backups would be used later in the week when the size and processing time of continuing differential backups becomes impractical. We will also schedule a single monthly backup for archival purposes.

Activity

1. If necessary, log on as **Administrator** to the Arctic.local domain with a password of **Password!**. Close any open windows.

2. Click **Start**, click **Run**, type **ntbackup**, click **OK**, and then click the **Advanced Mode** link.

3. Click the **Schedule Jobs** tab. Double-click today's date to start the Backup Wizard, and then click **Next**. Click **Next** to back up everything on this computer.

4. Click **Browse**. In the File name text box, type **D:\Backup\Weekly Normal.bkf**, and then click **Save**. Click **Next** and then click **Yes** in the dialog box to create the folder. The backup type should be set to Normal by default. Click **Next** and then check the **Verify data after backup** check box select it. Click **Next**, click the **Replace the existing backups** option button, and then click **Next**.

5. Type **Weekly Normal** in the Job name text box, and then click **Set Schedule**. In the Schedule Task drop-down list box, click **Weekly**. Check the **Monday** check box, and check the **Friday** check box (as shown in Figure 14-17). Click **OK**.

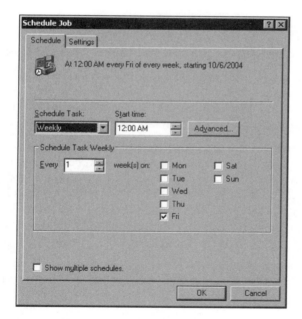

Figure 14-17 Schedule Job dialog box

6. In the Set Account Information window, type **Password!** in the Password and Confirm password text boxes. This account will be the user who has the authority to run the task. Click **OK**.

7. Click **Next** in the Backup Wizard. You are asked again for account information; this is the user that will run and own the backup. These users do not need to be the same, but you will continue to use the Administrator user. Type **Password!** in the Password and Confirm password text boxes, click **OK**, and then click **Finish**.

8. In the calendar, double-click the first Monday after the new schedule begins. Click **Next** and then click **Next** to back up everything on your computer.

9. Click the **Browse** button. In the File name text box, type **D:\Backup\Daily Differential.bkf** and then click **Save**. Click **Next**. Click the **Select the type of backup** drop-down list arrow, and then click **Differential**. Click **Next**, confirm that the **Verify data after backup** check box is checked, and click **Next**. Click the **Replace the existing backups** option button, and then click **Next**.

10. Type **Daily Differential** in the Job name text box, and then click **Set Schedule**. In the Schedule Task drop-down list box, click **Weekly**. Verify that the **Monday** check box is selected, and then check the **Tuesday** check box to select it. Click **OK**, type **Password!** in the Password and Confirm password text boxes, and then click **OK**. Click **Next**, type **Password!** in the Password and Confirm password text boxes again, and then click **OK**. Click **Finish**.

11. In the calendar, double-click the first Wednesday of the new schedule. Click **Next** to start the wizard, and then click **Next**. Click **Browse**. In the File name text box, type **D:\Backup\Daily Incremental.bkf** and then click **Save**.

12. Click **Next**. Click the **Select the type of backup** drop-down arrow, click **Incremental**, and then click **Next**. Check the **Verify data after backup** check box, if necessary, and then click **Next**. Click the **Append this backup to the existing backup** option button, and then click **Next**.

13. Type **Daily Incremental** in the Job name text box, and then click **Set Schedule**. In the Schedule Task drop-down list box, click **Weekly**. Uncheck the **Monday** check box, check the check boxes for **Wednesday** and **Thursday**, and then click **OK**. Type **Password!** in the Password and Confirm password text boxes, click **OK**, and then click **Next**. Type **Password!** in the Password and Confirm password text boxes again, click **OK**, and then click **Finish**.

14. The last job to add is a monthly copy to be kept offsite for archival purposes. Double-click the last Saturday of this month. Click **Next** to start the wizard, and then click **Next**.

15. Click **Browse**. In the File name text box, type **D:\Backup\Monthly Copy.bkf**, click **Save**, and then click **Next**. Click the **Select the type of backup** drop-down list arrow, click **Copy**, and then click **Next**. Click **Next**, click the **Replace the existing backups** option button, and then click **Next**.

16. Type **Monthly Copy** in the Job name text box, and then click **Set Schedule**. In the Schedule Task drop-down list box, click **Monthly**. Click the second option button, and use the drop-down boxes to select the **last Saturday** of the month, as in Figure 14-18, then click **OK**. Type **Password!** in the Password and Confirm password text boxes, click **OK**, then click **Next**. Type **Password!** in the Password and Confirm password text boxes again, and click **OK**. Click **Finish**.

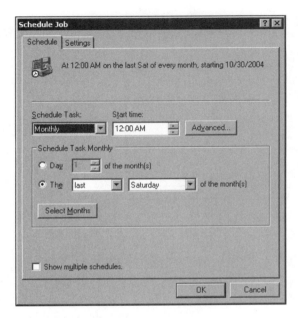

Figure 14-18   Monthly schedule

14

17. In the calendar (shown in Figure 14-19), you can click any scheduled event to confirm its properties. Close the Backup Utility.

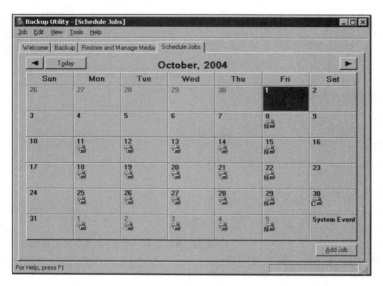

Figure 14-19   Calendar of scheduled backups

18. Click **Start**, click **Control Panel**, right-click **Scheduled Tasks**, and then click **Open**.

19. Double-click **Weekly Normal**. Notice the long command line in the Run text box. (The command can be read easier if you copy and paste into Notepad.) The important things to note are that Weekly Normal.bks (a backup selection file) was created and where it is located. If a backup fails to run, check that this file still exists.

20. Disable the backup tasks. On the Task tab, uncheck the **Enabled (scheduled task runs at specified time)** check box, and then click **OK**. Repeat with each scheduled backup task to disable them all. Close the Scheduled Tasks window.

Certification Objectives

Objectives for Microsoft Exam #70-293: Planning a Microsoft Windows Server 2003 Network:

- Plan a backup and recovery strategy.

REVIEW QUESTIONS

1. What is the extension for a backup selection file?

   a. .dbf

   b. .bkf

   c. .bak

   d. .bks

2. By default, how many hours will a scheduled backup job run before the task scheduler ends the task?

   a. 12

   b. 24

   c. 48

   d. 72

3. Backups cannot be directly saved to which of the following media?

   a. hard disk

   b. CD-R

   c. Zip disk

   d. tape

4. A member server could not schedule a backup of which of these types of data?

   a. everything on this computer

   b. selected data files

   c. Active Directory

   d. system state

5. The same backup job can be scheduled to run several times a day. True or false?

14

LAB 14.5 PREPARING FOR AUTOMATED SYSTEM RECOVERY

Objectives

The goal of this lab activity is to learn how to prepare for an Automated System Recovery (ASR) using Ntbackup.

Materials Required:

This lab will require the following:

- A Windows Server 2003 system installed and configured according to the instructions at the beginning of this lab manual

- One blank, formatted 1.44 MB floppy disk

- Approximately 1.8 GB free on the drive D

Estimated completion time: **45 minutes**

Activity Background

In order to be able to repair your server using the ASR feature, you must create an ASR backup after every significant configuration change. Upon completion of the backup, you will have a .bkf file, which can be saved to disk or removable media, and a floppy disk that contains information about the backup and disk configuration.

Activity

1. If necessary, log on as **Administrator** to the Arctic.local domain with a password of **Password!**. Close any open windows.

2. Click **Start**, click **Run**, type **ntbackup**, and then click **OK**.

3. Click the **Advanced Mode** link.

4. On the Welcome tab, click **Automated System Recovery Wizard**.

5. Read the Welcome page. Note that the ASR backup does not include your data, which must be backed up separately. Click **Next**.

6. In the Backup media or file name text box, type **D:\Backup\ASR backup.bkf**, click **Next**, and then click **Finish**. The backup (as shown in Figure 14-20) can take up to 90 minutes.

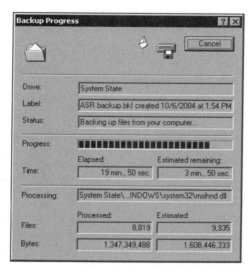

Figure 14-20 ASR backup progress

7. Insert the floppy disk when prompted (as shown in Figure 14-21), and click **OK**.

Figure 14-21 Requesting a floppy disk to restore the ASR backup

8. Once the backup is complete, close the status window. Close the backup utility.

9. Click **Start**, right-click **My Computer**, and then click **Explore**.

10. Double-click drive D, and then click the **Backup** folder. Notice the size of the ASR backup.bkf file. If necessary, click the **View** menu, and then click **Details**. Note that the backup is too large to fit on a 700 MB CD-R.

11. Click drive C, click the **Windows** folder, and then click the **repair** folder. Note the files asr.sif, asrpnp.sif, and setup.log. These are the same files that were copied to your floppy disk. Along with ASR backup.bkf, these are the files you will need to have available to restore your system using ASR.

12. Remove the disk from your computer. Close all windows.

14

Certification Objectives

Objectives for Microsoft Exam #70-293: Planning a Microsoft Windows Server 2003 Network:

- Plan a backup and recovery strategy

- Plan system recovery that uses Automated System Recovery (ASR)

REVIEW QUESTIONS

1. When should you perform an ASR backup?

   a. weekly

   b. annually

   c. anytime configuration is changed

   d. only when the server fails

2. An ASR set can be restored using which of the following recovery tools?

   a. Recovery Console

   b. installation CD

   c. boot disk

   d. safe mode

3. Which of the following files are required to restore an ASR set? (Choose all that apply.)

   a. asr.sif

   b. boot.ini

   c. asrpnp.sif

   d. [asr backup set].bkf

4. If the floppy disk is lost but you still have access to your server, where could you find the files you need to restore an ASR backup?

   a. c:\windows

   b. c:\windows\system32\drivers\etc

   c. c:\windows\repair

   d. c:\windows\dev\floppy0

5. An ASR Backup is created with which application?

  a. Backup utility

  b. Add or Remove Programs

  c. Computer Management

  d. Erd utility

14